PRINCIPIUM
SAPIENTIÆ

THE ORIGINS OF
GREEK PHILOSOPHICAL THOUGHT

ηαrper 🔥 τorchbooks

*A reference-list of Harper Torchbooks, classified
by subjects, is printed at the end of this volume.*

PRINCIPIUM SAPIENTIÆ

THE ORIGINS OF GREEK PHILOSOPHICAL THOUGHT

BY

F. M. CORNFORD

'TIMOR DOMINI
PRINCIPIUM SAPIENTIÆ'
PROVERBS i. 7

Edited by W. K. C. Guthrie

HARPER TORCHBOOKS ❦ The Academy Library
Harper & Row, Publishers, New York

PRINCIPIUM SAPIENTIÆ'

Printed in the United States of America.

This book was originally published in 1952 by the Syndics of the Cambridge University Press. It is here reprinted by permission of Cambridge University Press.

First HARPER TORCHBOOK edition published 1965 by Harper & Row, Publishers, Incorporated
49 East 33rd Street
New York, N. Y. 10016.

CONTENTS

PREFACE

THE work on which Cornford was engaged at his death was one by which he himself set great store. As a comparatively young man he had tried, in *From Religion to Philosophy*, to lay bare the pre-philosophical origins of philosophy among the Greeks. That book contains much that is still of value, but the progress of discovery and the increasing maturity of his own mind and enrichment of its store of reading and meditation had made him keenly aware that a fresh approach was necessary. The problem itself was one which absorbed him above all others in later as in earlier life; and the present work represents the results of his latest researches and reflexions upon it.

The manuscript of the book, which is unfinished, was submitted to Professor E. R. Dodds, in order that the decision—always a difficult one—whether to publish it posthumously should not be taken on one man's opinion alone. After reading it Professor Dodds wrote: 'I am strongly of the opinion that it ought to be published as soon as possible....Cornford would doubtless have pulled the threads together in a final chapter. He might also have provided certain rather thin chapters with more illustrative material. But even as it stands the book seems to me to throw important new light on the origins of Greek philosophical thinking, and it certainly contains pages as brilliant as any that he ever wrote.' He remarked, in addition, how Cornford's theory of the oriental origin of certain myths in Hesiod's *Theogony* seems to have been confirmed, in a way which would have delighted him, by the publication of the Hittite-Hurrian *Epic of Kumarbi*. (See his note on p. 249, below.) The questions of the general origin of myth in ritual, and of the oriental, and ultimately ritual origin of certain Greek myths in particular, illuminated as they have been by important additions to our collection of ancient Near Eastern religious texts, are under lively discussion today.[1] These questions

[1] Compare, for example, R. Dussaud, *Les Antécédents Orientaux de la Théogonie d'Hésiode*, Brussels, 1949, vol. 1, pp. 227–31, and references there. Theodore Gaster's book *Thespis*, 1950, deals with the same problems and has a full bibliography.

loom large in the second part of the present book, and Cornford's contribution to their development is certainly not one which should be withheld.

The final extant chapter (ch. XVI) is evidently incomplete, and there are some rough notes in manuscript for two more, with the titles 'Suppression of Death and Resurrection of the God' and 'India and China'. Since, however, the notes which the author left under the headings of the completed chapters do not always correspond to the contents of the chapters as written, but rather suggest earlier and abandoned schemes, it seemed wisest not to attempt any reconstruction. Though adding to the material, the notes do not strengthen the main argument.

The book appears to fall naturally into two parts, and an intention so to divide it is perhaps indicated by the opening words of Chapter X. This division has therefore been adopted. The first part is complete and speaks for itself. The argument of the second is also not difficult to extract, but since the author did not live to make a final summing-up, I have tried to summarize the main ideas in an appendix, using as far as possible notes left by the author himself.

W. K. C. GUTHRIE

June 1952

PART I
EMPIRICISM VERSUS INSPIRATION

CHAPTER I

PROBLEMS AND AIMS OF ANCIENT NATURAL PHILOSOPHY

IN his admirable survey of Hippocratic Medicine,[1] W. A. Heidel defended the ancient Greek men of science against the charge that they

were not in the habit of experimenting or that, if and when they did, it was solely in the interest of confirming conclusions arrived at by abstract reasoning. Thus Bacon, in the *Novum Organum*, asserted that we should give no weight to the fact that Aristotle in some of his works was concerned with experiments, because he had formed his conclusions before and made experiments conform with what he wished. In another connexion Bacon referred, obviously as confirmatory evidence for his contention, to the circumstance that Aristotle cited very few authorities and when he did so that he mentioned them only in order to refute or differ from them.

In reply, Heidel alleges 'the obvious fact that Bacon knew little of the way the human mind actually works'—a rather surprising charge to bring against the author of the *Essays* and of the *Aphorisms* on the four kinds of idol—

and had not reflected on the difference between arriving at conclusions and presenting them for the acceptance of others. Psychologists have sufficiently emphasized the processes by which one passes from direct observation of particulars to generalizations by noting similarities and differences, classifying and forming hypotheses which are tested and modified by experience; and they have shown that one proceeds experimentally throughout. What makes possible so crude a view as that implied by Bacon's statement is the fact that the mind commonly functions automatically, as it were, and that in consequence we are generally unaware of the steps it has taken in the march to its goal. Every scholar or scientist can bear witness to this; for, unless he has

[1] *Hippocratic Medicine, its Spirit and Method*, New York, 1941, p. 96. Heidel refers to Bacon, *Nov. Org.* aph. 63.

kept a minute dated record of his investigations, he will not be able to give a true account of the way he arrived at his conclusions. And it is no less obvious that one cannot judge by the form of exposition what labor of the mind has gone into a seemingly dogmatic or *a priori* pronouncement.

John Burnet argued to the same effect.[1] The reason why

we are told very little about observations and experiments in the accounts that have come down to us relative to the beginnings of science among the Greeks [is that] nearly all that we know on this subject comes from compilations and manuals composed centuries later, by men who were not themselves interested in science, and for readers who were even less so. What was even worse, these works were to a great extent inspired by the desire to discredit science by emphasizing the way in which men of science contradicted each other, and the paradoxical character of the conclusions at which they arrived. This being the object, it was obviously useless, and even out of place, to say much about the methods employed in arriving at the conclusions. It suited Epicurean and Sceptic, as also Christian, writers, to represent them as arbitrary dogmas.... Such being the nature of the evidence...it is obvious that all the actual examples of the use of sound scientific methods that we can discover will carry much more weight than would otherwise be the case. If we can point to indubitable examples of the use of experiment and observation, we are justified in supposing that there were others of which we know nothing because they did not happen to interest the compilers on whom we are dependent.

Both these critics suggest that, if we possessed the note-books of the early Greek philosophers with a minute dated record of their investigations (supposing they had troubled to keep one), we should find that they reached their conclusions, now only recorded as dogmatic pronouncements, by methods resembling those of the modern man of science, though with less consciousness of the need for caution in devising experimental tests. Behind this suggestion lies the assumption that the questions they asked themselves, the motives which prompted their inquiries, and the quarters to which they looked for the sources of knowledge, were the same then as now. This assumption is very naturally made by most historians of science, who, looking at the past from our own

[1] *Essays and Addresses*, London, 1929, p. 253.

standpoint, are interested in those features of ancient thought—atomism, for example—which can be historically linked to modern developments, just as they are concerned with alchemy chiefly for the sake of its anticipations of chemistry. The archaic features are ignored or dismissed as childish errors, excusable in the infancy of science. But if our aim is to abandon our own standpoint and to regain that of the ancients, we cannot afford to discard all the elements which seem foreign to our own ways of thinking, any more than the historian of religion can afford to discard as 'superstition' beliefs and practices which educated people in the civilized world have outgrown. Rather we should fix attention on elements which strike us as strange and unaccountable. We may find in them a clue to the attitude of mind we are trying to recover.

Burnet produces a single example of the use of experiment by a fifth-century philosopher—Empedocles' experiment with the *clepsydra*. The *clepsydra*[1] ('water-stealer') is described as 'a narrow-necked vessel having a broader base pierced with small holes'. The neck was held uppermost, and the hole in it could be closed by the thumb. It was used for lifting wine from the mixing-bowl.

With these vessels two distinct experiments were performed. (1) The vessel was lowered, empty, into water, as for its use in wine-serving, but with the thumb of the experimenter closing the opening at the top, and it was observed that until the thumb was removed no water entered through the holes in the bottom. (2) The vessel was allowed to fill with water, and the thumb placed over the opening. No water escaped through the holes in the bottom. When the thumb was removed the water dripped out.

Burnet describes these experiments as leading to the discovery that 'air was a substance having its own distinctive character' and that 'air consists neither of condensed fire nor of rarefied water'. I do not see how they could establish this latter point or prove anything more than that air is 'something'—a body which can resist pressure or sustain a weight—not 'nothing' or 'the void', with which it had earlier been confused. This is, no doubt, an important

[1] I borrow the description of the vessel and the experiments from W. K. C. Guthrie's note on Aristotle, *de Caelo*, 294 b 20 (Loeb translation), where an extant vessel of this type is figured.

truth; but it may be noted that the facts of the *clepsydra's* behaviour must have been already known to everyone who used it. All Empedocles did was to draw the explicit inference: 'the vessel cannot be simply empty: the air in it cannot be nothing at all.' He did not invent the *clepsydra* in a laboratory with a view to testing the hypothesis that air has some substance, and then abiding by the unforeseen result of his experiments. Anaxagoras is said to have demonstrated the same point by means of inflated wine-skins. But such skins were used in rustic sports, and every child knew that they resisted pressure when you jumped on them. To draw a clear-sighted inference from familiar experience is not the same thing as to practise the experimental method, as understood today.

As Burnet remarks, the *clepsydra* is used by Empedocles to illustrate his theory of respiration. His doctrine that the body transpires through pores all over the surface of the skin was used by Plato,[1] and after him by Diocles, to explain how respiration is maintained by a 'circular thrust'. The warm air breathed out by the mouth is replaced inside the body by cool air drawn in through the pores of the thorax. When this air inside is heated, it goes out again through the same pores and is replaced by air drawn in through the mouth. So the mechanical process goes on, with 'a motion like that of a wheel which swings now this way now that', driven by the heat of the internal fire. Now this theory could have been tested by anyone who would sit in a bath up to his neck in water and observe whether any air bubbles passed through the water into, or out of, his chest as he breathed. Why did no one try this simple experiment before dogmatically stating that this is how we breathe? It seems certain that it was never tried, either to prove or to disprove the doctrine.

Anaximenes affords another instance of an hypothesis which no one tested. He held that differences of heat and cold can be reduced to differences of density; steam is hotter and less dense than water, water hotter and less dense than ice. If that is so, a given quantity of water ought to fill less space when frozen. Had Anaximenes set a jar full of water outside his door on a frosty night and found it split in the morning, he might have found out that

[1] *Timaeus*, 78 B ff.

ice fills more space than water and revised his theory. But there is no sign that either he or any critic went to this length. The neglect is the more remarkable because a similar experiment, made for another purpose, is recorded by a Hippocratic writer: 'if in winter one pours a measured quantity of water into a vessel and sets it out of doors where it will freeze quickly, and on the morrow brings it into a warm room where it will melt as quickly as possible, one will find on measuring it that the quantity is considerably reduced.' [1] As will appear later, it is significant that the experiment should have been recorded by a doctor, and entirely neglected by the natural philosopher.

As against the one or two instances of so-called experiment which stand to the credit of the philosophers, Heidel has produced from the medical writers a long list of appeals to experience, which more or less approximate to what we should regard as really scientific experiments. Even in their case Heidel admits that 'experimentation had not yet attained either the fundamental importance or the systematic form it has now assumed' and that 'reasoning was for the most part by analogy'. There is, however, a marked contrast, so far as our evidence goes, between the natural philosopher and the physician. Empedocles himself was both philosopher and physician; and the *clepsydra* experiment, as we have seen, is associated with a physiological account of respiration as well as with the cosmological doctrine that air is a bodily substance.

Once we have observed this contrast, the reason is not far to seek. Medicine is, and always has been, a practical art, with a history stretching back for untold centuries before it came to have anything that we should recognize as a basis of scientific theory. The doctor was a 'healer' (ἰατρός), a craftsman in the public service (δημιοεργός), a chirurgeon, working with his hands (χειρουργός). He was always dealing with the individual patient, and had always before him the immediate practical end of curing him. Whatever preconceptions he may bring with him as to the nature of the human body and its diseases, he cannot escape the constant need to observe the symptoms of the individual case, to

---

[1] Heidel, *op. cit.* p. 113; Hippocr. *de Aere Aqua Locis*, VIII (ii, 36 Littré).

find out what is wrong and what needs to be done. His reputation and his income will depend on his success, not as a theorist, but as a healer.

Hence we can trace in the Hippocratic writings the impulse to build up a theoretical science on the basis of particular observations. The following is a brief summary of Heidel's account.[1] The *Epidemics* is still famous for its record of individual cases; and 'a most striking example of Greek observation and record in the field of medicine is the description of the great plague at Athens left by Thucydides, a contemporary of Hippocrates. He states that he himself had been smitten by it and gives his reason for recording the symptoms and course of the disease—that it may be recognized if it should ever recur.' The phenomena selected for observation must be significant for the physician's purpose. 'The ultimate object of the practitioner was naturally mastery over disease, and, just as inevitably, the proximate purpose was to determine its cause.' The Hippocratics approached their problems in a rational and clear-sighted way, recognizing that 'one must take account not only of the individual and his constitution, character, and habits but also of more general factors, such as the race and sex of the patient and the environment—climate, location and water supply and even social and political conditions'. 'Nothing is more characteristic of Hippocratic medicine than its insistence on the closest attention to the individual.'

The ideal of the Hippocratics aimed at a total unified picture of a diseased state.... In the *Epidemics*, especially in Book IV, the special case under consideration is almost always compared with others, and any such comparison must bring out differences as well as similarities. In any case, a classification presupposed a judgement as to what marks are typical or essential, and must consequently be founded on experience deemed sufficient. A disease thus described or defined becomes for the physician an entity with a character and presumable course that may generally be foreseen. Hence the Hippocratics regarded their diagnoses as essentially prognoses.

In two closely related treatises we find that 'one treatise states the matter positively, while the other asks a question. Instances occur

[1] *Op. cit.* pp. 61 ff.

in which both sources agree in asking questions, evidently because the data available were not sufficient to justify diagnosis or prognosis.... Nothing, it would seem, could better show generalizations in the making.' After reviewing a number of 'observations derived from experiments, whether made in the ordinary routine of life or in the practice of the industrial arts', as well as in medicine, Heidel remarks that 'relatively few can be definitely shown to have been undertaken with the avowed purpose of seeing just what would result'. On the other hand, if 'experiment' is used in a wide sense, an enterprising doctor, in the ordinary course of practice, will try the effect on his patient of a certain drug or regime, observe the result, and try another in case of failure. We come back to the point that the doctor's whole attitude to this question of observation, inference, experiment and generalization is determined by the fact that he is always faced with a definite problem from which he starts and to which he must return— what is wrong with this particular patient, why he is suffering, how he can be cured. In this respect the art of medicine is on the same footing as the industrial arts. In opening his case for experiment and observation as the unrecorded basis of Greek science, Burnet points to evidence of 'a great development of technical ability which could not have been acquired except by means of experiments'.

Herodotus tells us (III, 60) that Eupalinus of Megara constructed a tunnel through the hill above Samos, and this tunnel, of which he has left us a description, was discovered in 1882. It is about half a mile in length, but the levels are nearly exact. Quite apart from the observations that we still have in the Hippocratean corpus, which are not later than the fifth century B.C., we can hardly believe that the anatomical exactitude of Greek sculpture was obtained by *a priori* methods. These facts undoubtedly presuppose experiment and observation of a truly scientific character. (Burnet, *op. cit.* p. 253.)

No one has ever suggested that a knowledge of human anatomy can be gained without a close observation of human bodies. As it becomes more and more the sculptor's aim to reproduce the appearance of a human being—this was not his original purpose— so his observation will need to be more exact. Like the doctor, he has always a particular problem to solve in practice. If this problem is to copy an existing pattern, naturally he must study the pattern first; and in a school of sculpture, the necessary knowledge will accumulate; the results of many observations will be embodied in a generalized type or canon of the human figure. Eupalinus, again, had to construct a particular tunnel. He would use the measuring instruments already invented by craftsmen to meet their needs; and he would know a 'few rules derived from the *a priori* science of geometry. Also he would have behind him the experience of ·many generations of engineers, who had applied common sense and methods of trial and error to simpler problems. Any householder who is called in to remedy minor disasters, such as a burst pipe, has to think out contrivances which differ only in complexity from those employed on the one hand by Eupalinus driving his half-mile tunnel, and on the other by a chimpanzee piling one box on another in order to reach a bunch of bananas. The success of Eupalinus and the realism of the later sculptors show that the Greeks (like other peoples) could turn common sense and ingenuity to practical account and were capable of observing closely what interested them for practical purposes. But the question we are concerned with lies outside the fields of medicine and of the industrial and fine arts. It is the question whether methods of observation, generalization, and experiment were commonly used by the Ionian philosophers. They were not bringing their ingenuity to bear on healing the sick or driving tunnels or making statues. Their problems were not of the practical kind which daily force upon us the necessity of sharpening our wits to circumvent some mechanical obstacle. They could not be solved by 'experiment' in the loose sense of trial and error;[1] and,

---

[1] Some confusion is introduced into all this question by the ambiguity of 'experiment'. Heidel (*op. cit.* p. 101) goes so far as to apply the word to the use of a sounding-line, and even to introduce it into the text of Herodotus (II, 28): 'That the springs (of the Nile) are bottomless, he said, Psammetichus, King of Egypt, showed by *experiment*; for though he let down a rope of many fathoms' length he could not reach the bottom. Thus if the secretary told the truth about the *experiment* it only proved....' All Herodotus says is that the King 'had recourse to trial' (ἐς διάπειραν ἀπικέσθαι) and 'if the secretary was telling the truth about this' (εἰ ταῦτα γινόμενα ἔλεγε).

as we have seen, the philosophers neglected, to an extent which strikes the modern mind as astonishing, to check their statements by experiment in the scientific sense of putting to nature a question the answer to which could not be foreseen. The reason for this neglect will appear when we have considered what their problems were. Later[1] we shall examine the earliest Ionian system of which we have a sufficient description, the system of Anaximander, which set the pattern followed throughout the later course of Ionian speculation.

[1] In ch. x.

CHAPTER II

EPICURUS

IT will be one of our objects to gain a clearer idea of what is meant by 'mythical' thought, but it may be useful first of all to consider the final outcome of Ionian physics; for here the inward spirit and trend of this philosophy might be expected to emerge, as mythical representations come to be detected for what they are and discarded by advancing rationalism. This final outcome was the atomism of Epicurus, a system often hailed as the most scientific product of ancient thought. For our purpose we have ample information from Epicurus' own writings and from the poem of Lucretius. We must concentrate attention not so much on details as on the attitude of mind in which the philosopher approaches his subject.

It is true, indeed, and universally recognized that Epicurus' physical doctrine made no pretence of being the product of disinterested curiosity. Philosophy was to him 'a practical activity, intended by means of speech and reasoning to secure a happy life' by saving mankind from 'the two great terrors which might disturb their lives, the dread of the arbitrary interference of divine beings in the world and the fear of the punishment of the soul after death'.[1] On the other hand, these practical motives were precisely what led him to desire a purely 'rational' account of matters which seemed to him obscured by mythology and superstition. Hence modern men of science, looking among the relics of ancient thought for anticipations of their own methods and results, and finding a thinker who rejects mythology and preaches atomism, are apt to conclude that Epicurus must have been 'scientific', because he was a rationalist and a materialist.

Attempts have recently been made to represent the materialism of Epicurus as inspired by philanthropic motives. It is argued that belief in 'another world', whether in the idealist or the religious

---

[1] C. Bailey, *The Greek Atomists and Epicurus*, p. 233.

sense, was upheld by the aristocracy and the rich as a means of keeping the poor in their places: the proletariat was to be fed on delusive hopes of a better lot after death, which would cost nothing to their oppressors in this life. This view, however, finds no support in the writings of Epicurus himself or in the poem of Lucretius. I doubt whether a single sentence can be produced which implies the smallest interest in the economic disadvantages of the free workman or of the slave. On the other hand there is abundant evidence that Epicurus felt, and attributed to others, a horror of death and still more of 'something after death', associated with the religious, and in particular with the Platonic, doctrine that the world is governed by gods who are concerned with the reward and punishment of human conduct. Valuing untroubled peace of mind above every other so-called good, he had here an amply sufficient motive for embracing the gospel of materialism. Unlike the modern materialist he was not an atheist. It made him more comfortable to believe in gods who lived in Epicurean bliss, well outside the boundaries of this world of ours or any other world, in whose arrangement and workings they were not allowed to take any part. Having thus rejected both the argument from design and the demand for a divine justice, he left the existence of his gods unsupported by any proofs that would bear examination. His religion, in fact, was more purely dogmatic than the beliefs he denounced.

In other respects his materialism was as whole-hearted as materialism can be. In the Battle of Gods and Giants, he was of that party who

try to drag everything down to earth out of heaven and the unseen, literally grasping rocks and trees in their hands; for they lay hold upon every stick and stone and strenuously affirm that real existence belongs only to that which can be handled and offers resistance to touch. They define reality as the same thing as body, and as soon as one of the opposite party asserts that anything without a body is real, they are utterly contemptuous and will not listen to another word.[1]

Such was the final outcome of the Ionian tradition. At first, in the Milesian scheme, the ultimate 'nature of things', though

[1] Plato, *Sophist*, 246A.

bodily, had been alive and self-moved. Then, in the fifth century, its life had come to be distinguished as moving forces, still corporeal, but consisting of an extremely subtle and penetrating form of matter, comparable to the electric fluid of our ancestors. The suggestion of Anaxagoras, that the moving force might be an Intelligence capable of 'setting all things in order', had been taken up by Plato and built into the structure of his religion. Epicurus' reaction against a benevolent Providence entailed an extreme emphasis on the bodily nature of the real. He wished to believe in nothing but lifeless atoms moving mechanically in empty space, with the inevitable consequence that all the phenomena of life and consciousness, which cannot be wholly denied, must, so far as possible, be explained in terms of the contact and collision of atoms. Knowledge must somehow be reduced to sensation, and sensation to touch; for the real is body, and body is essentially the tangible.[1] Hence we arrive at the doctrine that all the objects of sense-perception are real, and all our perceptions of them true and infallible; for Epicurus thought that, once a single perception were called in question, there would be no ground left for trusting any perception, and knowledge would give place to complete scepticism. As Dr Bailey remarks, in his summary of this doctrine:

It is not difficult now to answer the question 'how is our knowledge of the external world acquired?' For the immediate corollary of the belief in the reality and truth of the perceptible world is the assertion that the one method of cognition of truth is sense-perception: sensation is the ultimate and only guarantee or criterion of truth. This is indeed the one fundamental principle of Epicurus' whole system.[2]

To anyone acquainted with the history of thought it will be obvious that this principle gives rise to a series of formidable problems, which Epicurus either ignored or answered in ways that no one would now accept. What concerns us is rather to discover whether the emphatic assertion of the truth of all perceptions led Epicurus to pursue in his physical speculations what

---

[1] Aristotle, *de Sensu*, 442a29 (Democr. A 119 (*Vors.*[5] II, p. 112)): 'They make all the objects of sense touchable; if this is so, each of the other senses is a kind of touch.' [2] *Greek Atomists*, p. 237.

we should consider a scientific method. Did he start always from careful observation of sense-data, formulate hypotheses which appeared to be in accordance with them, and finally bring these hypotheses to the test of further observation? Surely it is reasonable to demand this procedure of a man who declares that sense-perception is the ultimate criterion of truth—so reasonable that modern critics interpret Epicurus on the assumption that he thought of science as an attempt to discover laws of nature by this procedure.

Having laid such exclusive stress on sense-perception, Epicurus divided objects into three classes, according to the degrees in which they came within, or lay outside, the immediate reach of the senses. First come those fully perceptible things (πρόδηλα) of which we can gain a 'clear view' at close quarters; secondly, 'what goes on in the sky (τὰ μετέωρα) and under the earth', perceptible phenomena which cannot be examined at close range; and thirdly, things wholly imperceptible by the senses (ἄδηλα), such as the ultimate realities, atoms and void, which are accessible only to thought. We shall take these divisions in order.

(1) The discussion of immediate sense-perception moves within limits already traced by Plato in the *Theaetetus*. The materialist regards the mind as analogous to a waxen tablet, vacant at birth, and receiving impressions stamped on it by the impact of material images or 'idols' thrown off by the objects around us. Images of a number of similar objects accumulate in a sort of composite photograph, in which the individual peculiarities (say) of many horses have become merged in a general idea or concept, 'horse', called by Epicurus an 'anticipation' or 'preconception' (πρόληψις). This preconception is stored in memory and can be called up to enable us to conceive beforehand the general characteristics of something we wish to create, or to identify fresh images as they are presented to us. 'For instance, we ask "Is that standing yonder a horse or a cow?" To do this we must know by means of a preconception the shapes of horse and cow. Otherwise we could not have named them.' (*D.L.* x, 33.) While the object is still distant we may have an indistinct impression, but this, so far as it goes, has the infallible truth of sensation. Error comes in only

with the 'addition of judgment', when we assign the fresh impression of a horse to the preconception of 'cow' and judge: 'That is a cow.' Our judgment ought to be held in suspense, awaiting the confirmation of the 'clear view'. If confirmed by closer inspection, the judgment will be true.

Epicurus seems to have remained satisfied with this account of the scope of sensation and judgment, ignoring the later argument of the *Theaetetus* which had shown that it is far from adequate to cover all types of false judgment. What concerns us is to note that, in Epicurus' narrow view, 'inquiry' in this field of terrestrial objects seems to be confined to the identification of a freshly perceived object with a memory-image, and the verification of the judgment so formed by a closer inspection. Once the 'clear view' has settled the doubt between horse and cow, curiosity is satisfied. The atoms of the mind have established intimate contact with the material body outside.

Writers who assume that Epicurus was thinking like a modern man of science confuse this verification of a dubious judgment by the closer view with the experimental verification of a scientific hypothesis by recourse to fresh observation. But Epicurus is not describing a scientific method at all; he is describing a common-sense procedure which everyone follows in ascertaining whether a dimly seen figure is Jones or Brown. All that interests him is to defend sensation as infallible, because it is the senses that reveal the material world of tangible things, and tangible things are to be the only realities.

Had Epicurus been a man of science, he would surely have found the most promising field of inquiry in the region of these terrestrial objects within immediate reach of our infallible senses. Here we ought to be well equipped to set out upon the conquest of nature by observation and cautious inference, leading to the discovery of natural laws, and finally to the application of scientific knowledge to the improvement of material conditions. But no such prospect is opened up either in Epicurus' extant writings or in Lucretius. Lucretius deals at great length with the other two departments—the atomic cosmogony, and the celestial phenomena which we shall presently consider. Then at last he turns to terrestrial objects, the things around us. Here his interest seems to be confined to a short list of curiosities or wonders of the world, such as the rising of the Nile, the well of Juppiter Ammon which was alleged to be cold by day and hot by night, the attractive power of the magnet, and a few others. These curiosities had already figured in the system of Democritus and earlier Ionian speculations. Lucretius introduces this topic with a very curious remark (VI, 703 ff.):

There are also a certain number of things for which it is not enough to assign one cause; you must give several, one of which at the same time is the real cause. In the same way, suppose you see the lifeless body of a man lying some way off; it would be natural to mention all the different causes of death, in order that the one real cause of that man's death may be mentioned among them. For you would not be able to prove that he died by steel or cold or disease or perhaps by poison;[1] yet we know it is something of this kind that has befallen him. The same thing may be said in the case of a number of other things.

If I understand this passage rightly, it means that the real cause of a curiosity of this class cannot be ascertained by a close view, though Lucretius shows a preference for an atomistic explanation. There is no suggestion of forming a provisional hypothesis and then confirming or disproving it by experimental tests. The philosopher will not even visit the well of Juppiter Ammon and find out whether it really is hotter at night than by day. He will sit at home, thinking of all the causes which present themselves as possible, and he should prefer the one which seems most probable to an atomist; but at any rate, he may hope that 'the one real cause may be mentioned among them', and that will content him. There is, however, for these terrestrial curiosities, one and only one real cause. In this respect they differ from the celestial phenomena to which we shall presently turn.

But before leaving the terrestrial region, the important point must once more be emphasized. Apart from this list of curiosities

---

[1] Munro seems to misunderstand this clause. He translates: 'Thus you may be able to prove that he has not died....' Giussani takes it as above: 'There is one cause which is the real cause in this case, but you cannot be sure which of the possible causes it is.' So also Bailey.

inherited from the earlier Ionians, there seems to be no evidence that Epicurus regarded the things we can see and handle as a proper field for scientific inquiry. Nothing is said about collecting facts with a view to generalization. Neither Epicurus nor Lucretius invites the Epicurean to continue the admirable research into the natural history of animals and plants inaugurated by Aristotle and Theophrastus. Nor do they express the smallest interest in what is called the conquest of Nature, the attempt to grasp the working of natural forces in order to harness them to human needs and raise the level of material comfort. The arts of building, weaving, agriculture, metal-working, and so on, are mentioned by Lucretius as contrivances of human ingenuity, long ago arrived at in the early stages of civilization. It never occurred to the ancient Atomists that the atomic theory of the ultimate nature of things could have any bearing on their further development. And if it had occurred to them, Epicurus, at any rate, saw in the pursuit of wealth a misuse of human energy as disastrous as the pursuit of power. One reason why the ancient Atomists took not a single step towards the technique of modern science was that the practical motive, which has driven science to create that technique in the centuries since Galileo, was foreign to their minds. This is also the reason why they never tried to ascertain the laws of motion, the dominating concern of science in the sixteenth and seventeenth centuries. If you want to control Nature, these laws are the first things you need to understand. Epicurus was not seeking to control or to exploit Nature; for an accession of power and wealth would only have upset that peace of mind which he found in the simplest possible manner of life. If the happiness you desire can best be obtained by living on bread and water and wearing a homespun shirt, the sight of steam agitating the lid of a boiling kettle will not impel you to invent the steam-engine, the power-loom, and the tractor.

The upshot here is a curious paradox. This materialistic system, for all its insistence on the reality of tangible bodies revealed by the infallible senses, is least of all concerned with the things close around us and within reach of the 'clear view'. Much has been written in praise of the wealth of observation in the pages of

Lucretius; and no wonder, for it is in his descriptions of Nature that the poet finds congenial scope for his magnificent powers. But, from the standpoint of science, all this observation contributes no more than vague, unanalysed analogies which prove nothing and serve only to illustrate foregone conclusions. Despising mathematics, Epicurus never dreamed that the accurate measurement of quantities must enter into observation as understood by the man of science, and distinguishes it from the observation of Nature practised by the poet and the ordinary man. He seems to have thought that, for the practical purpose of leading an untroubled life, we can deal with the things around us by trusting our perceptions and using common sense. He may have regarded natural history as a harmless pastime for anyone who chose to amuse his leisure in that way. But no further enrichment of human happiness was to be looked for in the direction of such pursuits.

(2) We now leave the field of terrestrial objects which has furnished a few problematical curiosities. The rest of physics covers the same table of contents as the earlier Ionian systems. There is the chapter dealing with the ultimate nature of things and the evolution of an ordered world from an initial chaotic condition—cosmogony, including the origin of life. All this process must be accounted for in terms of atoms and void, which are entirely imperceptible by the senses. But we shall first consider the remaining province of the perceptible, containing objects which, although we can see them and even feel their effects at a distance, cannot be approached and handled at close quarters like the things around us. There are the things 'up in the sky' (μετέωρα), namely the heavenly bodies and atmospheric phenomena, and the things 'under the earth' (ὑπὸ γῆς). They form a separate class because in their case our judgments cannot be brought to the test of the close view. The discussion of these celestial and subterranean phenomena fills a much larger space in Lucretius' poem than those terrestrial curiosities we have just been considering. The reason for this concentration of interest is stated again and again. It throws a clear light on the Epicurean attitude towards physical speculation.

The clearest statement is to be found where Epicurus, in the Letter to Herodotus (§ 76), turns from cosmogony to this field, which it will be convenient to call by its old name, meteorology. He begins by rejecting two current explanations of the motions that take place up in the sky, the turnings, eclipses, rising and setting of the heavenly bodies, and atmospheric phenomena. We must not think that they are controlled or ordained by any divine being. A god is essentially an immortal being who enjoys perfect bliss. His happiness is not to be impaired by 'trouble and care, anger or kindness'; such activities and feelings occur only 'where there is weakness and fear and dependence on neighbours'. Secondly, the same requirement of untroubled bliss forbids us equally to suppose that the heavenly bodies are themselves divine and moved by their own wills. Either of these religious views would contradict our notion of divine happiness and 'cause the greatest disturbance in our souls'. The last words reveal the fundamental objection. Epicurus frankly admits that no other purpose is to be served by a knowledge of meteorology, or of any other branch of physics, than 'peace of mind and a secure confidence'.[1] Our own happiness would be destroyed by the theological belief that any sort of divine providence interferes in the workings of Nature, that thunder and lightning are tokens of divine anger, or that the rain falls by divine grace. On the other hand, our happiness is increased by believing in gods as free from care as we should like to be ourselves. The solution is to translate them, out of harm's way, to Islands of the Blest in the intermundane spaces outside the boundaries of any of the innumerable worlds. These are described in language traditionally associated with the abode of the gods from Homer onwards.

Although Epicurus defends his belief in the existence of gods on grounds which profess to be rational, he does not care to conceal the more human motive for both asserting their existence and denying their activity. On his own principles the religious views he forbids us to accept ought to be entertained as possible, since they are certainly not contradicted by the evidence of our senses. Plato, Aristotle, and the Stoics, all saw in the regular motions

[1] *Ep. to Pyth.* 85.

20

of the heavenly bodies the clearest evidence, not of any blind necessity of 'natural laws', but on the contrary of divine intelligence and will. So did Sir Isaac Newton in the very work which at last revealed those laws of mechanical motion of which the ancients had no inkling. 'It is not to be conceived', says the *Principia*,[1] 'that mere mechanical causes could give birth to so many regular motions.... This most beautiful system of the sun, planets and comets, could only proceed from the counsel and dominion of an intelligent and powerful Being.' If Epicurus thought otherwise, it was not because he could point to any observable phenomenon inconsistent with the religious view; nor had he any rational ground for assuming that the universe must be so constituted as not to disturb his own peace of mind. His attitude, accordingly, has no claim to be called scientific. It is not based on observation or the evidence of the senses, but dogmatic to at least the same degree as that of his opponents.

If the reader has any doubts upon this point, they may be dispelled by a consideration of the rule laid down by Epicurus as peculiarly applicable to meteorology. In this department he is not content with the negative principle, already sufficiently lax, that any explanation may be accepted as true, if it is not contradicted by sense experience. He goes further and tells us that, for celestial occurrences, *all* explanations which sense does not contradict must be accepted as true, because they actually happen in several different ways. It is not merely that their remoteness denies us the opportunity of deciding between the alternatives by means of a closer view. 'Even if in our world there should be only one true explanation of a given phenomenon, yet thanks to the "equal distribution" (ἰσονομία) of things in the whole universe, the other explanations will hold good in other worlds. They must then all be accepted equally.'[2]

In dealing with other departments of physics 'there is only one explanation which harmonizes with phenomena. This is not so with the things in the sky: they admit of more than one explanation of their occurrence and more than one account of their nature

---

[1] Gen. Schol. to *Principia*, Bk III, trans. Motte–Cajori.
[2] C. Bailey, *Greek Atomists*, p. 261, referring to *Ep.* II, 87.

which harmonizes with our perceptions.... To accept one and reject another which harmonizes just as well with the appearances, is to leave the path of physical speculation and relapse into myth.' We can obtain 'indications' from what goes on around us and can be closely observed; but what goes on in the sky cannot be closely observed and 'may be produced in several ways'.[1]

It is amusing to see how this dogmatist, in the very act of denouncing the dogmatism of 'myth', lays down a principle which is, to our minds, wildly unscientific. As Dr Bailey remarks, 'in this astonishing but wholly consistent conclusion lies the reason of the many curious passages in Epicurus' astronomy and meteorology which must strike any reader of the Letter to Pythocles or of the fifth and sixth books of Lucretius' poem, where again and again what we know to be the true explanation of a phenomenon is classed side by side with the most puerile hypotheses'. Eclipses of the sun and moon, for example, may be due to their extinction and rekindling, or to 'the interposition of some other bodies, either the earth or some unseen body or something else of this sort' (Ep. II, 96). Having rejected 'the slavish artifices (or technicalities) of the astronomers', the Epicurean does not think it worth while even to examine their reasons for believing that the sun's light is obstructed by the moon and for preferring this explanation to the view that the sun goes out for a while and lights up again. So long as eclipses are not taken to be omens of divine displeasure, it does not matter how they are caused. Any physical account is as good as any other for our peace of mind, and all accounts must be entertained. Again, after giving four alternative explanations of the motion of the stars, Lucretius concludes:

Which of these causes is in operation in this world, it is not easy to affirm for certain; but what can be and is done throughout the universe in various worlds formed on various plans, this I teach, and I go on to set forth several causes which may exist throughout the universe for the motions of stars; one of which however must in this world also be the cause that imparts lively motion to the signs; but to dictate which of them it is, is by no means the duty of the man who advances step by step. (v. 526.)

[1] Ep. II, 86–7.

It was not by following the Epicurean principle that astronomy had in fact advanced, more than a century earlier, to the true explanation of eclipses, accepted by all serious mathematicians. If Epicurus wished to rescue the common man from the superstitious belief in omens, he would have done better to master their demonstrations and explain them in simple terms, instead of denouncing them for 'dictating' a single explanation.

We can now detect the deeper reason for the special application of this extraordinary principle to meteorology. 'What goes on in the sky and under the earth' had long been regarded as the peculiar region of the visible world in which divine agency and intentions were revealed. It had become a commonplace that belief in the existence of gods had had its origin in two causes: dreams or waking visions, and meteoric and subterranean phenomena. Primitive men, said Democritus,[1] had been terrified by the sight of what goes on in the sky—thunder, lightning, thunderbolts, comets, eclipses of sun and moon—and thought that these were caused by gods. Lucretius repeats this. After mentioning dreams, which the Atomists accepted as valid evidence, he turns to the second source of religious belief:

Again they would see the system of heaven and the different seasons of the years come round in regular succession, and could not find out by what causes this was done; therefore they would seek a refuge in handing over all things to the gods and supposing all things to be guided by their nod. And they placed in heaven the abodes and realms of the gods, because night and moon are seen to roll through heaven, moon, day and night and night's austere constellations and night-wandering meteors of the sky and flying bodies of flame, clouds, sun, rains, snow, winds, lightnings, hail, and rapid rumblings and loud threatful thunderclaps. (v, 1183, tr. Munro.)

Lucretius goes on to enlarge upon the terror of divine anger supposed to be manifest in thunder, storm and earthquake. He professes to be disquieted not only by these exceptional outbursts,

---

[1] Democr. A 75 (*Vors.*⁵ II, p. 102). Cf. Aristotle, *frag.* 10: the conception of gods arose from two sources, the soul's experience of inspired divination in dreams, and ἀπὸ τῶν μετεώρων, the regular movement of the heavenly bodies.

but by the notion that the very regularity of the stars' courses may be due to divine will:

For when we turn our gaze on the heavenly quarters of the great upper world and ether fast above the glittering stars, and direct our thoughts to the courses of the sun and moon, then into our breasts burdened with other ills that fear as well begins to exalt its reawakened head, the fear that we may haply find the power of the gods to be unlimited, able to wheel the bright stars in their varied motion; for lack of power to solve the question troubles the mind with doubts, whether there was ever a birth-time of the world, and whether likewise there is to be any end; how far the walls of the world can endure this strain of restless motion; or whether gifted by the grace of the gods with an everlasting existence they may glide on through a never-ending tract of time and defy the strong powers of immeasurable ages. (v, 1204 ff.)

In confronting these terrors Epicurus found himself in a curious dilemma. On the one hand, there was the religious belief, to which Plato had lent all the weight of his authority, that the regular course of the heavenly bodies and of the seasons was the work of a divine Intelligence designing the best possible order for the world, and the older, simpler belief in a sky-god who sent the rain to fertilize the earth for man's benefit. In such a faith men had found it possible to find comfort and reassurance. But in the idea of Providence benevolent care for mankind was indissolubly linked with divine justice and the punishment of the wicked after death; and to Epicurus' timid soul the terrors of hell outweighed the consolations of faith. The gods, therefore, must be banished from the visible world and the soul proved to be mortal. Some purely physical explanation must be given of all those 'meteorological' phenomena which had already bulked so large in the Ionian philosophy. But here another terror lurked in the obvious alternative. To escape the rule of Providence is to fall under the iron hand of Fate. If the world is not governed by beneficent deities, must it not be subject to the even more terrible dominion of blind necessity? When we have escaped the prospect of immortality by reducing the soul to the level of dead matter in mechanical motion, the logical conclusion seems to be a complete determinism: every human thought, feeling, and action will be the inevitable result of causes pushing us from behind. The Stoics evaded this dilemma by embracing both alternatives and identifying Fate with Providence.[1] Epicurus felt it necessary to reject both. He deserves some credit for defying Fate and clinging to that belief in free will which all men, including most philosophers, have cherished in their hearts. The only metaphysical basis which his system permitted was found in the celebrated doctrine that the atoms, at any moment, can swerve, for no reason, from the vertical line of their fall through empty space. The materialist has thus ingeniously inverted the Platonic doctrine that all physical motion must be traced back to the self-moving power of the soul.

The point which now concerns us is that 'meteorology' was pre-eminently the field in which religion had found the evidences of divine intervention. It was, therefore, the citadel which Epicureanism must defend, at all costs, against both the enemies of our peace of mind: Providence on the one side and Fate on the other. This motive, perhaps unconsciously, dictated the desperate expedient of accepting as true *every* non-supernatural explanation, and refusing to be bound by any 'single cause'. The 'slavish artifices of the astronomers' threatened to strangle freedom in a network of causal necessity. It is certain, at any rate, that in the meteorological field Epicurus' procedure is as far removed as possible from the standpoint of modern science.

(3) We must now turn to the third department, of things wholly imperceptible by the senses. This includes the gods, and the ultimate constituents of the universe, atoms and their motions in the void. We shall find that Epicurus is no less dogmatic here than in the other parts of his system.

We have already seen how one of the two evidences for the existence of gods has been rejected: it is not to be inferred from 'what goes on in the sky'. There remains the evidence of dreams, which had already been accepted by Democritus and explained by the impact of images (*idola*) entering the pores of the body in

[1] Cf. Cicero, *Nat. Deor.* I, 20, 54–5.

sleep. These images are objects of 'mental apprehension', an act independent of the senses, but analogous to the perception of sensible things. It is unnecessary to go into the reasons which Epicurus gave for believing that we have a 'clear knowledge' of the anthropomorphic gods who appear to us in dreams, whereas visions of chimaeras or hippocentaurs are mere chance combinations of stray *idola* with no corresponding realities. It is obvious that the real motive behind Epicurus' theology is his determination that there shall be immortal and blessed beings, enjoying an existence of untroubled peace such as the Epicurean desired for himself. But for that determination, our dreams of the gods could be explained away just as easily as our dreams of chimaeras; and the Academic in Cicero's *de Natura Deorum* has no difficulty in tearing the doctrine to pieces. Epicurus' theology, which his most ardent admirers do not care to defend, offers only the thinnest pretence of a 'scientific' character.

Apart from the gods, the department of the wholly imperceptible includes the ultimate constituents of the universe, atoms and the void. The atoms, of course, are essentially tangible body; it is only their extremely minute size that prevents our limited senses from perceiving them. But they are entirely beyond even the distant view that we have of things in the sky.

Here the claim of Epicureanism to be 'scientific' is put to the supreme test. A system which professes to rest on the testimony of the infallible senses might be expected to put forward only a tentative hypothesis about the wholly imperceptible, and to re-commend suspense of judgment, since without the apparatus of a modern laboratory no theory of the nature of atoms could be confirmed by any sort of experimental proof. But Epicurus' attitude is exactly the reverse of this sceptical caution: he is more dogmatic in this field than in either of the other two. As we have seen, our judgments on the things immediately around us were to await the confirmation of the close view; and in dealing with meteorological phenomena we were to keep our minds open to every possible explanation. But when we come to these objects of which the senses can give us neither a close nor a distant view, 'this multiplicity of causes and explanations has passed away.

There is no hesitation as to the true explanation, and in no single instance is there a suggestion of a possible alternative: Atomism is not one among several possible theories of the universe, nor with regard to any of its details is there a hint that any other view than that expounded by Epicurus himself could be true.'[1] Epicurus is content to assert roundly that his atomism is the only theory consistent with phenomena.

How is this extreme dogmatism to be accounted for? In replying to this question, Dr Bailey seems to combine two really incompatible accounts of the mental processes supposed to be involved in arriving at the certain truth about atoms and void. He is perhaps elaborating a confusion which existed in Epicurus' own mind. At first, Dr Bailey speaks of sense-perceptions providing us with 'signs' for a *start in our investigations* and suggesting *inferences* to the invisible. The work is then carried on by thought alone, and '*hypothesis must be framed on the basis of phenomena*'. Thought is 'a movement of the mind, which by the combination and comparison of previously existing images creates new images by a kind of "visualization"'. 'The *hypotheses* of thought must be tested by being referred back to sensation. Confirmation (ἐπιμαρτύρησις) is no longer possible, because the "clear view" of sensation is no longer possible, but phenomena may contradict (ἀντιμαρτυρεῖν), and if so *the hypothesis must be rejected as untrue*. At each stage then in the process of scientific reasoning *thought must be checked by sensation*.'[2]

But, as Dr Bailey sees, this account, which sounds so like the procedure of modern science, is not given by Epicurus himself, and it does not fit the results actually stated. The atomic theory is not a hypothesis which can be checked by sensation, nor is there any question of its being rejected as untrue. Dr Bailey himself has pointed this out, and he proceeds to put forward what is really a quite different description of the process of thought, and one which does explain the dogmatic certainty of Epicurus. The data for thought in this field cannot be directly supplied by sensation; for the ultimate realities, the atoms and space, cannot from their very

---

[1] C. Bailey, *Greek Atomists*, p. 265.
[2] *Ibid.* pp. 423–6 (my italics).

nature throw off 'idols'. The mind is dealing no longer with the images of sense-perception, but wholly with mental concepts. The concept is 'clear' in the very special sense of being 'self-evident': it is not formed arbitrarily by the loose and erratic operation of 'opinion', but is immediately grasped by an act of 'mental apprehension' (ἐπιβολὴ τῆς διανοίας). This operation might be called in modern terms 'the immediate intuition of a self-evident proposition': the mind 'looks' and sees a new picture that is perfectly 'clear' and could not be otherwise than it is. 'The whole of scientific thought is then to Epicurus a chain of such self-evident or "clear" concepts, grasped by the act of "mental apprehension" each in their due order; its "uniqueness" of truth is as inevitable as that of the science of mathematics. At each step we directly apprehend an image that is itself a precise and certain reproduction of imperceptible realities.'[1]

Dr Bailey hardly seems to be aware of the incompatibility of these two accounts; or else he is loyally reproducing a confusion made by Epicurus, who tried to believe that mental apprehension, grasping a clear view of the imperceptible, was a process of the same nature as sense-perception, whose clear view of a near object is a guarantee of absolute truth. In dealing with the things around us the clear view of the senses decides on the truth or falsity of our judgments. But in the region of the imperceptible a preliminary judgment, e.g. as to the way in which atoms move, though it may be based on some sensible analogy, cannot be refuted or confirmed by appeal to sensible experience. The decision rests with the self-evident conception, clearly seen by mental apprehension.[2]

In any case, the second account is the one which corresponds to Epicurean practice. Consider the argument whereby Lucretius introduces and establishes the atomic theory. He deduces it from a few axioms: nothing can come out of nothing; nothing can perish into nothing; bodies which cannot be seen nevertheless exist and act upon other things; without a void there could be no motion, and no differences in weight between bodies of the same size. These are examples of the self-evident truths immediately grasped by mental apprehension, though he supports them

[1] *Greek Atomists*, pp. 427–9.   [2] *Ibid.* p. 570.

by appealing to a wealth of facts which anyone can observe. Advancing from such premises, Lucretius arrives at all the conclusions about the nature and behaviour of atoms. The procedure is not such as to recommend itself to a modern man of science, who has witnessed the downfall of countless systems and theories based on postulates which claimed to be perfectly clear and self-evident. For many centuries astronomy had to accommodate the self-evident truth that the heavenly bodies must move in circles, because the circle is the most perfect figure.

The dogmatism of Epicurus about the imperceptible is thus seen to rest upon the belief in the infallibility of 'mental apprehension'. The nature of this activity has been carefully discussed by Dr Bailey. The word ἐπιβολή, translated by 'apprehension', primarily means the *projection* of the mind *towards*, or *turning* the attention *to*, some object, whether sensible or intelligible, so as to obtain a clear view or apprehension of it. This is no mere matter of passively receiving impressions or images thrust upon us by external objects. The materialist is prone to emphasize this passive aspect of cognition, which he can explain, however inadequately, by a theory of 'idols' composed of material particles entering the sense-organs and striking upon the material particles composing the soul. He cannot, however, give any account of the processes of thought without recognizing a movement in the opposite direction, a spontaneous and voluntary projection of the mind upon objects which cannot present themselves by an inflowing stream of impressions. The Epicurean in Cicero's dialogue says that we should not feel the need to postulate divine workmanship in the universe, if we could see the unbounded immensity of space in all directions, 'into which the mind strains and projects itself and travels so far and wide that it can see no ultimate shore on which it could find rest'. Lucretius uses the same metaphor, speaking of infinite space 'to which the intelligence (*mens*) yearns to look ever forward, and which the free projection of the mind traverses in its flight'.[1] Dr Bailey remarks that this projection of

----

[1] Cicero, *N.D.* I, 20, 54, in quam *se iniciens* animus et *intendens* ita late longeque *peregrinatur*; Lucr. II, 1046–7, quo prospicere usque velit mens atque *animi iactus liber* quo *pervolet* ipse.

the mind into infinite space is exactly the notion, as he has explained it, of the 'mental examination of a scientific concept'.[1] But, as we shall soon see, we have here something more than a mere metaphor. Metaphors, indeed, often deserve a closer scrutiny than they receive. Almost all our philosophical language is unconsciously metaphorical; and even when terms are still felt as metaphors, they may be used to conceal awkward gaps. Sometimes we find that a so-called metaphor enshrines a thought that was once meant literally. In the present case, the 'projection' of the mind, 'travelling' far and wide in its 'flight', is one of these fossilized thoughts. It represents a conception of mental activity that is really foreign to the materialist's empirical view of knowledge as built up from the impact of sense-impressions. How can this theory of incoming idols explain the power of thought to grasp the immensity of empty space, which could never despatch so much as a single idol? The Epicurean falls back upon a metaphor whose original meaning was that the mind has the power of escaping from the body and ranging at will on a flight into the unseen world. Epicurus' dogma of a soul consisting of atoms, which must be dispersed and lost as soon as they leave the body, forbids him to accept the literal sense of his words; but he perpetuates the metaphor to hide from himself and his readers the inability of his system to explain in its own materialistic terms the powers of the mind. Space cannot send idols into the mind; the mind cannot maintain its existence outside the body. Space should therefore be entirely unknowable; but since its existence and infinity are indispensable to the system and we can in fact think of infinite space, though we cannot imagine it, he is glad to borrow the language of a theory of knowledge based on a totally different view of the mind's nature and powers.

It is hard indeed to suppose that the earlier Ionians had established a genuinely scientific method, if it could be so entirely ignored by those who adopted atomism.

[1] *Greek Atomists*, p. 576.

CHAPTER III

THE EMPIRICAL THEORY OF KNOWLEDGE

THE argument of the last chapter has led us to see, in Epicurus' epistemology, a combination of two opposite theories of the sources of knowledge. As a materialist he aimed at building up all knowledge on the sure foundation of the senses, whose clear perceptions he would not allow to be discredited. All the furniture of the mind was to be derived from this source by the accumulation of impressions from the world outside, forming composite notions. The spontaneous activity of thought in manipulating these notions was to be reduced, so far as possible, to a power of fixing the attention and thus gaining a 'clear view' analogous to the close inspection which warrants the truth of sense-perception. Yet, when he came to objects and truths in the most important field, the wholly imperceptible, he was compelled to fall back, though under cover of a metaphor, on a belief in the power of the mind to project itself outside the body and apprehend wisdom which can never be revealed through sense. It is now time to disentangle these two opposite theories of the sources of wisdom and to trace their history. We shall begin with the empirical theory, which has the better claim to be called 'scientific'.

The clue leading us to the origin of this theory is furnished by the medical writers of the Hippocratic corpus. In particular, the author of the treatise *On Ancient Medicine*, who may have been Hippocrates himself, was clearly conscious of a profound opposition between the dogmatic method of the natural philosopher and the empirical method of the physician. His protest against the importation of the philosopher's procedure into his own art of healing is illuminating.

He opens at once with his attack on writers and lecturers who, in discussing medicine, base their whole discourse on an assumption or postulate, asserting that all disease is ultimately due to one or two factors—'heat, cold, moisture, dryness, or whatever else they may fancy'. This dogmatic starting-point leads them to make many statements which are manifestly false; but their worst fault is their failure to recognize that medicine is an art with a long-established existence of its own, whose value is acknowledged by all who invoke its services on the gravest occasions and hold its practitioners in high honour. The very differences among physicians in skill and experience are proof that the art is securely based on research and the discovery of facts.

Hence I claim that it has no need of empty postulates such as are inevitable in dealing with insoluble problems beyond the reach of observation (τὰ ἀφανέα τε καὶ ἀπορεόμενα), for example, what goes on in the sky and beneath the earth (περὶ τῶν μετεώρων ἢ τῶν ὑπὸ γῆν). If a man pronounces some opinion he has formed on how these things are, it cannot be clear either to himself or to his hearers whether what he says is true or not; for there is no test that can be applied so as to yield certain knowledge.

Here, more than a century before Epicurus, we find the characteristic scope of natural philosophy defined as limited to insoluble problems byond the reach of observation: the two main departments in which Epicurus admitted that the senses could give us no clear view, meteorology and the ultimate constituents of matter, 'heat and cold or whatever they may fancy'. Hippocrates (if we may so call the writer) considers that in these fields speculation must inevitably be dogmatic, laying down unfounded assumptions which cannot be brought to any test. We have seen, in studying Epicurus, how just the criticism proved to be.

Hippocrates goes on to contrast his own art with this arbitrary procedure. Medicine, he says, has for a long time past been completely furnished with a starting-point and a procedure of its own, which have led to many admirable discoveries. All that remains to be discovered will be found out, if the inquirer is competent and will start from a knowledge of the discoveries already made. If he follows any other method, he will only deceive himself and others. There is no need of remote and abstract assumptions. The doctor is dealing with the actual sufferings of ordinary men. He should discuss with them their symptoms in language which laymen can understand, and explain what is wrong with them and why they get better or worse. Then they will understand and remember what they are told. But if you fail to get on to this footing of mutual understanding, you will not arrive at the true state of the case. 'For this reason also medicine has no need of any postulate.'

Hippocrates proceeds to define what he believes to have been the starting-point of the medical art. Mankind originally lived like the brutes on fruit, wood and grass. The sufferings caused by this crude diet led to the invention of cooking, which combines strong and uncompounded elements with weaker ones, so as to suit man's constitution. These discoveries of a healthy form of nourishment constituted the art of medicine in its earliest shape; and fresh discoveries of the same sort are still being made by those whose function it is to keep the body in health. Remedial medicine arose from the fact that the sick require a different diet from that which suits the healthy. This led to further modifications of regimen adapted to the needs of various types of patient. Some may need stronger, some weaker forms of nourishment; excess in either direction may be dangerous. No absolute standards of measure and weight can be fixed; the only 'measure' is the individual patient's reaction. The best physician is he who makes the smallest mistakes in either direction. In some departments medicine has reached a high pitch of exactness; the old-established method should not be blamed because perfect accuracy has not been reached at all points.

Hippocrates now returns (ch. xiii) to the contrast between the empirical procedure he has described and the *a priori* dogmatism imported into medicine by natural philosophy. He attacks the new-fangled method of those who take as their starting-point a postulate, e.g. that all diseases are due to an excess of heat or cold or dryness or moisture, and must be remedied by counteracting each of these with its opposite: hot with cold, cold with hot, and so on. Hippocrates objects: (1) that, supposing a patient has suffered from crude diet and been cured by taking cooked food, you cannot say whether it is the heat or the coldness or the dryness or the moisture that has been removed from the diet; (2) that there is no such thing as an absolute 'hot' which can be administered to redress 'coldness'; a man must take hot water, or hot wine, or hot milk, and the water, wine, and milk will have different properties of their own, which will have more effect than the heat; (3) that experience shows that heat and cold have less effect in the body than any of the other 'powers'. In contrast to this philosophical theory of four abstract opposites, Hippocrates maintains, as the old-established result of discovery, that the human body is 'seen' to be composed of a vast number of things—saline, bitter, sweet, acid, astringent, insipid, etc.—possessing active properties[1] of all sorts, varying in quantity and strength. When these things are blended and compounded, they are not obtrusive or harmful; when any one of them is isolated and stands alone, it becomes apparent and does harm. Similarly, the harmful foods are those in which one of these properties is uncompounded and too strong. In normally cooked food, these too potent properties have been diluted and compounded into a single simple whole. 'A man is in the best possible condition when there is complete coction and rest, with no particular power displayed.'

This polemic against natural philosophy is very illuminating when we consider the history that lies behind it. The abstract conception, that bodies are composed of opposites and that their preservation is due to some sort of balance or blending of the hostile powers, their destruction to the wrongful prevalence of one opposite over the other, was first formulated by the philosophers. In studying Anaximander's system we shall find the four cardinal opposites mentioned by Hippocrates—hot and cold, moist and dry—playing a leading role in cosmogony. They can be identified with the four seasonal powers of summer and winter, rain and drought; and, in the order of space, they become the four elements of Empedocles, fire, air, water, earth. Anaximander had, moreover, the notion of a 'just' balance, periodically redressed when one power pays the penalty of its aggression to its opponent. But from this point philosophy and medicine begin to take different

---

[1] Or 'powers', δυνάμεις. A 'power' in the human body is defined as 'the intensities and strengths of the humours', ch. XXII.

ways; and we can name the physician who began the reaction against the philosophers. Alcmaeon of Croton in Southern Italy belongs to the early fifth century. He was in touch with the Pythagorean school in his native city, but 'most of his doctrines are medical, though he sometimes states a physical theory, as when he says that "most human things go in pairs"' (*D.L.* VIII, 83). In other words, he applied the physical doctrine of opposites to the constitution of the human body, with which he was concerned as a physician. Aristotle,[1] however, notes how he differed in two ways from the Pythagoreans. They had a list of exactly ten opposites, ten being the perfect number in their mathematical system. Alcmaeon admitted an indefinite number, just as Hippocrates maintains a 'vast number' of opposed powers as against the four opposites of the philosophers of his time. Secondly, Alcmaeon's opposites are less abstract and cosmic than the ten Pythagorean pairs: limited and unlimited, odd and even, one and many, right and left, male and female, rest and motion, straight and curved, light and darkness, good and evil, square and oblong. Alcmaeon, we are told, taught that health was preserved by an equality of the powers: moist, dry, cold, hot, bitter, sweet, *and so forth*; the sole domination of one opposite causes disease. Health is a duly proportioned blend of the qualities. Hippocrates adds to this indefinite list the names of other powers: saline, acid, astringent, insipid, and a 'vast number' more. The essential point is that the lists contain only sensible properties, whose presence in the body is directly perceived by sight, touch, and taste. These, says Hippocrates, the first discoverers of medicine (probably a reference to Alcmaeon himself) *saw* to be the constituents of the human body; any one of them when not duly compounded becomes *apparent* in its isolation. He amends Alcmaeon's list by omitting the old cosmic powers, hot, cold, moist and dry, on the ground that they cannot be visibly isolated like the others, but are always actually found in association with other qualities, and it is these others that cause disease. But this is a minor point. He accepts Alcmaeon's main doctrine as securely based on sensible experience, not on the 'empty postulates' of philosophy.

[1] *Met.* A 5, 986 a 22 ff.

35

The same attitude towards the intrusion of natural philosophy into the domain of medicine is taken in another treatise, *On the Nature of Man*, parts of which were ascribed to Hippocrates' son-in-law, Polybus. The author opens by saying that his work will not interest those accustomed to hear discussions of the human constitution which travel outside the range of medicine. He is not going to assert that man consists of air or fire or water or earth or anything else that cannot be plainly seen to be a component of the human body. He will set aside the underlying dogma that all reality is one thing; those who assert it cannot agree what this one thing is—air, or fire, or water, or earth—and the proofs they allege amount to nothing. When they debate in public, victory goes to the man with the most glib tongue; whereas it ought always to rest with him who knows the facts and can state his knowledge correctly. The writer then turns from these philosophic dogmatists to the physicians themselves, and attacks doctors who, though they do indeed point to constituents, such as blood, bile, and phlegm, which are visibly present in the body, are misled into adopting the philosophic postulate that man must consist of one thing only. 'They say that man is one thing, to which each of them gives what name he pleases; this one thing changes its form and power under constraint of the hot and the cold, and becomes sweet, bitter, white, black, and of every sort of quality.' He argues against this attempt to derive all the visible humours with their characteristic properties from any one of them. He takes his stand on what he considers to be the observed fact that

man's body has in itself blood, phlegm, yellow bile, and black bile; these make up the nature of his body and account for his feeling pain or enjoying health. His health is at its best when these things are duly proportioned to one another in respect of compounding, power, and bulk, and when they are blended in the best way. Pain is felt when one of them is in excess or defect or becomes isolated in the body instead of being compounded with all the others.

He appeals to various effects which can be observed in the treatment of wounds and illnesses.

It does not matter, for our purposes, that the Hippocratic physician seems to us moderns to have fallen, like his opponents, into the dogmatic snare. What matters is that he refuses to take as the starting-point of medical doctrine the physical or metaphysical postulate of the philosophers that all reality, and therefore the human body, must ultimately consist of one or more things which are not visibly present in the body. His own doctrine of the four humours was, in his eyes, founded on the direct evidence of the senses and supported by much accumulated experience of successful treatment.

The reason for this attitude towards *a priori* philosophy is, as we have said, not far to seek. We have already noted[1] that medicine was from the outset a practical art, long before it felt the need to develop anything resembling a scientific basis for its procedure. Hence, unlike the natural philosopher speculating on matters beyond the reach of observation, such as the origin of the world and 'what goes on in the sky and beneath the earth', the doctor is forced to start from the observation of individual cases, to note the symptoms, and to find out, if he can, what has gone wrong and how it can be set right. So far as we can see, it was in Alcmaeon's time, about the beginning of the fifth century, that medicine became sufficiently free from its magical phase to realize clearly the paramount claims of careful observation. The Hippocratic school is deservedly famous to this day for the minute records of individual cases preserved in the books on Epidemics. Such records were consciously designed to furnish the indispensable basis for generalized rules of art: 'In this case and in this, such and such a remedy proved helpful in this *kind* of fever.' Even if no remedy had been found, in each case the doctor's prognosis, the course and crises of the malady, and its outcome, were faithfully noted down. There remained the question of causes: why is this body out of order, and why does this remedy do good or prove useless? So, at the end, not at the beginning, comes the inquiry into the nature of man, the constitution of his body, the elements and 'powers' visibly present in him and needing to be adjusted and restored to equilibrium by the application of counteracting 'powers' present in substances administered from outside.

[1] P. 7 above.

It is in medicine, moreover, that we find the beginnings of a genuinely experimental procedure. Experiment starts with the trial of this or that remedy on some individual patient, to see whether it will work. It is a practical weapon, indispensable to the physician, but without any application, under ancient conditions, to the problems of the earliest natural philosophers. It was the doctors who first interrogated Nature with an open mind, prepared to accept the answer she gives and to modify their practice accordingly. Of all the recorded examples of anything resembling an experiment in this sense, the great majority occur in the medical writers.[1]

What now concerns us is the fact that the physician approached the question of the nature of man as it were from below, advancing towards it from what seemed to him the certain facts observed in particular cases. It was at this point that medicine came into conflict with natural philosophy, which had reached its theories of man's nature from the opposite quarter, descending to it from above. The philosophers began with cosmogony, inheriting the traditional problems implied in cosmogonical myths. How did a world order arise out of some primal unity or chaos? What was the original state of things? Were all things once nothing but water, or air, and are they at all times ultimately composed of a single element? How can what goes on in the sky be explained in natural terms? How did life arise, if it was not created by some god but came spontaneously out of the interaction of the elemental powers? So they arrived at theories of plant, animal, and human life. The nature of man thus came at the end of a long chain of reasoning from their original postulates;[2] and when they began, in the fifth century, to take an interest in medical questions, their

___

[1] Cf. the extracts from Heidel's account, pp. 8 f. above.

[2] As Aristotle remarks, *de Sensu*, 436a18: 'Since sickness and health can occur only in animate beings, the first principles of health and disease must fall within the province of the physicist. Hence practically all natural philosophers *end* with the subject of medicine; and physicians who pursue their art in a more philosophic spirit start their treatment of medicine from truths of natural philosophy.' At *de Resp.* 480b22 ff. the two disciplines are again described as different, but having a common boundary where the philosophers *end* and the more sophisticated physicians start.

doctrines of man's physical constitution were predetermined by their general theory of the constitution of all bodies in the universe. Man must be composed, like everything else, of water, or air, or the four elements, or atoms. Modern writers constantly speak of fifth-century philosophers as coming to take a prevailing interest in 'biology' or 'physiology', as against 'physics'. But we ought to realize that no such sciences had any independent existence. The field was divided between natural philosophy (or 'physics') and medicine, and the conflict arose at the boundary which they reached from their opposite standpoints—the nature of man.

Hippocrates himself was well aware of this. In *Ancient Medicine* (xx) he speaks of certain physicians and philosophers who tell us that no doctor can know medicine and treat his patients properly unless he knows the nature of man.

Their argument points to philosophy, like that of Empedocles and other writers on Nature who have described what man is from the beginning, how he first came into being and of what elements he was constructed. But, in my view, all that philosophers or physicians have written on Nature has no more to do with medicine than with painting. I also hold that medicine is the only source of clear knowledge about Nature; and that no one can attain to the certain knowledge of what man is, of the causes of his coming into being, and all the rest, until medicine itself has been properly comprehended.

He goes on to specify the right approach to these questions. The physician should start from the observed effects of various diets and habits of life on individuals. We are not to be content with unqualified statements, such as 'cheese is a bad food, because a surfeit of it causes pain'; we must know the nature of the pain, why it occurs, and what constituent of the human body is harmfully affected. Individual constitutions differ, according to the prevalence of this or that humour; and cheese will suit some temperaments, not others.

Such being the typical attitude of the physician towards the study of Nature, we should expect him, when he came to formulate a general theory of knowledge, to find the sources of knowledge in observation of facts by the use of the senses. Aristotle, himself the son of a practising physician, outlines this type of epistemology in the opening chapter of the *Metaphysics*. The faculty of sensation is common to all animals; and in some of them sensation gives rise to memory, making them more intelligent and, if they have the sense of hearing, capable of being taught. In man many memories of the same thing finally result in a unified experience.

Art comes into being when from many notions by experience a single general judgment about a class of similar objects is produced. Thus the judgment that this remedy benefited Callias when suffering from this disease, and also benefited Socrates, and so on in many individual cases, is a matter of experience; whereas to judge that it has done good to all persons of a certain constitution, marked off as a single class, when suffering from this disease, e.g. to phlegmatic or bilious people in a burning fever—this is a matter of art.

For purposes of practice, experience may be even more successful than theory without experience; because experience is knowledge of individuals, art of generalizations, and all action and production are concerned with the individual: 'the physician does not cure "Man", except incidentally, but Callias or Socrates or some other individual who happens to be a man.' On the other hand, we associate knowledge and understanding rather with art than with mere experience, which knows only the fact, but not the reason. So knowledge or wisdom in the full sense comes last with an understanding of causes. The senses are authoritative about particulars; they tell us that fire is hot; but they cannot tell us why it is hot. Wisdom is always regarded as concerned with the first causes and principles of things.

It is not for nothing that the illustrations given in the above description are all taken from the art of medicine. This theory of knowledge, as built up from the ground-work of sensation and perception, had already been mentioned by Plato among the speculations which had interested Socrates in his youth.[1] He had wondered whether the organ of thought is the blood (as Empedocles said) or air or fire; 'or whether it is none of these, but it is the brain that gives us our perceptions of sight, hearing, and smell, and from these arise memory and judgment, and from memory

[1] *Phaedo*, 96 B.

and judgment, when it has come to rest, arises knowledge'. The author of this doctrine is known to be none other than the physician Alcmaeon, who taught that man is distinguished by the possession of understanding from the animals who have only sensation; and that all the senses are linked together in the brain. Hence disturbance of the brain injures the senses and the power of thought.[1] Alcmaeon even tried, by dissection, to trace the 'pores' connecting the sense-organs with the brain.

The whole theory is recapitulated in the Hippocratic *Precepts* (ch. 1), following upon the injunction to attend, in medical practice, not to plausible theory but to experience combined with reflection. 'For the sense-perception, coming first in experience and conveying to the intellect the things subjected to it, is clearly imaged, and the intellect, receiving these things many times, noting the occasion, the time, and the manner, stores them up in itself and remembers.'[2] Theory should take its start from the experience that comes to it and proceed to infer its conclusions from phenonema. Our nature is compulsorily stirred and instructed by the great variety of facts; the intellect then takes over from it these impressions and later leads us to truth. If it starts, not from a clear impression but from some plausible fiction (postulate), we shall lose ourselves in a blind alley. The doctor must be persistently occupied with facts, not hesitating to question his patients. 'For so I think the whole art has been set forth, by observing some part of the final end in each of many particulars, and then combining all into a single whole.'

Another reference to the theory may be traced in Plato (*Gorg.* 501 A) where he contrasts the true art of medicine, 'which has studied the nature of the body it cares for and the reasons for its

---

[1] This view, that man is intelligent so long as the brain is still, is adopted by the Hippocratic author of *The Sacred Disease*, XVII, and alluded to in Plato's *Cratylus*, 437 A, where ἐπι-στήμη is derived from ἵστησιν ἐπὶ τοῖς πράγμασι τὴν ψυχήν, and Aristotle, *Phys.* 247 b 10, τῷ γὰρ ἠρεμῆσαι καὶ στῆναι τὴν διάνοιαν ἐπίστασθαι καὶ φρονεῖν λεγόμεθα, and *Post. An.* 100 a 7.

[2] Translated by Dr W. H. S. Jones (Loeb ed. of Hippocrates, vol. 1, p. 306), who thinks that the language of chs. 1 and 11 of the *Precepts* betrays Epicurean influence; but Heidel (*Hippocr. Medicine*, p. 73) maintains that there is nothing here that might not well have been said by any thoughtful Greek at the middle of the fifth century. He refers to *Dialexeis* 9 (*Vors.*[5] 11, p. 416).

operations, and can give an account of all these things', with the irrational practice of the confectioner, which can produce pleasure (not health) because by mere experience (without art) it has 'preserved a memory of what usually happens'.

The evidence all points to the conclusion that the empirical theory of knowledge was a medical theory, first formulated by Alcmaeon. It arose naturally from reflection on the actual procedure of the practising physician. It dates from the time when the most intelligent doctors were feeling the impulse to disentangle their art from its magical antecedents. This was the same impulse towards rationalism that had already driven the Milesian philosophers to disengage cosmogony from its mythical trappings. But whereas the philosopher had recourse to abstract postulates about the original state of things, the physician, with his attention constantly fixed on individual cases needing to be dealt with practically, moved in the other direction, from observed particulars to generalizations.

Under ancient conditions, moreover, medicine was the only practical art that was impelled by its immediate interests to build up something that we can recognize as the embryonic form of empirical science. In the last hundred years natural philosophy (as it used to be called) has come to be known as 'natural science' and even simply as 'science', as if its characteristic method of observation, hypothesis ānd experiment were the only means of arriving at knowledge, and the habits of matter in motion were the only things that can be known. Since the term 'science' has now acquired these arrogant associations, the application of it to the natural philosophy of Greece is perpetually misleading the reader, since it at once suggests to his mind the whole apparatus of the modern laboratory and the whole outlook of its denizens. It also suggests a long list of specialized departments—physics, chemistry, biology, philosophy and so on—and these specialist names are frequently used in histories of ancient philosophy as if these several disciplines had already been distinguished. All these illusions should be dismissed from our minds. The only discipline before the time of Aristotle which can safely be described as 'natural science' at least in a nascent stage is medicine. This was clear enough to Aristotle himself. When he set his three pupils or colleagues, Theophrastus, Eudemus, and Meno, to write the histories of earlier thought, he divided the field into (1) metaphysics and natural philosophy, (2) mathematics, and (3) medicine. Evidently he felt the force of the Hippocratic contention that medicine stood alone as a long-established art with a starting-point and procedure of its own, independent of, and even opposed to, the principles and procedure of the physicists and metaphysicians and of mathematics.

We can also see why none of the other practical arts of antiquity showed any tendency to develop into a science. Medicine, as we have seen, had its point of contact with natural philosophy where the two met in the question of the 'nature of man'. But there was nothing whatever to connect the arts of building, weaving, agriculture, pottery and so on with the speculations of the philosophers about the origin of the world and the ultimate constituents of matter. It could not occur to anyone's mind that the debate whether matter consists of atoms or of the four elements could have any bearing on the invention of more efficient types of loom or plough. The common idea that the Ionian philosophers in particular aimed at the 'conquest of Nature' and the harnessing of natural forces to industrial production is due entirely to the confusion of their aims and methods with those of the modern man of science since the Renaissance. The Ionians were not setting out to discover 'laws of nature' with a view to setting the forces concerned to drive machines and thereby raise the level of human comfort. If this had been their aim, they would have had to follow the physician's procedure. They would have started with careful observation of facts and advanced to generalizations, with constant recourse to experiment, to see whether their conclusions would work. But we find nothing of this sort. The 'experiments' recorded as having been made by natural philosophers are very few, and they hardly deserve the name. They are, in fact, illustrations of foregone conclusions.[1]

Of all the natural philosophers, the Atomists, as being the most

[1] Cf. the *clepsydra* and wineskins of Empedocles and Anaxagoras above, pp. 5 f.

materialistic, made the most gallant attempt to carry through the empirical theory of knowledge presented to them by the physicians. They would have liked to build up the whole of knowledge on the basis of sense impressions produced by the 'idols' thrown off by particular tangible bodies. Our purpose in reviewing the system of Epicurus was to show how his actual method of reaching all his most important doctrines was totally inconsistent with this notion of how knowledge is obtained. His mind was irresistibly dominated by an opposite conception which he shared with all the other philosophers. To this we must now turn.

CHAPTER IV

ANAMNESIS

W HEN Plato founded the Academy, shortly after his return from his first visit to Italy and Sicily (388–387 B.C.),
he already possessed something that might be called a
system of philosophy, if the word 'system' did not carry the
suggestion of a body of thought that has been rounded out and
closed in a final form. Such a suggestion is false to the whole spirit
of Platonism, which, to its author, always remained a philosophy
in the proper sense, a pursuit of wisdom. Some of the adventures
of this pursuit are recorded in the great dialogues of the middle
period: the *Meno, Phaedo, Symposium, Republic* and *Phaedrus*. Taken
as a whole, these dialogues set forth a theory of knowledge and of
its objects which is recognized by the general judgment of ancient
and modern scholars as characteristically Platonic. The *Meno*,
which may be safely regarded as the earliest of the five works
above-mentioned, is concerned with the way in which knowledge
is acquired. This question is now linked with the immortal
nature of the soul, the foundation stone of the new edifice. In the
Phaedo attempts are made to prove that the soul not only will
survive the death of the body, but has already existed before it
became incarnate. At the same time, it is asserted that the Forms
or 'Ideas', which are the true objects of knowledge, are equally
independent of the particular concrete things that embody them,
or images of them, in the sensible world. The Theory of Forms is
already expanding into a metaphysical theory of the nature of
things, such as Aristotle tells us lay beyond the range of Socrates'
speculation. In so far as it is possible to indicate a point where the
thought of Socrates passes over into the far-reaching vision of
the universe that we call Platonism, we have here reached that
threshold.

We can, moreover, make out what it was that enabled Plato to
advance so far beyond his master. There is, indeed, a sense in which

the whole of Platonism is an expansion and completion of the Socratic doctrine, Goodness is knowledge. The theory of Ideas gives to this formula a more definite content by adding a clearer conception of the nature of knowledge and of its objects; it tells us also how this knowledge is gained. But this development does not arise solely from reflection on the Socratic formula. The new light comes from another source, already indicated in the *Gorgias*, namely the mathematical and religious philosophy of the Pythagoreans. The Platonic theory of Ideas is described by Aristotle as a variety of Pythagoreanism, its peculiar features being due to reflection on what was implied in Socrates' attempts to define moral terms. In his eyes Platonism was, in fact, rather Pythagoreanism modified by Socratic influence than Socraticism modified by Pythagorean influence. This view of the historical perspective has an authority which cannot be shaken by anything less than a proof that it is inconsistent with the Platonic writings. In my opinion, no such proof has ever been produced.

Before turning to the new solution of the problem of knowledge presented in the *Meno*, it is well to remind ourselves that to a disciple of Socrates this problem meant, in the first place, the problem of that knowledge which Socrates had identified with goodness. The theory of Ideas is sometimes treated as if Plato had set out to discover a theoretical justification for what is now called 'science'. We must cling to the fact that in Plato's time no one of the imposing array of specialized natural sciences as now conceived and established—physics, chemistry, geology, botany and so on—had any existence. It cannot, therefore, have been the purpose of the theory of Ideas to provide them with a 'methodology'. We learn, moreover, from Aristotle that Plato in his youth had adopted the Heraclitean principle that all sensible things are in a perpetual flow of change, so that there can be no knowledge of them: and Aristotle adds that in later life he held fast to this opinion. Plato was not seeking a basis for any science of the sensible world; he was, in the first instance, seeking to give an account of that knowledge which must direct the conduct of human life. The objects he discovered were not laws of nature, if by that we mean formulas describing the sequence of sensible phenomena, or anything of that sort. The theory grew upon his hands into a doctrine of an intelligible 'nature of things', consciously opposed to the materialism which identified reality with the elementary components of tangible bodies. But in its inception it was rather a theory of Ideals to regulate moral conduct. Socrates had been convinced that all men, if their minds could be cleared of the mists of prejudice and false beliefs, would see the true end of life and could not then fail to desire it. But they cannot be just until they know what Justice is. The theory of Ideas asserts that Justice and other such ideals are eternal objects of thought which can be known and which possess universal and unconditional validity. They are not part of the furniture of your private world or of mine; nor are they arbitrary conventions of society. They form a common world independent of us all. They are, in fact, the absolute objects of the Socratic knowledge on which all virtue depends.

The *Meno* opens abruptly with an old question: how is goodness acquired? Is it innate, or formed as a habit by exercise, or can it be taught? Socrates observes that before we ask how goodness is to be acquired, we ought to know what it is. The definitions suggested by Meno fail to stand criticism; and he complains that Socrates is like the electric fish which benumbs its victims. At this point a dialogue of the earliest type would have ended in a confession of failure; but in the *Meno* this part is only prefatory. Plato goes on to raise the general question: how is it possible, in such an undertaking, to proceed further? From our failure to define the common character in a number of things called 'virtues', it appears that we do not *know* the thing we are looking for. How, then, is it possible to look for it, and how can we ever tell whether we have found it or not? This problem had been crudely formulated, possibly by some sophist who criticized Socrates' search for definitions. It demands an answer.

It seemed quite clear to Plato that knowledge of the kind that Socrates sought, knowledge of the meaning of moral terms such as 'goodness' or 'virtue', could never be accounted for by the apparatus of the empirical theory of knowledge. Goodness cannot be perceived by any sense, and a definition of it cannot be distilled out of accumulated impressions of colours, sounds, and so on, stored in the record of our personal experience. The *Meno*, moreover, contains evidence of a newly awakened interest in mathematics, the only abstract science then existing which had developed a systematic logical procedure for the discovery of new truths. Whether independently or through contact with the mathematicians of Cyrene and Southern Italy, Plato came to recognize that mathematical objects are not the concrete things around us, but objects of thought known by the mind when, as the *Phaedo* says, it withdraws from the senses to think 'by itself'. Arithmetic and geometry consist of a system of truths which do not even hold good of the visible and tangible things of sense, and which cannot be proved by reference to such things. They belong to a supersensible world, accessible to our intelligence, but not to the organs of sight or touch or hearing.

This was not entirely a fresh discovery. Protagoras, who championed the world of appearance against the Eleatic denial of its reality, had written an attack on mathematics in which he argued that lines and figures such as geometry defines are not to be found in the actual world: a straight ruler does not touch a circular body only at one indivisible point.[1] We hear from Aristotle of some Pythagoreans who had drawn no distinction between mathematical solids and physical bodies, but argued as if geometrical demonstrations applied directly to natural objects. Protagoras' polemic was bound to bring home to the more philosophical mathematicians that they had all along been dealing with concepts, simpler than percepts and free from the imperfections of material things. Plato, at any rate, had clearly grasped that the numbers of arithmetic are not identical with collections of things, and that the lines, planes and solids of geometry are ideal objects to which material bodies can only approximate. He further saw that these mathematical objects have all the characters which make them knowable in a way that sensible things can never be known. They are perfect and exact, having neither more nor less content than is expressed in their definitions. They are exempt from time and change: nothing that is true about the sphere or the triangle can ever cease to be true at some other time because the object has

[1] Aristotle, *Met.* B 997 b 35.

changed in the interval. Finally, the knowledge we have of their properties can 'give an account' of itself; the properties are deduced by a rigid chain of reasoning, such that anyone who has understood the premisses must see the certainty of the conclusions. The name of knowledge cannot be refused to such a system of eternal objects and necessary truths.

Further, if these objects can be known, they must surely be real; for 'the perfectly real' must be identical with 'the perfectly knowable'.[1] The power of thought has broken through the surface of fleeting appearances and disclosed beyond it an objective 'nature of things' of a quite different order from the material elements or atoms of the physicists.

Now, if these real objects of thought are not to be found in the physical world and cannot be extracted from it, how do we come to know them? How is it that the geometer, shutting his eyes and thinking about objects he can never have seen or touched, can discover fresh truths he has not heard from any teacher? Whence does this knowledge come? Plato argued that it must come out of the mind itself; it is raised into consciousness by some process analogous to that whereby we recall some object we have formerly been acquainted with and have forgotten. This is the famous doctrine that 'learning', the process of acquiring knowledge in the full sense, is Recollection (*Anamnesis*).

Socrates brings foward this doctrine as furnishing a possible solution of the problem raised by Meno: how can we look for something we do not know, and how can we tell when we have found it? Socrates has heard it from 'men and women who are wise in divine matters', 'priests and priestesses who have been concerned to give an account of their proceedings'. It has also been stated by many inspired poets, including Pindar.

They say that the soul of man is immortal; now it comes to that end which men call dying, and now it is born again, but it is never destroyed. We ought therefore, they say, so long as we live to keep ourselves as pure as we can.

For as for those from whom Persephone exacts the penalty of the ancient woe, in the ninth year she gives up their souls again to the

----

[1] *Rep.* v, 477A.

sunlight in this world above. From these come noble princes and men swift in strength and highest in wisdom; and for all time to come men call them pure heroes.[1]

Since, then, the soul is immortal and has been born many times, since it has seen all things both in this world and in the other, there is nothing it has not learnt. No wonder, then, that it is able to recall to mind goodness and other things, for it knew them beforehand. For, as all reality is akin and the soul has learnt all things, there is nothing to prevent a man who has recalled—or, as people say, 'learnt'—only one thing from discovering all the rest for himself, if he will pursue the search with unwearying resolution. For on this showing all inquiry or learning is nothing but recollection.

In order to convince Meno that knowledge can be gained without teaching, Socrates conducts his experiment with one of Meno's slaves, who has never been taught geometry. By means of questioning he elicits from the slave the solution of a not very easy problem, the construction of a square which shall be double a given square. (This involves the theorem about the square on the hypotenuse, which the ancients ascribed to Pythagoras himself.) Socrates claims that he is not teaching or imparting information: he only asks questions. The slave is producing his own opinions. At first, his opinions are wrong; but, still by questions, he is led on to see his mistakes and to produce true opinions. It is possible, then, to possess, somewhere in one's mind, true opinions about things one does not know. If the slave were repeatedly put through the demonstration, these opinions would be converted into knowledge. This means that he would come to see clearly the necessary connexions of reason and consequence and to feel that complete certainty which no argument could shake. He would not merely believe the conclusion, as he now does; he would know it. By the same method, he might be made to produce knowledge of 'the whole of geometry and all the other mathematical sciences' (μαθήματα, 85 E).

In conclusion, Socrates argues that the slave, not having learnt geometry in this life, must have acquired his knowledge before he was born, or indeed have possessed it always. 'And if the truth

---

[1] Pindar, Dirges, frag. 133.

of things is at all times in the soul, the soul must be immortal.' Socrates adds, however, that he is not prepared to defend this theory at all points, though he is satisfied that we shall be the better for not allowing ourselves to be debarred by any objection from inquiring after things we do not know. Plato's dramatic method leaves us in uncertainty as to the extent of this reservation. It might mean no more than a warning to the reader not to suppose that the real Socrates had accepted the doctrine of immortality and reincarnation which he says he has heard. Or it might mean that Plato himself, though convinced of the soul's immortality and of its access, through pure thought, to the truth about reality, is not committed to the whole theological scheme of reincarnation and the myths associated with it.

That Plato himself was convinced of the pre-existence of the soul, its inherently immortal nature, and its power of recollections, is clear from the *Phaedo*, where the theory of Recollection is re-affirmed and supported by fresh arguments. The experiment in the *Meno* is there alluded to, not by Socrates, but by the young Theban Kebes, who reminds his friend Simmias of 'one admirable argument, that when people are questioned, if the questions are well framed, they will give a true account of anything. They could not do so unless they had in them knowledge and a right account of the matter. If you confront them with geometrical diagrams and things of that sort, it becomes abundantly clear that this is so.' The words 'if the questions are well framed' may possibly point to some uneasiness in Plato's mind. The experiment conducted on the slave might be criticized on the ground that many of Socrates' questions are leading questions. At any rate, Plato now offers another proof, which dispenses with the intervention of a questioner, recollection being occasioned by acts of perception. The conclusion reached is that our knowledge of such a concept as absolute equality must have been obtained before birth. It cannot be derived from sense-perception because our senses never show us two perfectly equal things. The sight of approximately equal things revives the thought of perfect equality—an ideal standard which they seem to be striving after and of which we judge that they fall short. The weak point in the argument lies in the statement that we make such judgments, implying acquaintance with perfect equality, as soon as we begin to use our senses; whereas in truth such judgments are highly reflective and not made by infants. It seems quite clear, however, that Plato thought the argument valid. It provides the one substantial proof of pre-existence in the first part of the dialogue and it is accepted and reaffirmed by all parties to the discussion.

In the Meno the theory of Anamnesis was put forward to escape the sophistic dilemma: either we know a thing, and then there is no need to look for it; or we do not know it, and then we cannot know what we are looking for. The dilemma assumed that the only choice is between complete knowledge and blank ignorance. Anamnesis provides for degrees of knowledge between these two extremes.

There is, in the first place, unconscious knowledge, which may be present in our minds without our being aware of it or ever having been aware of it since we were born. The contrast between latent knowledge and blank ignorance is familar in common experience. We are often sure that we know a certain person's name, but cannot recall it. The information is somewhere 'at the back of our mind' and we know enough about it to reject suggestions felt to be incorrect. If we leave it alone, it appears to force its way into consciousness. All this, of course, is a matter of the ordinary memory of past experience. But there is some analogy with the effort of the Meno to grasp the meaning of the term 'virtue' or 'goodness'. We have never yet known the full meaning in this life, but the question 'What is virtue?' does mean something to us: if the word 'virtue' corresponded to a complete blank in our minds, we could not discuss the question or reject suggested definitions as inadequate. The state of mind is described by Laches where he says: 'I am really annoyed that I cannot express what I have in my mind. I seem to myself to have a notion of what courage is, but somehow it has escaped me just now, so that I cannot formulate it and say what it is.'[1] Our experience is somewhat similar

---

[1] Laches, 194 B: ὡς ἀληθῶς ἀγανακτῶ εἰ οὑτωσὶ ἃ νοῶ μὴ οἶός τ' εἰμὶ εἰπεῖν. νοεῖν μὲν γὰρ ἔμοιγε δοκῶ περὶ ἀνδρείας ὅτι ἔστιν, οὐκ οἶδα δ' ὅπῃ με ἄρτι διέφυγεν, ὥστε μὴ συλλαβεῖν τῷ λόγῳ αὐτὴν καὶ εἰπεῖν ὅτι ἔστιν. Cf. Euthyphro, 11 B.

when the mind is, as Plato says, 'pregnant' or 'in labour with' some thought which is pressing to birth. In this case what is striving to come to the surface is not some single item of past experience, such as a temporarily forgotten name registered somewhere in the ordinary memory. It is a more complex thought or idea which has never yet been present to consciousness. Socrates' method of asking questions, compared in the *Theaetetus* to the midwife's art, aims at raising such thoughts to the conscious level. It relieves the painful labour of the mind by bringing its own contents to birth; it does not put into the mind anything that was not already there.

Here is the difference between learning from a teacher and discovering truth for oneself, on the prompting of some external stimulus. The teacher 'hands over' information—transfers it from his mind to the learner's. But in Recollection, there is, as Socrates said, 'nothing to prevent a man who has recalled only one thing from discovering all the rest for himself, if he will pursue the search with unwearying resolution'.

Probably Plato had observed what happened in his own mind when he made a discovery. We cannot account for such an occurrence, if we confine ourselves to the bald dilemma: we must either know a thing or not know it—either be fully conscious of it or in a state of blank ignorance. We must take into account Plato's third factor, unconscious knowledge. A new theory or generalization appears to grow and take shape at the back of the mind. We have only enough inkling of it to guide attention to the right quarter. The embryo theory seems to gather force in the submerged region and to strive for expression. In the moment of discovery, it breaks into full consciousness with an effect of sudden illumination, overwhelmingly convincing and self-evident.

In a letter of 1841, Robert Mayer described his discovery of the conservation of energy. Mayer was not a physicist, but a doctor; he was on a voyage, working at physiology. He writes:

If one wishes to be enlightened about physiological matters, some knowledge of physical processes is indispensable, unless one prefers to work from the metaphysical side, which is immensely distasteful to me. I therefore kept to physics, clinging to the subject with such ardour that, although it may seem ridiculous to say so, I cared little about what part of the world we were in. I preferred to remain aboard where I could work uninterruptedly, and where many an hour gave me such a feeling of being inspired in a way I can never remember having experienced either before or since. A few flashes of thought that thrilled through me were immediately diligently pursued, leading again in their turn to new subjects. Those times are passed, but subsequent quiet examination of what then emerged, has taught one that it was a truth which can not only be subjectively felt, but also proved objectively; whether this could be done by one who has so little knowledge of physics as I have, is a matter which obviously I must leave undecided.

Heim, in his book on Energetics, expresses the opinion:

that Robert Mayer's new thought did not gradually detach itself, by dint of revolving it in his mind, from the conceptions of power transmitted from the past, but belongs to those ideas that are intuitively conceived, which, originating in other spheres of a mental kind, surprise thought, as it were, compelling it to transform its inherited notions conformably with those ideas.[1]

These quotations illustrate a kind of experience that Plato must certainly have had; there must, indeed, have been some moment when the theory of Ideas itself flashed upon his mind and illuminated the problem of a knowledge independent of sensible experience. The pieces of the puzzle suddenly fitted together: what was implied in Socrates' attempts to define universal terms, and the *a priori* discovery of geometrical truth. All this could be explained if mathematical and moral concepts are eternal objects of thought, to be known without the intervention of the senses; and if the knowledge of them is not distilled or extracted from the changing things of sense, but recovered out of a memory always latent in the soul.

So far, we have been able to illustrate the doctrine of *Anamnesis* from experiences universally recognized, but capable of explanations which do not involve the acquisition of knowledge before birth, without the use of the senses. We must next consider the

[1] These quotations are borrowed from C. G. Jung, *Analytical Psychology*, trans. C. E. Long, London, 1920, p. 411.

features of the doctrine which go beyond what would now be commonly admitted.

Obviously it is only knowledge of a certain kind that can be thus recovered. Historical knowledge in the widest sense—the facts and events of human or natural history—is not contained in the inner consciousness. We are not born with the knowledge that the battle of Marathon was fought in 490 B.C., or that fire burns if we touch it. Such facts are learnt by sensible experience, or taught by various sources of information; and they are registered in the ordinary personal memory. To these records Plato refuses the name of knowledge. They constitute what, in common with the empiricists, he calls 'experience which merely preserves a memory of what usually happens', in contrast with 'art' which understands the nature of its object and the reasons for its procedure.[1]

It is clear that in Plato's middle period his attention was concentrated on mathematical truth and those moral ideals the knowledge of which, as sought by Socrates, was to regulate conduct. The essential feature of these objects, that which makes them in the full sense knowable, is their eternal and unchanging nature. They are outside and beyond the flow of time and becoming in which everything the senses can perceive is involved. All previous philosophy had been the search for some permanent and unchanging 'nature of things'; but the physicists had imagined that this was to be found in some ultimate form of matter. Plato, having accepted Heracleitus' intuition that nothing in the sensible world is exempt from change, but every form of matter is perpetually dying and being reborn in a different form, could only declare that the permanent reality was immaterial and accessible only to pure thought. In the objects of mathematics and in the moral forms he recognized realities having these necessary attributes. Knowledge, accordingly, was limited to our apprehension of them.

All this means, of course, that the memory containing this knowledge is not the personal or individual memory, the waxen

[1] *Gorg.* 501 A: τριβῇ καὶ ἐμπειρίᾳ μνήμην μόνον σωζομένη τοῦ εἰωθότος γίγνεσθαι.

tablet of the empiricist, which registers sense-impressions that have flowed in upon us since birth and all the information we have 'learnt' in the ordinary sense. The memory implied in the doctrine of *Anamnesis* is an impersonal memory. Its contents are the same in all human beings. Any two persons who have clearly conceived the definition of the triangle and proceed to reflect upon it will be led to discover exactly the same truths about it, or, if they differ, the one can convince the other of his mistake. The only difference between individuals will lie in the extent to which the latent knowledge has been recovered. According to the *Meno*, the whole of knowledge can be recovered in this way. 'All reality is akin': the structure of truth forms a single coherent system, in which the parts are linked together by logical necessity. The recovery of a single link is enough to lead the mind on to further truths without limit.

It has long been recognized that the close connexion of *Anamnesis* with reincarnation and with mathematics points to Pythagorean sources. Where the belief in reincarnation exists, it is held that the soul must have forgotten its previous lives and its experiences in the other world, as the souls in the myth of Er drink of the River of Unmindfulness before returning to be born again. But some souls drink more of the water, some less. This means that the less forgetful spirits can recover during this life some part of the forgotten knowledge. In popular belief, in present-day Burma for example, the Buddhist quite commonly remembers enough of his previous life to identify the dead person whose soul has passed into his own body. The belief in this form appears in the legend of Pythagoras. Empedocles[1] describes him as 'a man of surpassing knowledge, who had won the utmost wealth and wisdom and was well skilled in all manner of works; for whenever he reached out with all his mind, he easily saw everything that is, in ten, yea, twenty lifetimes of men'. The last words here may refer to the tradition that Pythagoras, like the Buddhist, could recall his previous incarnations.[2] But the passage as a whole suggests much

[1] Empedocles, B 129 (*Vors.*[5] I, p. 364). Rohde, Diels, Delatte, Burnet and others agree that the reference is to Pythagoras.
[2] See Heracleides Ponticus *ap.* D.L. VIII, 4 (*Vors.*[5] I, p. 100).

more than this—not a mere recollection of past experiences in this world, but the 'utmost wealth of wisdom', a vision of 'everything that is', gained in a state of exaltation when the powers of the mind were stretched to their furthest extent. Empedocles' description is, in fact, compatible with Socrates' view of the range of recoverable knowledge in the *Meno*; and it is at least possible that Pythagoras himself regarded the mathematical discoveries that came to him in moments of intensely concentrated thought as revelations 'seen' when his spirit had thrown off the trammels of the flesh and visited the unseen world. This possibility will appear more probable in the light of our later argument. But we cannot tell how far the doctrine of the *Meno* goes beyond Pythagorean tradition as known to Plato.[1]

The point in which Plato unquestionably agrees with the Pythagoreans is the belief that the human soul is an independent substance which has existed before it entered its present bodily habitation and will exist again apart from the body after death. It is, moreover, not merely indestructible but conscious and intelligent, in possession of knowledge which it has not obtained through the bodily senses. The purpose of the *Phaedo* is to recommend this belief in a separate intelligence (νοῦς χωριστός) concurrently with the equally unfamiliar belief that the objects known by this intelligence are Forms separate from material things (χωριστὰ εἴδη). The protreptic discourse of Socrates, which precedes the argumentative portion of the *Phaedo*, opens with a definition of death which prejudges the question of survival. Death is defined as 'the deliverance of the soul from the body': 'to be dead' means that 'the body has come to be by itself in separation from the soul, and the soul by itself in separation from the body' (64 c). In accordance with the religious doctrine to which Socrates has already appealed, the animal pleasures are condemned as chaining the soul to its material associate. The senses—even sight and hearing—are no better than a hindrance to thought. The soul that is in love with wisdom takes flight from all fellowship with the body. Its one desire is to gather itself together out of the body and

[1] This question has been discussed by A. Cameron, *The Pythagorean Background of the Theory of Recollection*, Wisconsin, 1938.

withdraw by itself to contemplate realities the senses cannot reveal. This is that 'purification', followed by the vision of truth, which the mysteries enjoin. In this world, at the best, the withdrawal can be but imperfectly achieved. Bodily death will be the final and complete deliverance.

Thus the conversation in the *Phaedo* opens, not with argument, but with a passage of religious eloquence upon the meaning of life and death, in which the author's conviction has plainly carried him beyond the domain of rational proof. Doubts are raised later, and arguments devised to counter them. Recollection is again offered as a proof of pre-existence: the soul which can exist apart from the body is the element in us which thinks and knows the Forms which exist apart from material things.

It is only when this conception of the rational soul and the objects of its thought has been clearly brought before the reader's mind, that one of the young Thebans puts forward the materialistic view of the soul or vital principle as a mere 'harmony' or 'adjustment' of the physical opposites comprising the body. Such a soul could not exist independently; but pre-existence has by this time been established by the proof of Recollection, which is bound up with the existence of the Forms (92 D). And about the existence of the Forms Plato has no serious doubts.

The harmony doctrine is closely related to the medical theory of health as the balance or due proportion of opposite 'powers' in the body; indeed it seems to identify the soul with the healthy condition of the living body, disease being an upsetting of the balance, which, if it goes beyond a certain point, will entail the dissolution of the bodily elements in death. Plato's doctrine of the separately existing intelligence is sharply opposed to this, just as, on the side of the objects of intelligence, his separate and eternally existing Forms are contrasted with the images which, according to the empirical epistemology, flow into our senses from material bodies. The medical-empirical apparatus of materialism seemed to Plato utterly inadequate to account for the knowledge which we certainly obtain in mathematical discovery, as well as for the knowledge of absolute moral standards on which 'virtue', in the full Socratic sense, depends.

To return now to the *Meno*. As we remarked earlier, the dilemma which was to be solved by *Anamnesis* assumed that there were no degrees of knowledge intermediate between complete knowledge and blank ignorance. The experiment with the slave showed that this was not so: his mind contained beliefs which he had never been taught and which could be awakened by questioning. Some of these beliefs were true, some false. Even the true ones could not be called knowledge until the slave should have been taken through the demonstration many times and come to see the necessary connexions. He would then not merely be thinking correctly; he would know with unshakable certainty (85 c). Towards the end, Socrates returns to this point. A true belief may be as useful a guide to action as knowledge: a man who is correctly informed about the road to Larissa will get there as well as one who knows the road by having travelled over it himself. But his belief will be insecure; a second informant might persuade him that he had been misdirected. True belief is converted into knowledge by 'reflection on the reason', binding a whole set of true beliefs into a coherent system. And this work of reflection, says Socrates, 'is recollection, as we agreed earlier' (98 A). The reference is to the passage where all reality was said to be 'akin', so that, when the mind has picked up a single link in the chain, there is nothing to prevent it from discovering all the rest for itself. This history of mathematical discoveries would illustrate how isolated theorems, such as the Pythagorean proposition itself, had been divined by acts of intuition, but the task of proving them had forced mathematicians to follow the chains of reasoning back, through more 'elementary' propositions, to the original definitions and axioms. It thus appears that *Anamnesis* is a long, if not an endless, process. Starting from the awakening of a single correct belief or (to look at it in another way) a single act of intuition, the work of reflection or reasoning (λογισμός) may continue indefinitely until, if that were possible, the whole logical structure of truth should have been recovered.

Nothing short of the goal could be called knowledge in the fullest sense. As the *Republic* points out, even the entire structure of geometry depends on premisses which may have been unwarrantably assumed to be self-evident and ought really to be guaranteed by deduction from the highest of all principles. Plato is now coming to conceive the knowledge which is true virtue as involving nothing less than an insight into the whole structure of reality, to be reached by arduous training in mathematics and moral philosophy, leading to a vision of the ultimate Form which irradiates the universe with the light of truth.

At the end of the *Meno* Socrates returns to the question: can virtue be taught? The theory of *Anamnesis* had given a totally new meaning to 'teaching' and 'learning', but we are left to think out the consequences for ourselves. They come to this. (1) All knowledge worthy of the name is recovered out of our own minds. No 'teaching' in the usual sense is needed: the midwife's art of Socrates will bring latent thoughts to birth, and his elenchus will clear away the false ones. The knowledge on which true philosophic virtue depends will be gained by this process; but it cannot be 'taught' in the ordinary sense.[1] (2) Ordinary teaching and learning mean the 'handing over' of information from one person to another (93 B). A system of morality laid down by philosophers on the strength of their own knowledge could be taught to the citizens of a state under their control. This would never be more than 'true belief'; but it would be a sufficient guide for action, and would amount to the lower or 'popular' kind of virtue.

Finally comes the suggestion that comparatively good statesmen are guided, not by knowledge or wisdom (φρόνησις), but by a sort of inspiration, like that of the seer and the poet, who 'in their rapt condition say many true things, but do not *know* what they mean'. They have not intelligence (νοῦς), but are 'possessed by divine inspiration'. This suggestion is not explicitly connected with

---

[1] The ostensible conclusion of the *Meno* (98 D–E) disguises this result, by resuming the argument that virtue cannot be knowledge, because, if it were, it must be 'teachable' (διδακτόν), and there are in fact no teachers of it (i.e. the Sophists who profess to teach virtue cannot do so). This argument deliberately ignored the distinction between 'teachable' (διδακτόν) and 'recoverable by recollection' (ἀναμνηστόν) which Socrates had just established (87B–C). The fact that the Sophists cannot 'teach' virtue does not prove that virtue is not knowledge of the sort that is recollected under Socratic questioning. As in other early dialogues the true conclusion is masked.

Anamnesis, but it is based on the same analysis. The inspired states-man is acting on one of those true beliefs or intuitions which arise in our minds but have not been co-ordinated and justified by 'reflection on the reason'. The interesting point is the comparison of such intuitions to the inspiration of the poet and the seer. The further consideration of this comparison in the next chapter will lead to the conclusion that the Theory of Recollection represents a view of the sources of knowledge much older than the medical-empirical doctrine that knowledge comes through the senses.

CHAPTER V

SEER, POET, PHILOSOPHER

WE have now before us some picture of the two com-
peting theories of the sources of knowledge and some
indications of their respective origins. The Platonic
theory finds the ideal type of knowledge in the eternal objects and
coherent logical structure of geometry. Discovery in this field
can be indefinitely pursued by concentrated thought without
reference to visible and tangible things. It seemed plain that in
this advance pure thought was tracing out the order of an unseen
reality inaccessible to the senses, not extracting or abstracting
knowledge from an influx of sense-impressions. The *Phaedo* and
other dialogues of the middle period leave no doubt that, in
Plato's mind, this theory of knowledge is indissolubly bound up
with a firm belief in an immortal soul or intelligence, which itself
belongs to the world of unseen reality and is only temporarily
housed in the body with its senses and animal desires. So much of
the doctrine of *Anamnesis* was certain and (as Plato hoped) demon-
strable truth.

Enveloping it is a fringe of 'mythical' belief derived from the
religious side of Pythagoreanism. The kinship of all life—divine,
human, and animal—provides a scale of being along which the
migrating soul may rise or sink according to its merits. This belief
is retained and valued for its moral significance: it affords a hope
of divine justice to redress the manifest inequalities of merit and
reward in this life. Transmigration also offered the prospect of
escape from the wheel of rebirth to the company of the gods, on
condition that the soul shall have kept itself 'pure'. In the *Phaedo*
itself we can trace the stages whereby the notion of purity had
advanced from a mere ceremonial avoidance of uncleanness to
the conception of the intelligence withdrawing from the contagion
of its bodily associate and drawn by its love of wisdom and knowledge to the contemplation of truth.

In diametrical opposition to *Anamnesis* stands the empirical theory of knowledge which regards all general notions as creatures of the individual mind, somehow built up out of, or abstracted from, a multitude of similar sense-impressions. In Aristotle's outline of this theory the next step was to be the generalization based on experience; and knowledge in the full sense would be reached with the further apprehension of the reason or cause. The whole account appeared to be founded on the actual procedure of the more scientific physicians, who started with individual observations and inferred from them their general conclusions as to the causes of disease. But even the best of them did not succeed in confining their speculations within these cautious limits. We find them in the same breath making the most sweeping assertions, which no observation could warrant. They will affirm, not as a tentative hypothesis, but with full dogmatic confidence, that all diseases are caused by lack of equilibrium in the four humours. No doubt they thought that their success in dealing with excess or defect of this or that humour by means of drugs and regimen confirmed their assumption; but the assumption itself was really just as dogmatic as the assumption of Empedocles that all bodies consist of four elements, which they denounced as baseless. There is a similar, or even wider, gap between the principles and the practice of Epicurus. As we saw in considering his system, while he professed to base the entire structure on the evidence of the infallible senses, the doctrine of unseen reality—atoms and void—was not offered as a scientific hypothesis which might need modification in the light of further experience and observation, but as an unchallengeable truth deduced from the immediate 'mental apprehension' of perfectly 'clear' concepts and self-evident propositions. The ultimate truth, in fact, is directly revealed to the intelligence; the witness of the senses is called in afterwards. They cannot positively confirm the truth about a reality which is altogether beyond their range. We are satisfied that their testimony does not contradict the pronouncement of the intellect. The senses serve, not as the source, but as the *criterion* of truth.

Our review of Epicureanism was undertaken for the purpose of showing that the Ionian philosophy of nature was no less dogmatic in its final outcome than it had been in its beginnings at Miletus. In the interval there had been much discussion of the question whether man can attain to certain knowledge, and, if so, in what fields and by what means. This problem had not troubled the Milesians. The sixth-century philosopher had felt no doubts about his own 'mental apprehension' of self-evident truths. Lucretius has well described this attitude where he compares the pronouncements of the pre-Socratic philosophers to the oracles of Apollo! He hails the poetry of Empedocles as the voice of inspired genius, setting forth his glorious discoveries in such a way that he hardly seems born of mortal stock. He, and others inferior to him, have been divinely inspired to discover many truths, and 'have given, from their heart's inmost shrine, responses with more sanctity and much more certainty than any delivered by the Pythian prophetess from the tripod and laurel of Phoebus'.[1]

It is true that, when they came to the ultimate nature of things, these oracles of philosophic wisdom had missed the truth. But such failures did not shake Lucretius' confidence in the inspired intuitions of his master, which he describes in precisely the same language. Embarking upon his own account of the origin of the world, he foretells its future destruction, and complains that it is hard to produce conviction by words, 'as is the case when you bring to the ears a thing hitherto unexampled, and yet you cannot submit it to the eyesight nor put it into the hands, through which the straightest highway of belief leads into the human breast and quarters of the mind'. He will, however, speak out and 'pour forth decrees of fate with more sanctity and much more certainty than any delivered by the Pythian prophetess from the tripod and laurel of Phoebus' (v, 97 ff.). Thus Epicurus is exalted as the one true prophet among many, who were nevertheless often endowed with more than mortal wisdom, in respect of matters where the truth could not enter the mind by the common highway of belief through the senses.

Lucretius' poetical insight discerns, behind Epicurus' seemingly prosaic and materialistic doctrine of 'mental apprehension', an analogy with the intuitions of the inspired seer or prophet. The

[1] Lucr. I, 731 ff.

64

kinship, or even identity, of these phenomena had been explicitly recognized by Democritus, who, as Professor Delatte[1] has shown, was the first to put forward a scientific (i.e. materialistic) account of enthusiasm. Summing up his argument, Delatte concludes that according to Democritus, poetic genius, intuitive divination, the second sight manifested in dreams, the mystic's commerce with the divine, and certain nervous and mental affections are all due to an abnormal, specially ardent and emotional temperament, in which the psychic atoms are constantly animated by very lively motion. Such a disposition enables men to enter into communication with beings of a like fiery and animated character, above all with those great 'spectres' vulgarly called gods and demons, and to receive from them effluences producing forcible impressions. The reception of these spectres charged with ideas, emotions, and impulses confers on such men, for a time and in a certain degree, the character of the beings whence they emanate; and it is in a crisis of superhuman exaltation, resembling madness, that works of art are created and mysterious truth is revealed in communion with the divine. If he reduced gods and demons to the rank of natural and even material existence, on the other hand he retained their superhuman power and their intervention in human affairs, and so preserved for the religious factor a considerable role in the explanation of phenomena popularly considered to be supernatural.

The most interesting statement bearing on this subject tells us that, according to Democritus, irrational animals, the wise (σοφοί) and gods have an extra sense, over and above the five senses.[2] In the irrational animals this extra sense is, no doubt, part of what we call instinct. 'The wise' in fifth-century Greek would include poets and seers as well as sages and philosophers. Accordingly, as Rohde saw, this statement would connect with the inspiration of poet and seer that philosophic intuition which Democritus called 'true-born wisdom' (γνησίη γνώμη).[3] This faculty comes into play at the point where the 'bastard knowledge' of the five senses fails;

---

[1] A. Delatte, *Les Conceptions de l'Enthousiasme chez les Philosophes Présocratiques*, Paris, 1934.
[2] Aet. IV, 10, 4= *Vors.*⁵ 68 [55] A 116 (vol. II, p. 111). Delatte, *op. cit.* p. 52.
[3] Democr. B 11 (*Vors.*⁵ II, p. 140).

and it reveals the great principle of the constitution of the world, atoms and void. Democritus prayed that he might meet with favourable spectres of the gods, who could affect man for good or evil and reveal the future in dreams. Hence his disciples could compare him to a prophet, calling him the Voice of Zeus; and tradition represents him as a contemplative ascetic, shunning society, and subject to accesses of madness.

Epicurus concealed or denied his debt to Democritus; but here we can recognize in its earlier and more vivid form the 'projection of the mind', taking its flight from the body to travel in the region of the unseen. We can also see the justification for Sextus' remark that Plato and Democritus both held that the only realities were the objects of intelligence (νοητά). Cicero, likewise, brings the two philosophers together as agreeing that no man could be a great poet who was not inspired with divine madness.[1]

'I have often heard it said', writes Cicero, 'that there cannot be a good poet without a fiery spirit touched with the afflatus of something resembling madness—a sentiment which is to be found in the writings of Democritus and Plato.' Democritus' words are preserved by Clement: 'Truly noble poetry is that which is written with the breath of divine inspiration (μετ' ἐνθουσιασμοῦ καὶ ἱεροῦ πνεύματος).' Plato's are in the *Phaedrus*: 'He who knocks at the doors of poetry untouched by the madness of the Muses, believing that art alone will make him an accomplished poet, will be denied access to the mystery, and his sober compositions will be eclipsed by the creation of inspired madness.'[2] The context of this sentence will further illustrate the association of poetic and prophetic inspiration with the intuitive wisdom of the philosopher.

First, a word about the setting of the conversation. Socrates meets Phaedrus, who has been hearing a discourse by Lysias. They walk out along the Ilissus and sit down under a plane-tree. This is the only Socratic dialogue of which the scene is laid in the open country. Socrates remarks that such surroundings are strange to him: he never leaves the city, because fields and trees have nothing to teach him. On this occasion, however, he breaks out in admira-

[1] Cicero, *de Div.* I, 80; *de Or.* II, 194; Horace, *Ars Poet.* 295.
[2] Democr. B 17 and 18 (*Vors.*5 II, p. 146); Plato, *Phaedr.* 245 A.

tion of the trees and grass, the fragrance of the flowering shrubs, and the shrill music of the cicadas. The place, too, is consecrated to Achelous and the Nymphs. Socrates gradually falls under its inspiration and speaks in lyrical language, which, as the astonished Phaedrus notes, is very unlike his usual manner. Throughout the dialogue, up to the prayer to Pan at the close, we are not allowed to forget the influences of nature and of inspiration which haunt the spot.

This singularly elaborate and beautiful setting is symbolic. Socrates is taken out of the surroundings which he never left and subjected to influences which he never felt. Within the limits of his dramatic art Plato could not have indicated more clearly that this poetic and inspired Socrates was not known to his habitual companions. The poetry and inspiration come from a side of Plato's own temperament which was not satisfied by the usual discourse of the ironic dialectician. The attitude of the historic Socrates towards the poets is defined in the *Apology*. He had cross-examined them about the meaning of their works in the hope of 'learning' something from them. But these men, who were looked up to as authorities on religion and morals, could not 'give an account' of what they meant. 'So I soon recognized that it was not by conscious wisdom (σοφία) that they wrote, but by some instinctive genius or inspiration, like seers or soothsayers, who do not know what they are saying.' Inspired genius would not yield knowledge of the kind that Socrates wanted—explicit knowledge able to state its rational grounds. Socrates concluded that the poets knew no more than he did, and he had no further use for them. Like the fields and trees, they could teach him nothing.

The transformation effected in the *Phaedrus* had already been heralded in the *Phaedo*. There again the conversation is prefaced by a significant passage. Curiosity had been excited about certain poems which Socrates was reported to have set to music during his imprisonment. He explains that, often in his past life, he has been visited by a dream, always with the same message: 'Socrates, compose music: make that your business.' Until now he had supposed that music meant philosophy—'the highest form of music'; and by philosophy he had understood the search for wisdom that could give an account of itself under critical examination. But since the trial, waiting for the sacred ship to return from its mission to the island of the Delian Apollo, he has wondered whether the dream might not mean music in the ordinary sense. So, to be on the safe side, he set himself to compose poetry. First he wrote in honour of the god whose festival was postponing his death. Then, remembering that a poet must deal not in rational arguments, but in myths, and being himself no myth-maker, he took the only myths he could remember and began to versify—of all things—the fables of Aesop.

This incident may be historical; but Plato is working as an artist, and he chose to make it the point of departure for the whole conversation (which cannot be historical) because he saw in it a meaning. This recurrent vision warning the untiring dialectician to work at music and poetry came from an element in human nature which had found no outlet in the cross-examination of other men's beliefs. The emissary of the Delphic Apollo had forgotten that Apollo was leader of the Muses, and the philosophic Muse was not the only one. The theme is touched again, later in the dialogue, where Socrates calls himself the fellow-servant of the swans, the birds of the Delian Apollo, who never sing till the day of their death, when they are inspired with mantic power to foresee the joys of another life.[1] We are meant to understand that the

[1] At *Phaedo* 85 B Socrates calls himself ὁμόδουλος τῶν κύκνων καὶ ἱερὸς τοῦ αὐτοῦ θεοῦ; hence his mantic power comes from his master and also his power of meeting death with good courage. I cannot agree with Burnet's note that 'we know from the *Apology* that Socrates regarded himself as consecrated to Apollo by the answer given to Chaerephon at Delphi'. When this answer was reported to Socrates he was puzzled and set out to refute the oracle (ἐλέγχων τὸ μαντεῖον) by discovering someone wiser than himself. This put him to much trouble; but he found himself obliged to 'support the god' (βοηθεῖν τῷ θεῷ, 23 B) and became very poor because of his 'service' (λατρείαν) to the god, which has left him no leisure. The *Phaedo* nowhere refers to the Delphic oracle as the source of Socrates' mission, and his conception of philosophy has changed from the cross-examination of others, perhaps to be continued in Hades, to a rehearsal of death, a purification of the soul from the body to fit it for the revelation of truth. The burdensome service of the Delphic god, as described in the *Apology*, would not make Socrates ἱερός. We have been reminded at the beginning of the *Phaedo* of the law that the city must be kept pure and no criminal executed during the absence of the sacred ship on its mission to Delos. He had refused to escape from the prison, just as man, the slave of the gods, must not escape by suicide

music we hear in the *Phaedo*, this swan-song of Socrates which overpasses the limits of sober agnosticism, had not been heard from his lips in the past seventy years. Otherwise, when he wanted myths to set to music, he might have found some theme more inspiring than the beast fables of Aesop. And this Socrates, after saying that he was no myth-maker, ends with a long myth about that other world, symbolized as an earthly paradise. By such means Plato has contrived to convey, through Socrates' own mouth, that he is carrying his master beyond the limits of his historic self as presented in the *Apology*. Indeed, the protreptic discourse forming the first episode in the conversation is presented as a revised Apology, 'more persuasive than the speech I made in my defence before the judges'.[1]

In that speech Socrates had declared that he knew nothing about any after-life in an unseen world: death, for all he knew, might be

from the prison of the body till the gods release him. Does ἱερός suggest that Socrates was set apart under a taboo, like a ἱερεῖον or a ἱερόδουλος dedicated to Apollo, not to be touched till the festival was over? At Rome a criminal under sentence of death was *consecratus* to Dis Pater or some other god, and called *sacer*. In Euripides. *Alc.* 74, Thanatos says he will cut off a lock of Alcestis' hair (as from a sacrificial victim), ἱερὸς γὰρ οὗτος τῶν κατὰ χθονὸς θεῶν/ὅτου τόδ' ἔγχος κρατὸς ἁγνίσῃ τρίχα. Virgil, *Aen.* IV, 696, Dido's struggling soul cannot escape, *Nam, quia nec fato merita nec morte peribat, Sed misera ante diem, subitoque accensa furore, Nondum illi flauum Proserpina vertice crinem Abstulerat, Stygioque caput damnaverat Orco.* Juno sends Iris to cut the lock, which is *Diti sacrum*, and so release her soul. Both Alcestis and Dido are dying before their fated day and by an undeserved death; hence they are not yet consecrated to Dis in the ordinary course. Socrates also is dying *nec fato merita nec morte*. He has been waiting for his release at the hands of the god to whom he is dedicated. Is there also, perhaps, an allusion to the religious manumission of slaves? Enfranchisement was sometimes performed before an altar with the deity as witness. This was especially frequent in the cult of Apollo. 'At Delphi such a form of manumission might be called an ἀνάθεσις (dedication) and the person thus manumitted became ἱερὸς καὶ ἀνέφαπτος, sacrosanct, that is to say, as touching his liberty.' But a large number of inscriptions of the second century B.C. at Delphi represent Apollo in a different light, as a principal in the transaction, himself purchasing the slave, not in order to retain him in the temple as ἱερόδουλος, but to set him free (Farnell, *Cults*, vol. IV, pp. 177 f.).

[1] 63 B: χρή με πρὸς ταῦτα ἀπολογήσασθαι ὥσπερ ἐν δικαστηρίῳ... πιθανώτερον πρὸς ὑμᾶς ἀπολογήσασθαι ἢ πρὸς τοὺς δικαστάς; D: ἅμα σοι ἡ ἀπολογία ἔσται; E: ὑμῖν τοῖς δικασταῖς βούλομαι ἤδη τὸν λόγον ἀποδοῦναι; and at the end, 69D: ταῦτα οὖν... ἀπολογοῦμαι; E: εἴ τι οὖν ὑμῖν πιθανώτερός εἰμι ἐν τῇ ἀπολογίᾳ ἢ τοῖς Ἀθηναίων δικασταῖς.

a blessing, whether it were a dreamless sleep or a migration into another place where he might meet and cross-examine the famous dead. Now his tone is changed: he is convinced that he is going into the presence of 'other gods', who are good masters. The lover of wisdom, least of all men, will shrink from death; for death is the deliverance of the soul from the body, whose senses and lusts are a hindrance to the acquisition of wisdom.

And so again in the *Phaedrus*, Socrates, under a wholly un-accustomed influence of inspiration, is set to compose poetry very unlike a versified Aesop, a 'dithyrambic hymn to Eros', which opens by exalting above rational sobriety the divine madness of the poet, the seer, and the lover of wisdom.

The first half of the dialogue contains three speeches: a sophistic love-letter by Lysias; a complementary sophistic speech by Socrates and the Recantation. The theme common to all three is the contrast between rational sobriety (*sophrosyne*) and the irrationality of passion (*Eros*). We are given three different views of this contrast and of the meaning of the terms contrasted.

Lysias' speech is a love-letter from a suitor who is not in love, but urges that, being in his sober senses, he should be preferred above his rivals who are carried away by passion. This frigid composition, whether it be a genuine work of Lysias or not, is a sophistical exhibition of paradox which provides Plato with a starting-point. The imaginary suitor speaks of love as a malady: 'Lovers themselves admit that their wits are disordered; they know they are foolish, but cannot control themselves' (231 D). His own state of rational sobriety is the sort of sobriety that is never carried away by passion to forget its own interests, but is always cool and calculating. At the same time what he is asking for is the satisfaction of his own sensual desire. Lysias' doctrine (if you take it seriously) is that the deliberately selfish sensualist is less dangerous to the equally self-interested object of his pursuit than the lover inspired by passion, who is liable to be carried away and to behave imprudently. To Plato this so-called sobriety is the exact opposite of virtue. Reason is enslaved to the lowest form of desire—sensual appetite unredeemed by passion—instead of converting all lower desires to its own service. If there is any element in animal desire that is capable of a different orientation, it is precisely that element which Lysias' sobriety excludes as foolish extravagance, losing sight of self-interest and immediate pleasure; the element in Eros which, as Diotima taught, causes even animals to sacrifice self-preservation to the immortality of the race and starve themselves to feed their young, and which moves men to give up their lives for the sake of immortal fame that they can never enjoy. As Diotima says: 'You will marvel at the irrationality of human ambition, unless you understand what I say.' It is this touch of divine irrationality that Lysias' sober egoist will never understand. He is Plato's 'despotic man' whose whole nature is dominated by the lowest part of the soul.

The ostensible object of Socrates' first speech is to rival Lysias and supply the other side of the same argument. Lysias has given the encomium of the non-lover; Socrates will give the supplementary denunciation of the lover. The style is intentionally artificial and false, because in a sense the speech itself is false and afterwards recanted by Socrates. But it is important to see what it is that Socrates recants.

Lysias had not defined Eros. Socrates makes good the omission, defining Eros as Lysias conceives it: 'excessive desire for pleasure in bodily beauty, carried beyond the bounds of rational conviction'. This is the only kind of 'love' the speech is concerned with—the kind that Lysias meant: animal lust which outruns the prudent considerations of conventional morality. The denunciation is powerful, and is not retracted later; what will be denied is that this is the only kind of Eros. It is that species of desire which refuses to be detached from pleasure in the physical beauty of the individual person, and so makes the Greater Mysteries of Diotima's speech impossible. It is cut off from the apprehension of moral and intellectual beauty and from the final vision of Beauty itself. Sobriety also is defined in carefully chosen terms. This is not the sobriety of Lysias—the calculated cunning of reason enslaved to appetite. It is the moderation approved by conventional morality. Our nature is pictured as torn between contrary impulses: the innate appetite for pleasure and 'an acquired belief aiming at what is best'. In the struggle sometimes one impulse prevails, sometimes the other. The victory of 'acquired belief' is called sobriety or moderation. Eros is a species of excess, gluttony being another. This is the popular view of 'temperance' or 'self-control', holding excessive passion in check, in spite of occasional lapses, with a view to what is 'best' for us in a worldly sense. So Aristotle's continent man has the right opinions, but suffers from a conflict in which irrational appetite is normally kept in subjection to rational rules of conduct. He has not the genuine virtue described in the *Republic* as a harmony of all desires, secured by the reorientation of desire itself. In this speech desire or appetite is treated as a dangerous force which 'drags us irrationally towards pleasures, and when it establishes its ascendancy is called excess'. This is the false, or at least inadequate, conception of Eros which Socrates will recant as blasphemous. Eros, as we learnt in the *Symposium*, is not evil in itself, but neutral, taking its value from its object, evil only when misdirected.

Socrates breaks off this speech at the point where his lyrical rhapsody threatens to pass into heroic verse; a moment more and he will be rapt out of his senses by the inspiration of the Nymphs to whose influence Phaedrus has deliberately exposed him. He receives a warning from his divine sign, whose voice he seems to hear forbidding him to depart before he has purified his conscience of an offence against deity. His soul, he says, is prophetic enough to divine that, like Lysias, he has sinned in speaking of Eros, who is either a god or at least something godlike, as evil.

The Recantation includes the myth of the journey of the soul to seek truth in another world; but this is prefaced by two passages which are not mythical in form: the classification of the kinds of divine madness, and the demonstration of immortality.

Socrates starts once more from the contrast between sobriety and madness. The two earlier speeches have assumed that there is only one kind of madness and that madness is an evil. But there is a madness which is a gift of heaven and the cause of the greatest goods. (It is the very madness which has, at this moment, taken possession of the soul of Socrates and transfigured him out of his normal, supremely sober, character.) Of this divine madness there are four species.

The first is the entranced condition of the priestesses who deliver the oracles at Delphi and Dodona and of the Sibyl and all other prophets who have the power of divination by divine possession (μαντική ἔνθεος). When thus inspired, they can foretell the future to the great advantage of those who consult them for private or public interests; whereas in their sober senses they are powerless. In accordance with a universally recognized distinction, this intuitive divination of truth inaccessible to the normal faculties is contrasted with the rational procedure of augury. The contrast is repeatedly defined by Cicero. Augury he describes as an art of great antiquity, which has amassed an incredible amount of lore from long observation of the sequence of events and of their relation to signs and omens given by sacrificial victims, lightning, portents, or the stars. This art is independent of any impulse of divine operation (*de Div.* I, 109). In our passage Plato describes it as an inquiry into the future by means of omens and other signs, deriving insight and information from the reasoning faculty by unaided human belief. The procedure, in fact, is that of a pseudo-science, with an alleged empirical origin in observation. Acting by traditional rules, the human intelligence draws inferences about future events from a recognized code of signs supposed to indicate the intentions of a god. It is like deciphering a cryptogram by means of a key.

'Mantic inspiration', on the other hand, is the gift of Apollo (*Phaedr.* 265 B), who, as Homer tells us, endowed the seer Calchas with knowledge of past, present and future (*Il.* I, 70). The extent of this knowledge is an important point. Divination or prophecy of this inspired kind is quite as much concerned with the past and the hidden present as with the future;[1] whereas the interest of augury is mainly confined to the forecast of coming events. Recapitulating Plato's doctrine, Cicero reminds us that this visionary power of surveying all time and existence is possessed by the soul in sleep. 'When it is called away from the contagion

[1] As Bouché-Leclercq observes, *Divination*, vol. I, p. 8. Virg. *Georg.* IV, 392 (of Proteus): novit namque omnia vates, quae sint, quae fuerint, quae mox ventura trahantur; Ov. *Met.* I, 517 (Apollo speaking): per me quod eritque fuitque estque patet.

of its bodily associate the soul remembers the past, discerns the present, and foresees the future; for the sleeper's body lies as if dead, while his spirit is alive and in full vigour' (de Div. I, 63). In the Republic (IX, 571 D), the dreams of lawless appetite, the beast which has shaken off the control of reason, are contrasted with those of

a man sound in body and mind, who before he goes to sleep, awakens the reason within him to feed on high thoughts and questionings in collected meditation. If he has neither starved nor surfeited his appetites, so that, lulled to rest, no delights or griefs of theirs may trouble that better part, but leave it free to reach out, in pure and independent thought, after some *new knowledge of things past, present, or to come*; if, likewise, he has soothed his passions so as not to fall asleep with his anger roused against any man; if, in fact, he does not take his rest until he has quieted two of the three elements in his soul and awakened the third wherein wisdom dwells, then he is in a fair way to grasp the truth of things, and the visions of his dreams will not be unlawful.

Still more, as Cicero, recalling the *Phaedo*, goes on to remark, will the spirit possess this knowledge when death has altogether delivered it from the body. Hence its divine power is much greater when death is approaching. Socrates, it will be remembered, told the judges who had condemned him that he would prophesy to them, for he was 'already in that case when men are most prophetic, namely when they are about to die'.[1] On the same occasion Xenophon's *Apology* refers to the classic instances of the dying prophecies of Patroclus to Hector (*Il.* XVI, 851) and Hector to Achilles (*Il.* XXII, 356). Throughout the conversation in the *Phaedo* on the day of his death, Socrates, as we have seen, is to be thought of as inspired with a 'mantic' wisdom which sees beyond the confines of rational disputation, and he ascribes his power to Apollo.

The *Phaedrus* goes on to describe a second form of prophetic madness, the gift of Dionysus. Divination here is concerned with

[1] Plato, *Apol.* 39 c; Xenophon, *Apol.* 30; *Phaedo* 84E. Other references will be found in A. S. Pease's edition of Cicero, *de Div.* I, p. 206. The belief, as he shows, is very widespread.

the past and present. It is exercised to discover the 'ancient wraths' of offended spirits whose vengeance has caused hereditary maladies and afflictions. Prophetic madness reveals the means of 'deliverance' and 'absolution from present evils', having recourse to prayers and service to the gods in rites of purification and initiation. The elaborate sentence characterizing this Dionysiac or initiatory madness (μανία τελεστική, 265 B) introduces many terms associated with cathartic procedure both in medicine and in the mysteries. They might be illustrated at length from the *Oresteia*, where the hero, driven mad by the 'ancient wrath' which has haunted his ancestry, is purified and absolved by Loxias, the 'physician-seer, reader of portents, and purifier of houses'.[1]

In the half-light between myth and history we can discern this combination of attributes in the legendary figure of Epimenides. As Bouché-Leclercq observes,

it matters little whether there ever really existed a Cretan wonder-worker, born at Phaestos, living at Knossos, and called Epimenides. The most living and active element in religious history is not men but ideas, and an abstract entity round which a certain number of these ideas group themselves acquires an intenser life and a reality more active than material reality. Epimenides represents one of these moral forces, and as such is really one of the actors in religious history. The Cretan prophet is, above all, a purifier, a purifier of souls and even of lifeless objects. In his hands, the aim of divination was not so much to unveil the future as to discover in the past those forgotten errors of which present evils were the consequence. According to Aristotle, he said himself that he did not divine future events, but past happenings which remained unknown (*Rhet.* III, 17, 10). Not that he meant to limit the domain of prophecy in this way. In order to postpone the Persian Wars for ten years, he must have been able to read the fatal date in the book of Destiny.[2] He also predicted the defeat of the Lacedaemonians by the Arcadians at Orchomenos; but his special mission ordinarily turned him towards the past. This is not the primitive and essential role of Apolline divination, which borrowed Cathartic from other cults, but

[1] Aesch. *Eum.* 62: ἰατρόμαντις...τερασκόπος...δωμάτων καθάρσιος.
[2] Compare the postponing of the plague at Athens for ten years by Diotima (*Symp.* 201 D)—her only claim to be an historical character! She also is a mystagogue.

never succeeded in gaining a monopoly of it. Accordingly, Epimenides seems not to have been known originally as a prophet of Apollo. His prophetic enthusiasm came rather from the Nymphs or from Zeus.[1]

It was the Nymphs who gave him the magical food which dispensed him from eating for the rest of his life; and no doubt it was they who revealed to him the curative virtues of plants and made him a second Melampus. The cave where he slept recalls the mysterious colloquies of Minos and Rhadamanthys with Zeus on Ida. But Apolline religion took Epimenides into its service. The Athenians, haunted by phantoms and by the plague, in expiation of the murder of Kylon were told by the Delphic oracle to have recourse to the good offices of the Cretan purifier, and Epimenides introduced the cult of Apollo, hitherto an aristocratic cult, into the national religion of Athens. At the same time he appeased the Erinyes, reformed the mysteries and conferred on Solon, who was to consolidate and achieve the work, a sort of supernatural investiture.[2]

Third comes the 'madness of possession by the Muses, which, seizing upon a tender and virgin soul, rouses it to ecstasy in song and poetry, marshalling countless deeds of the men of old for the instruction of posterity'. This is the inspiration which 'eclipses the sober compositions' of the uninspired.

Once more we note that the vision of the Muses, like the prophetic vision of Epimenides, is turned towards the past, not, however, to trace out the sources of present evils, but to illustrate the examples of heroic virtue. The Muses are the daughters of Memory. The poet of the Catalogue of the Ships (*Il.* II, 484 ff.) calls on the Muses, in their Olympian home, to 'put him in mind' of all who went to Troy; 'for ye are goddesses, and are present (πάρεστε) and know all things, while we only hear the report of fame and know nothing'. As a man among men, the poet depends on hearsay; but as divinely inspired, he has access to the knowledge of an eye-

---

[1] The prophetess in the prologue to the *Eumenides* does not forget that Apollo himself is the prophet of Zeus, who 'caused his mind to be inspired with the diviner's art', or that the Corycian cave was a haunt of the Nymphs in a region possessed by Dionysus.

[2] Bouché-Leclercq, *Divination*, vol. II, pp. 100–2.

witness, 'present' at the feats he illustrates. The Muses are, in fact, credited with the same mantic powers as the seer, transcending the limitations of time. At Delphi, where the exhalation rose from the fountain by the old oracular temple of Earth, they had their shrine as the 'assessors of prophecy', because the oracles were delivered in verse.[1] Poetry was the language of prophecy.

They it was who once taught Hesiod sweet song, when he was feeding his sheep under holy Helicon. And these were the first words spoken to me by the divine Muses of Olympus, daughters of Zeus, the lord of the aegis: 'O shepherds who abide in the fields,[2] evil things of shame, mere bellies! We know how to tell many fictions that wear the guise of truth, but we know also how to declare the truth, when we will.' And with these words the eloquent daughters of great Zeus gave me a staff, a branch of the flourishing bay-tree, that I might celebrate the things that shall be and that have been aforetime. They bade me hymn the race of the Blessed ones who are for ever, and of themselves to sing always, first and last.[3]

So Hesiod begins with the Muses, who 'tell of things present, past, and future'—the same words in which Homer described the mantic gift of Calchas the seer. And what the Muses reveal to the poet's vision is the origin of the world and the birth of the gods. The daughters of Memory put him in mind of the very beginnings of time past, of which the common man knows nothing but by hearsay.

The invocation of the Muse has long since become a worn-out artifice. If an eighteenth-century poet meant by it anything at all, he must have felt that he was calling upon his own powers of imagination (as we call it), and he could no longer mistake the pictures he summoned up for genuine memories of the past. But must we say the same of the blind Milton?

[1] Plut. *Def. Orac.* XVII, 402 C.
[2] ποιμένες ἄγραυλοι has a verbal echo in Luke ii, 8, 'There were shepherds abiding in the fields (ποιμένες ἀγραυλοῦντες) keeping watch over their flocks by night', when the angel revealed the good tidings, though Luke may have been thinking not so much of Hesiod as of his contemporary, the shepherd Amos.
[3] Hes. *Th.* 22–34.

Sing, Heav'nly Muse, that on the secret top
Of Oreb, or of Sinai, didst inspire
That Shepherd, who first taught the chosen Seed,
In the Beginning how the Heav'ns and Earth
Rose out of Chaos....
And chiefly thou O Spirit, that dost prefer
Before all Temples th' upright heart and pure,
Instruct me, for Thou know'st; Thou from the first
Wast present, and with mighty wings outspread
Dove-like satst brooding on the vast Abyss
And mad'st it pregnant: What in me is dark
Illumine, what is low raise and support;
That to the highth of this great Argument
I may assert Eternal Providence,
And justifie the ways of God to men.

Descend from Heav'n Urania, by that name
If rightly thou art called, whose Voice divine
Following, above the Olympian hill I soare,
Above the flight of Pegasean wing.
That meaning, not the Name I call: for thou
Not of the Muses nine, nor on the top
Of old Olympus dwell'st, but Heav'nlie borne,
Before the Hills appeerd, or Fountain flow'd,
Thou with Eternal wisdom didst converse,
Wisdom thy Sister, and with her didst play
In presence of th' Almightie Father, pleas'd
With thy Celestial Song. Up led by thee
Into the Heav'n of Heav'ns I have presum'd,
An Earthlie Guest, and drawn Empyreal Aire,
Thy tempring; with like safetie guided down
Return me to my Native Element....

So much the rather thou Celestial light
Shine inward, and the mind through all her powers
Irradiate, there plant eyes, all mist from thence
Purge & disperse, that I may see & tell
Of things invisible to mortal sight.

What Milton prayed for was as much the vision of the seer as
the inspiration of the poet, the knowledge of a Spirit which 'from

the first was present', a revelation which, as he believed, was to be found not only in the canonical books, but in the Wisdom literature, the Cabala, and 'thrice great Hermes'. This Spirit, he declared, was wont to inspire his

> prompted song else mute,
> And bear through highth or depth of natures bounds
> With prosperous wing full summ'd to tell of deeds
> Above Heroic, though in secret done,
> And unrecorded left through many an Age,
> Worthy t'have not remain'd so long unsung.

The lines above quoted reproduce, in every feature, that claim to hidden knowledge of the past, as well as of the present and future, which, as we shall see, is regularly advanced by the seers and poets of the heroic and post-heroic ages in many different lands. In Greece those ages are respectively represented for us by Homer and Hesiod. The two poets stand out like island peaks towering above a sea whose surface hides all the other links in a submerged chain of mountains. Until very recently scholars have neglected all the evidence that can be drawn from parallel ages elsewhere to throw light upon their thought. Hence it has not been realized that their belief in their own prophetic inspiration was as genuine as Milton's. When they called upon the Muses, who were 'present and knew all things' to tell them what they, as common mortals, could learn only by hearsay, it is likely that their meaning was more serious than we ordinarily suppose. They would feel like Ion the rhapsode, who when he recited how Odysseus leapt on the threshold and poured out the arrows at his feet to slay the suitors, or how Hector parted from Andromache, thought that 'his soul, rapt out of himself by inspiration, was present at the events he described in Ithaca or Troy'. They would have accepted the whole theory of inspiration which Socrates suggests to Ion: that poets work, not by art, but by divine possession. 'The god deprives them of their sober senses and uses them as instruments, like singers of oracles and inspired seers, in order that we who hear them may know that it is not they who speak things of such high worth, but the god himself who speaks to us through them.'[1]

[1] Plato, *Ion*, 535 B, 534 C.

In the *Phaedrus* the rest of Socrates' recantation is devoted to the fourth species of divine madness, which comes upon the lover, transported by the sight of beauty, and wings the soul for its flight into the region of eternal truth. In the *Meno* and *Phaedo* the most substantial argument in proof of immortality was drawn from the power of the soul to regain knowledge—especially mathematical knowledge—revealed to it before birth. Such knowledge is not to be extracted or abstracted from sensible experience. The senses and their objects could at most provide hints and promptings to awaken recollection. This doctrine is repeated in the *Phaedrus*, but here the emphasis falls at first on the moving power of the soul in the living creature. The soul is defined as the only thing capable of moving itself, and hence the source and fountain of all motion in the universe. The whole context seems to imply (though this is not explicitly stated) that the moving force in the soul is desire, Eros; for desire is the type of motion which reaches forward to its object and is not pushed from behind by an antecedent mechanical cause. As the *Republic* (580) taught, each of the three parts of the soul—appetitive, passionate, rational—is characterized by its peculiar form of desire: the love of sensual pleasure, the love of honour, and the love of wisdom. Any one of these three desires may dominate the other two and so shape the three lives of the money-getter, the ambitious man, and the philosopher. In the symbolism of the *Phaedrus* the three parts are represented by the two horses of the soul-chariot and Intelligence, the charioteer. The chariot is winged, and before the soul sinks to inhabit an earthly body, the power of its wings enables it to accompany the procession of the Twelve Gods, which passes outside the sphere of the visible heavens to contemplate truth in the supra-celestial region of colourless, shapeless and intangible reality. Only Intelligence can be initiated into this 'most blessed of all revelations'; and Intelligence is hindered and troubled by the unruly struggling of the horses. In the turmoil the soul's wings are broken and it sinks downwards into its earthly prison-house, to undergo a round of incarnations until Eros can restore to Psyche the wings she has lost.

'The nature of wings consists in their power to raise heavy things aloft to the region where the gods dwell; there is no bodily part more closely akin to the divine; and the divine is beauty, wisdom, goodness' (246 D). Of these three aspects of the divine, the *Republic* was concerned with goodness and with wisdom or truth. In the *Phaedrus*, as in the *Symposium*, the significant aspect is beauty. We learn, more explicitly, that beauty is that aspect of the divine which is manifest, though dimly, within or through the world of sense. The perception of beauty which comes through the bodily eyes and causes the distraction of love is also the first occasion for the awakening of *Anamnesis*—that mysterious memory of truth once seen by every human soul before it became incarnate. And the awakening of *Anamnesis* is the beginning of philosophy.

The passage where the sensuous intuition of beauty is linked with *Anamnesis* runs as follows (249 B ff.):

The soul which has never seen the truth can never come into human shape. For man must have understanding by way of what is called the 'form'—a unity gathered by reflection from many acts of perception; and this is recollection of the things formerly seen by our soul when it travelled in the divine company, despising the things we now call real and looking upwards to true reality. Hence it is just that only the mind of the philosopher should get wings; for he is always, so far as he can, dwelling in memory on those things, the contemplation of which makes divinity divine. So the man who makes a right use of these means of recollection is always being initiated into the perfect mystery, and he alone becomes truly perfect; and being exalted above human interests to converse with the divine, he is rebuked by the world as a madman, for the world cannot see that he is possessed by divine inspiration.

And so all this discourse is concerned with the fourth kind of madness, whereby a man, when the sight of beauty in this world reminds him of real beauty and his wings begin to grow, longing to fly upwards but powerless to do so, like a bird gazing at the sky and careless of the world below, is charged with being distraught. And the discourse comes to this: that of all the forms of divine inspiration, this proves to be of the highest origin and the best, both for its possessor and for one who shares it with him; and that it is by being touched with this madness that one who is enamoured of a beautiful person is called a lover.

For, as we said, every human soul has by nature beheld the things that are; else it could not have come into the human creature; but it is not easy for every soul to recover the memory of them from things on earth. It is hard for such as had then but a brief vision of that other world, and for those who, after their fall hither, had the ill fortune to be turned by evil conversation to unrighteousness and to remain in forgetfulness of the holy things which then they saw. Few indeed remain in whom the power of memory is sufficient; but these few, whenever they see some likeness of the things in that other world, are struck with amazement and lose their self-possession, though they know not what this condition means, because the perception is not sufficiently clear. Now Justice and Temperance and all things else that are of value to the soul have no indwelling light in their likenesses on earth, and it is hard even for the few, when they approach the copy, to discern darkly, through dim organs, the features of the original. Beauty, however, was then visible in her splendour, when, in happy company, ourselves attending Zeus and others following some other divinity, we saw a spectacle of beatific vision and were initiated into the most blessed (as it may lawfully be named) of all revelations....

Let this, then, be our tribute to the power of memory, for whose sake I have spoken thus at length, as looking back with longing to the visions of that former life. Among them, as we have said, Beauty shone; and, since we came hither, we have seen the unrivalled clearness of her radiance through the clearest of the senses—sight, whose perceptions are keener than any others that come to us through the bodily organs. Wisdom is not visible to the eyes. If Wisdom gave us any manifest image of herself, coming in the same way through sight, she would inspire a marvellous passion, and so would all the other lovely realities; but Beauty alone has this prerogative—to be clearly apparent and lovely beyond all.

The identification of Eros, as the desire which has for its object the beautiful,[1] with the passion for knowledge or wisdom which is 'philosophy' had already been made in the discourse of Diotima. Desire, she argued, implies a lack of its object; Eros, therefore, must lack beauty and goodness. In calling Eros a great god Socrates, like Agathon, had confused desire with its object.[2] (It is indeed true that Aphrodite and Eros as an ideally beautiful woman and youth represent the desirable, not desire itself.) But Eros is not ugly or base. Just as true belief, though it falls short of

---

[1] At *Charm.* 167E it is assumed that τὸ καλόν is essentially the object of ἔρως.
[2] *Symp.* 204C: ᾠήθης...τὸ ἐρώμενον Ἔρωτα εἶναι, οὐ τὸ ἐρῶν. διὰ ταῦτά σοι οἶμαι πάγκαλος ἐφαίνετο ὁ Ἔρως.

knowledge, is intermediate between wisdom and ignorance, so Eros, though lacking the beauty and goodness of a god, is nevertheless one of those spirits (daemons) which are intermediaries between the divine and the mortal. The function of the world of spirits is to act as messengers conveying to the gods the prayers and sacrifices of men and to men the commands of the gods and the blessings they send in return for sacrifice. So the interval is filled and the universe bound together. 'This is the channel through which pass all divination and all priest-craft connected with sacrifice and ritual and every sort of spell and magical practice.' There is no direct contact between the divine and the human, but all converse between gods and men, whether waking or asleep, is carried on through this channel. Hence one who is wise and skilled in these matters is called a genius (*daimonios*[1]), in contrast with those whose skill lies only in vulgar arts and handicrafts. No god is a lover of wisdom or desires to become wise, for he is wise; nor yet is wisdom desired by anyone else who has it. On the other hand, wisdom is not desired by the ignorant, who are too dull to be conscious of any deficiency in wisdom or goodness. The love of wisdom resides in those who are neither wise nor ignorant, but between the two; and one of these is Eros.

In the next section of her discourse (204 c ff.) Diotima develops the theme that Eros, the passion for wisdom, is also the passion for immortality. Eros desires to possess beauty and goodness, or in other words, happiness; and this is a universal desire felt by all men at all times: however much they may mistake the nature of happiness and seek it where it is not to be found, their true and inmost will is bent upon what is really good.[2] The name Eros has been misappropriated by one species of desire, sexual passion, just as 'poetry', which should include all creation, is limited to mean metrical composition. Eros properly denotes 'all desire for good

[1] From Homer onwards δαιμόνιος is frequently used in apostrophizing persons, usually with a touch of protest or irony, as 'marvellous', 'miraculous'. Here the context gives it a more serious sense, including something like our notion of a man of poetical or spiritual genius.

[2] At 205 A this true 'wish' for what is really good, and not merely seems good, is called by its proper name βούλησις (cf. Ar. *E.N.* III, 1113 a 15 ff.), with reference to Socrates' doctrine that no one is willingly, or wittingly, a wrong-doer.

things and for happiness'. Moreover, it desires to possess these goods for ever. Eros is accordingly a desire for immortality.

The operation of this passion for immortality is seen in the animal impulse to perpetuate the succession of mortal individuals by generation; in the ambition for fame after death; and in the desire to beget spiritual children, seen in the poet and creative artist, and above all in the legislator, like Solon or Lycurgus, whose institutions seek to educate the whole community in goodness.

Here Diotima pauses. The words with which she resumes her discourse are significant: 'Into these Lesser Mysteries of Eros, you, Socrates, may perhaps be initiated; I know not whether you are capable of the perfect revelation, the end to which they lead. I will not fail, on my part, to do my best to express it; you must try to follow, if you can.'

I incline to agree with those scholars who read in this sentence Plato's intention to mark the limit reached by the historic Socrates. Socrates had been the prince of those who beget spiritual children in the minds of others and help them to bring their own thoughts to birth. Had he gone further? Immortality in all the three forms so far described is the immortality attainable by the mortal creature who can perpetuate his race, his fame, his creative work, his thoughts, in other mortal creatures who live after him. The individual himself does not survive; he dies, and leaves something behind. Immortality in these kinds, though it should endure while time lasts, is still an immortality in time, not in an eternal world. All that is contained in the Lesser Mysteries is true, even if there be no other life and no immortality for the individual soul. The vision of another world—the eternal world of the Ideas—is reserved for the Greater Mysteries that follow. Plato means, I believe, that the historic Socrates was not admitted to this final revelation. I should perhaps say, consciously admitted. Plato is not indicating any imperfection in his master. His own philosophy is, from one point of view, an explanation of the life and death of Socrates. What Plato adds is a theory, an explicit statement of what seemed to him implicit in that life and death. Here I take him to mean that this theory is his own; and from the other point of view, which we have taken in this chapter, the Socrates who sits at the feet of the seer Diotima is the transfigured Socrates of the *Phaedo* and the *Phaedrus*.

The line which at this point divides the Lesser from the Greater Mysteries corresponds to the line dividing the two stages of education in the *Republic*. The earlier books of that dialogue describe the simultaneous training of soul and body, or rather of all the three parts of the soul, by means of music and gymnastic. In this lower education every citizen must share. It is a training of the soul for life in this world. The higher education of the later books, reserved for the philosopher, is a training of the Reason, turning the eye of the soul away from the phantoms of the Cave towards the light of truth. In the *Republic* the two stages are separated by a long discussion of other matters, and the connexion between the end of the lower education and the starting-point of the higher is not obvious. The *Symposium* supplies the connecting link. The Greater Mysteries of Eros begin where the musical education of the *Republic* ends; namely in the passion for beauty and goodness as revealed in an individual person. The purpose of that lower education is to produce in the soul reasonableness, the rhythms of harmony and grace, and simplicity of character. These qualities, it is hinted, are images, existing in individual souls, of the eternal ideals of temperance, courage, and the other virtues. Such an image, says Socrates, is 'the loveliest object of contemplation to him who is able to behold it'. It inspires the passion of love in the 'musical man'. The love of beauty in an individual person is meant, though the physical side of this passion is expressly excluded. 'Music', Socrates concludes, ends where it should end, in the passion for beauty.

Now in Diotima's discourse the Greater Mysteries of Eros take this for their point of departure. They describe the conversion of Eros from the love of a single beautiful person to the love of Beauty itself. The upward journey of emotion runs parallel to the upward journey of the intellect in the mathematical and dialectical studies of the *Republic*. The intellect soars from the world of sense to the source of truth and goodness; but the wings on which it rises are the wings of desire for the source of beauty. The true self, the divine soul, is not a mere faculty of thought and dispassionate contemplation of truth; it has its own principle of energy in the desire kindled by goodness in the guise of the beautiful. The intimations of immortality already discernible in the lower forms of Eros are now confirmed when its true nature is disclosed as a passion for immortality in an eternal world.

In the ascent there are four stages. The love which is fixed upon the beauty of a single person must first be detached from its object and from physical beauty. The individual object is lost to sight in the perception that all physical beauty is one. Next the soul learns to value, above bodily beauty, beauty of the mind, and to perceive the unity and kinship of all that is morally lovely, honourable, and of good report—a sense which the Greek word for beautiful never lost. In the third stage we pass to intellectual beauty, such as pervades the whole structure of mathematical knowledge—that unearthly beauty of ordered truth and divine necessity, which a living mathematician has called supreme—'a beauty cold and austere, like that of sculpture, without appeal to any part of our weaker nature, without the gorgeous trappings of painting or music, yet sublimely pure, and capable of a stern perfection such as only the greatest art can show'.[1] At last by the strength gathered in these regions of contemplation, the soul becomes capable of a revelation that comes, if it comes at all, 'suddenly'. Plato here borrows from the Eleusinian mysteries the language of the Sacred Marriage and of the final revelation, when the ancient symbols of divinity were disclosed to the purified initiate in a sudden blaze of light. The soul is united with the divine Beauty, and itself becomes immortal and divine. The offspring of the marriage are not phantoms of goodness like those images of virtue which first inspired love for the beautiful person. The child of Love and Beauty is true virtue, dwelling in the soul that has become immortal, as the lover and the beloved of God.

There is no shadow of external evidence that either Socrates or Plato was ever visited by the mystical experience in its advanced form of ecstasy or trance. The state of rapt musing into which Socrates sometimes fell is mentioned at the beginning of the *Symposium*, where it makes him late for dinner, and towards the

[1] Bertrand Russell, *Mysticism and Logic*, p. 60.

close in the speech of Alcibiades. But the description makes it clear that Socrates was then simply absorbed in thinking out some problem which puzzled him: the condition has little in common with the loss of ordinary consciousness in the experience of time-less being. Concerning Plato, all that can be said is that he possessed, like the Euripides who wrote the *Bacchanals*, that power of poetic and religious imagination which could enter into the meaning of mystical enthusiasm; and further that there are intimations of immortality falling short of ecstasy and trance. The *Symposium* and the *Phaedrus* prove that Plato had moments of illumination, of seeing into the life of things, resembling those which inspired Wordsworth's ode. But there is nothing to show that Plato, any more than Socrates, ever passed into the condition of mystical ecstasy.

On the other hand, we have seen how the agnostic Socrates of the *Apology* and the earlier dialogues was subtly transfigured in the *Phaedo* and the *Phaedrus* to become the spokesman of the con-verted Plato. The perfect philosopher is inspired by Apollo to be the prophet of immortality and by the Nymphs to be the poet of Eros. He reveals a theory of divine madness which is the Platonic counterpart of Democritus' materialistic explanation of intuitive divination, poetic genius, and the 'genuine wisdom' of the philosopher. In Plato the soul which is detached from the body is the rational intelligence, moved by its own characteristic desire to recover the antenatal vision of truth; and from a worldly stand-point this desire has the appearance of irrationality, because it implies a disregard of all worldly interests.

The next point to be established will be that neither Democritus' theory nor Plato's is a novel invention. The three types which they bring together—prophet, poet and sage—had originally been united in a single figure. Here we shall find the ultimate reason why the philosophers of the historic period deliver their oracles as men having an authority transcending common experience.

CHAPTER VI

SHAMANISM

IN the *Phaedrus* the four species of divine madness are associated with four different divinities; but in the *Cratylus* (405) we find them united as attributes of Apollo and the Muses. In respect of his prophetic function Apollo is *Aplous* (= ἁπλοῦς), the speaker of truth. As purifier of the soul by means of mantic fumigations, washing, and aspersion (καθαρτικός) and of the body by healing medicines (ἰατρικός), he is the god who washes away (ἀπολούων) and delivers (ἀπολύων) from evil. The musical explanation of his name is clearly prompted by Pythagorean ideas, since it connects music with astronomy and brings in the harmony of the heavens (πόλοι). The god causes the heavens to revolve together (ἁ = ὁμοῦ, πολῶν) in a harmony, like concord in song. Finally the love of wisdom is represented by the derivation of Muse from μῶσθαι meaning 'inquiry and philosophy'.[1] The accompanying derivations of Leto and Artemis seem also to belong to the same complex of ideas. Leto signifies that gentleness of disposition (τὸ ἥμερόν τε καὶ λεῖον τοῦ ἤθους) which is a mark of the philosopher (*Rep.* 375). Artemis stands for a chaste and sober character and a knowledge of virtue.

All this combination of ideas is manifestly Platonic and Pythagorean: Apollo was the special god of the Pythagoreans, and the Academy was consecrated to the Muses and their Leader, whose birthday in Thargelion was celebrated as the official fête of Plato himself.[2] Taken together, the derivations in the *Cratylus* recall the relation of Apollo to the Socrates of the *Phaedo*, who, while in the Delian god's keeping, composes poetry and music in his honour, and is inspired with mantic power to foresee the happiness that

---

[1] Strabo x, 3, 10: μουσικὴν ἐκάλεσεν ὁ Πλάτων, καὶ ἔτι πρότερον οἱ Πυθαγόρειοι, τὴν φιλοσοφίαν. *Rep.* 548 B: τῆς ἀληθινῆς Μούσης τῆς μετὰ λόγων καὶ φιλοσοφίας. *Phileb.* 67 B: τῶν ἐν Μούσῃ φιλοσόφῳ μεμαντευμένων λόγων.

[2] Wilamowitz, *Platon*, I, p. 271.

awaits him when death shall have completed the purification of his soul from the senses and lusts of the body to receive the full revelation of wisdom in the company of the gods.

But our present concern is with the evidence showing that the union of prophet, poet and wise man in the same person is no novel invention of Plato or of Pythagoras. Apollo was, after all, a god; and his cults and myths exhibit a bewildering congeries of attributes over and above those which figure in the complex we have just considered. We come nearer to earth and to history if we turn to the human figure of Orpheus, who, like the Hyperborean god, appears to have come to Greece from the far north. Orpheus, as Hermias remarks,[1] combined all the forms of divine madness, as founder of mysteries, prophet, poet and son of the Muse Calliope, and instructor of Musaeus. There are other kindred figures, more or less thickly veiled in a cloud of supernatural legend. Bakis, inspired by the Nymphs, purified and healed the women of Sparta when attacked by madness, and predicted the invasion of Xerxes. Musaeus, whom the Eleusinian family descended from Eumolpus of Thrace claimed as an ancestor, son of a Nymph or of a Muse or of Selene, was reputed author of a theogony and of oracles in verse. Onomacritus represented him as flying through the air, by the favour of Boreas. The Hyperborean Abaris went round the world carrying his arrow (or flying on his magic arrow through the air), prophesied, and delivered Sparta from a plague. Aristeas of Proconnesus travelled in spirit far from his body, died and came back to life, and attended Apollo at Metapontion in the form of a raven. He was credited with poems, including a theogony, and his gift of prophecy was perpetuated in the bronze laurel at Metapontion, from which issued a voice that sent diviners into ecstasy. Like the rest he is connected with the countries of the far north. In Thrace again we find the confused legend of Salmoxis, who retired, like Minos and Epimenides, to seek inspired wisdom in an underground chamber (barrow?), or alternatively was a god to whom the Getae, believers in immortality, periodically sent a messenger by throwing him into the air to be transfixed by spears in his fall. The Hellespontine Greeks made out to Herodotus that

---

[1] *In Phaedr.* 244 A (p. 88. 25 Couvreur; Kern, *Orph. Fr.* p. 51).

Salmoxis was the slave of Pythagoras at Samos. Later, he was alleged to have been an inspired prophet who taught the Getae and even the Celtic Druids to believe in immortality, and to have become a god by apotheosis.[1]

In all these mythical or semi-mythical or legendary figures we encounter some of the features we have already seen combined in Epimenides.[2] We may recall Bouché-Leclercq's observation that what matters for religious history is not so much the question whether an individual man called Orpheus or Epimenides or Salmoxis ever existed as the fact that a certain set of attributes belong together, and cohere in a recurrent type. It would be an Euhemeristic fallacy to imagine that such a type had its origin in the crystallization of a number of separate attributes round a single historic personality. We should rather conceive them as constituting a universal function, like that of priest or king, which may be embodied in any number of individuals and transmitted through a succession. To gain further light on the functionary now in question we must follow the indication which points to the extreme northern fringe of the mediterranean world.

Beyond the horizon of the ancient Greeks there exists abundant evidence for the combination prophet-poet-sage, and the implied belief that all exceptional wisdom is the prerogative of inspired or mantic persons who are in touch with the other world of gods or spirits. We are concerned with a certain phase of social development which exhibits a constant character, though in different countries it may appear at widely different dates in the world's history. More particularly the phase in question has been described as covering the heroic and post-heroic ages—a phase in which literature has reached a considerable degree of development but is still orally transmitted or confined to a small lettered class.

The Thracians, it will be remembered, marched with Teutonic peoples on the north and with Celtic peoples on the west. It is tempting to suppose that they may have formed a link in early times between the

[1] Hippol. *Refut.* 1, 2. The references for all the legends mentioned above will be found in Bouché-Leclercq's *Divination*, II, pp. 95 ff.

[2] P. 75 above.

ancient mantic systems of the southern portion of *Eurasia*, as the cult of Othin and other features of Norse religion bear witness to an ancient link between Teutonic and Celtic manticism on the one hand and the shamanism of northern Asia on the other.[1]

Following this indication and starting in the west, we encounter among the ancient Gauls the class of mantic persons including 'bards' (poets), seers (*vates*, μάντεις) and druids. The difficulty experienced by Roman writers in clearly distinguishing their functions may be a sign that the three types were still, as we should expect, more closely allied by their common mantic powers than the corresponding types in Greek and Roman society. The bards were poets and singers who celebrated the epic deeds of famous men. The seers practised augury and foretold the future from sacrificial omens. Superior to both were the druids, who are said to have undergone a long training in natural philosophy and theology and in antiquarian lore. They also, according to Strabo, exercised judicial functions. They were not a caste, but some were of noble birth, like Cicero's friend Divitiacus, a druid who claimed a knowledge of natural philosophy and also a power of divining the future.[2] In Ireland the counterpart of the druid is the *fili*, who 'must originally have been a seer; but in early historical times he had become a scholar and (professional) intellectual man, versed in the cultivation of learned poetry. The growth of native philosophy was cut short by Christianity; but there is evidence enough to show that, like the Welsh, it was essentially mantic' (*G.L.* III, 891). In Wales *Awenithion* denoted persons who prophesied in ecstasy or frenzy, *awen* being the prophetic or poetic spirit in a man. Prophecy and poetry, in fact, were not distinguished, both being gifts of *awen*, as of the Muses in Greek. *Awen* also, like the Muses, supplied information.

---

[1] N. Kershaw Chadwick, *Poetry and Prophecy*, Cambridge, 1942, p. 12. In this short book Mrs Chadwick has summed up a great mass of evidence collected and discussed by Mr Chadwick and herself in the three stout volumes of *The Growth of Literature*, Cambridge, 1932. I owe almost all the evidence produced in this chapter to their invaluable collection, which merits the very serious attention of all students of literature.

[2] Cic. *de Div.* I, 90. The other chief sources are Strabo, IV, 4, 4; Diod. V, 31; Caesar, *B.G.* VI, 13 ff.; Amm. Marc. XX, 9, 8.

Throughout the ancient languages of northern Europe the ideas of poetry, eloquence, information (especially antiquarian learning) and prophecy are intimately connected.... Gnomic lore and mantic and mystical lore of various kinds belong to the same circle of activities.... Hesiod's poems...covered a very similar series of interests.

Celtic literature is particularly rich in information relating to the more technical side of manticism, the signs by which the youthful sage is recognized in early life, the youthful education and upbringing of the seer, his rule of life and professional dress and accessories, his ascetic training and preparation for his calling. More important still are the stories which tell of his later spiritual experiences—his adventures in the spirit world, the various stages through which his spirit passes to its divine vision. Hardly less interesting are the accounts, often fragmentary and obscure, but strangely consistent, of the seer's technique for bringing himself into the inspired condition. We note the preliminary period of seclusion, the stimulating food and drink, the necessity of absence of distraction, the assistance rendered by his companions. These and all other elements in the mantic process and the mantic experience are described with a wealth of technical terminology which proves that among the early Celtic peoples the inculcation of poetic inspiration and the entire mantic art were developed and elaborated to a degree for which we know no parallel.

The most interesting figure in Norse mantic tradition is that of the God Othin. He is *fjölkunnigr*, 'extremely knowing', with the implication of supernatural knowledge, and he is gifted with the power of shape-changing. He is the *thulr* of the gods, the inspired poet and seer, as well as the giver of poetic inspiration and of mantic wisdom.[1]

Othin is the 'High One' referred to in the opening of the Norse *Hávamál*, Part II: 'It is time to chant on the chair of the prophet (*thulr*), at the spring of Fate. I saw and kept silence, I saw and pondered, I listened to the speech of men. I heard runes spoken of—nor did they keep silent about the interpretation thereof— at the Hall of the High One. In the Hall of the High One I heard such words as these.' This is followed by precepts, mystical matter, and a list of spells. Othin is the speaker, and the whole poem is to end in a revelation from him. The milieu is a sanctuary (*G.L.* I, 618).

[1] *Growth of Literature* I, 636f.; *Poetry and Prophecy*, pp. 6, 10.

With this revelation we may compare the *Gylfaginning* (ecstasy or mantic vision of Gylfi), the first part of the Prose Edda written by the Icelandic scholar and statesman Snorri Sturluson, who died in 1241. A King named Gylfi makes his way to Asgarðr in disguise. He enters a hall and sees there three 'high-seats', occupied by persons whom he questions on cosmogony and on the characteristics and doings of the deities. They reply at length in what may perhaps be called a systematic exposition of Norse theology. At last Gylfi hears crashes round him and finds that the hall has disappeared and that he is standing alone out in the open.

The *Gylfaginning* is followed by the *Skaldskaparmál* or 'Diction of Poetry', and the *Háttatal* or 'List of Metres'. The *Prose Edda* as a whole seems to have been designed as a handbook for the study of poetry. But the question which interests us here is how far the *Gylfaginning* preserves a tradition of the method of teaching practised in heathen times. In any case the resemblance to the session of the (Polynesian) *whare wananga*[1]...is noteworthy (*G.L.* III, 902).

Mrs Chadwick concludes a brief survey of the Greek, Celtic, Teutonic, and Norse evidence with the remark that

it is clear that the function of the seer was practically universal in early Europe. For centuries before Christ it was important in the south—in Thrace, in Greece, and doubtless in Etruria. During the Roman period and the Dark Ages it was held in high estimation in central Europe. Long before the close of the first millennium it had left a rich store of legends to the Celtic and Teutonic populations of the outer fringes of Europe.

The fundamental elements of the prophetic function seem to have been everywhere the same. Everywhere the gift of poetry is inseparable from divine inspiration. Everywhere this inspiration carries with it knowledge—whether of the past, in the form of history and genealogy; of the hidden present, in the form commonly of scientific information; or of the future, in the form of prophetic utterance in the narrower sense. Always this knowledge is accompanied by music, whether of song or instrument. Music is everywhere the medium of communication with spirits. Invariably we find that the poet and seer attributes his inspiration to contact with supernatural powers, and his mood during

[1] See below, p. 97.

prophetic utterance is exalted and remote from that of his normal existence. Generally we find that a recognized process is in vogue by which the prophetic mood can be induced at will. The lofty claims of the poet and seer are universally admitted, and he himself holds a high status wherever he is found. In addition to all this we find a common vocabulary of technical terms which goes back to early times. (*Poetry and Prophecy*, p. 14.)

As we move farther eastwards we find that the practices reflected in Celtic, Teutonic and Norse legend are still in use among the peoples of northern Siberia. Othin, indeed, has been described as 'the divine *shaman* of the Norse pantheon', whose affinities are to be sought in northern Asia. The *shamans* and *bakshas* of these regions are of peculiar interest for our purpose, because they are responsible for spiritual and intellectual poetry, as distinct from the poets and reciters of the poetry of entertainment and celebration. Thus they illustrate the background of Hesiod's didactic poetry rather than that of the Homeric Epos.

The *shamans*[1] and *shamankas* (female seers) are found among the Tatars and other Siberian peoples who have not adopted Buddhism, Mohammedanism or Christianity; the *bakshas* among those which have embraced Islam, e.g. the Kazaka and Turcomans. They are described by a recent investigator as 'singers, poets, musicians, diviners, priests and doctors, the guardians of popular religious traditions, and the preservers of ancient legend'. The *shaman* is the intermediary between his fellow tribesmen and the spirit world. He offers their prayers to the spirits of the sixteen heavens or to Erlik Khan, the black ruler of the dead in the underworld. He conveys the tribal sacrifice to the highest god, and conducts the souls of the dead to their last abode in Erlik's realm. On his spiritual journeys he is often mounted on a bird or transformed into a bird, perhaps symbolizing the communal soul of the tribe. His manifestations take the form of a combined extempore performance (usually the drum), song, dancing and some mimesis. The dance is rapid and exhausting, but perfectly controlled, though apparently abandoned and wild. In dramatic monologue the *shaman* represents his journey to the Heavens or to the underworld,

---

[1] The following account of the *shamans* is taken from G.L. III, 192 ff.

on the back of a goose or a horse, with one or more companions. The journey is long and difficult. The *shaman*, as *psychopompos*, encourages his companions to the goal, and returns alone, glad to be back in this world. The whole performance, song, dance and acting, is by the *shaman* alone. Stimulants are used. Before he begins, a long silence of the whole audience helps him to concentrate on spiritual matters. At the annual horse sacrifice, the greater his power, the more heavens he can penetrate, up to the sixteenth, where he addresses the highest god, learns whether the sacrifice is accepted, and receives prophecies about the weather and the harvest and injunctions about sacrifice. At the end he sinks down exhausted, and, after a silence, seems to awake from sleep. A second religious drama represents his journey to the underworld conveying the souls of the dead. He describes his travels from the place of the performance, over steppes and mountains, to a hole in the ground, the 'jaws of the earth', leading to the underworld. After crossing the sea by a hair, he reaches the abode of Erlik Khan, which resembles a Buddhist monastic settlement, with great dogs and a porter who takes presents. He is admitted to audience with the great Khan, a typical oriental despot. There is some comic acting of the drunken god, who, overcome with wine and presents, gives his blessing and reveals the future. The *shaman* returns, riding his goose. Among the Yakuts the autumn festival, dedicated to the 'black' spirit, takes place at night.

It is important to realize that the *shaman* has not degenerated into a vulgar witch-doctor or medicine-man. The intellectual life of the community is almost wholly vested in the *shamans*. They are not a separate caste or class; they live and work like anyone else, though they are more given to solitude and are said to have a strange look in their eyes which often appears clearly in photographs. In contrast with the priests of more advanced communities, who hold office, hereditary or derived from a central authority, the *shaman* has no organization. His claim is based on divine inspiration, proved by his superior spiritual, intellectual and artistic gifts. The 'call' often comes in adolescence or early manhood, from a dead ancestor in the form of vision or dream, or as the result of an illness. He must be able, with a fresh mind and well-stored memory, to extemporize the libretto of his performance, on traditional lines already familiar to his audience, but composed afresh for every recitation. About his education there is little evidence; but the outlines are traditional, learnt partly by observation of older *shamans*, partly by a period of special instruction by them. At his inauguration an older *shaman* addresses him with mythological and mantic information and precepts on his conduct in his new calling. In general, however, he claims that his knowledge and power come, not by his own efforts or from men, but by inspiration. This revealed knowledge covers the whole field of human experience and consciousness, the past, the hidden present, and the future, including historical and 'scientific' information. Castrén[1] records the following statement by a *shaman*: 'God has appointed that I must wander both beneath and upon the earth, and has bestowed on me such power that I can comfort and cheer the afflicted, and on the other hand I can cast down those who are too happy.... I am called Kögel Khan and I am a *shaman*, who knows the future, the past, and everything which is taking place in the present, both above and below the earth.' V. V. Radlov, a highly experienced and acute observer, states that poetry and saga relating to the Heavens and to cosmogony and supernatural matters were largely obtained by him from the recitations of *shamans*. Tatar sagas represent the seer as maintaining his prestige by his knowledge of native natural science or philosophy and his skilled use of poetic diction. The Yakut *shaman* is said to have a poetic vocabulary of 12,000 words, as against some 4000 words in daily use.

Farther east, 'everywhere throughout the Pacific the most ambitious and imaginative forms of poetical composition, as well as all intellectual matter, are directly derived through inspired seers or other persons endowed with divine ecstasy, from the spirit world' (*Poetry and Prophecy*, p. 25). In this region the equivalents of the *shaman* are the Marquesan *tohungas*, 'the repositories of all the ancient chants and the composers of extempore ritual embodying the intellectual life and oral, historical and genealogical records of this singularly intellectual people'; the priestesses of

[1] *Nordische Reisen u. Forschungen*, IV, 256.

Pele in Hawaii, who claim to be permanent embodiments of the divinity; the inspired priest-kings of Mangaia; the *arioi* of Tahiti, a highly specialized guild who enacted ritual dramatic poetry connected with the life of the gods and cosmogony; the priest-seers (*kaulas*) of the Marquesas; the seeresses of the Sea Dyaks in North Borneo, whose ritual chants represent spirits passing to and fro as the emissaries of the seeress between the world of mortals and the spirit world, and the seeress herself conducting souls to the land of the dead.

One further point may be noted. At the stage where all exceptional knowledge, outranging the daily experience of the common man, is obtained by inspiration, it constitutes a body of wisdom which is sacred or 'mysterious'. This is the case, for instance, with the *tohungas* of Polynesia, of whom we read (*G.L.* III, 458):

In order to secure the best conditions for the preservation and transmission of oral traditional learning, certain institutions have been developed in various island groups, known as *whare*, such as the *whare wananga*, *whare kura*, etc. The word *whare* means literally 'house'.... In practice the *whare* was in the nature of a 'school', or course of instruction in native learning. The word *wananga*...means inspired knowledge which is part of the divine or spiritual experience of an inspired person; but in fact all knowledge was regarded as *tapu* or in some measure sacred by the Polynesians in general. The association of the *tohunga* and his spiritual and intellectual experience is very close. In other words, the Polynesians do not distinguish, as we do, between secular and spiritual knowledge and experience....

Our fullest information relates to the *whare wananga* of the Maori, in which the traditional oral learning of the Maori was carried on by *tohungas* who appear to have belonged to several orders. The learning itself was guarded with the utmost jealousy and secrecy, being regarded as exceedingly *tapu*. The desire was to hand on the traditional lore with as little change as possible. Great ceremony attended the courses, while the pupils were subject to much ritual and *tapu*....It is said that the pupils had to undergo a preliminary teaching amongst their own tribe before entering the *whare wananga*. The scholars were selected from among the 'young lads' who showed a disposition towards learning, and had been observed to be accomplished in telling stories. Only young lads belonging to families of good standing were taught by the *tohungas* the higher knowledge which was regarded as fitting for the chiefs and priests, especially knowledge relating to religion, cosmogony, traditional history and other antiquarian matters.

The parallel which this account presents, in many essential aspects, to the view of knowledge held by the Pythagorean brotherhood should not be overlooked.

In India the complex 'prophet-poet-sage' is neatly illustrated by the word *kavi*, 'poet', which also means 'seer'—the original meaning, as is generally thought—and in the plural denotes 'the wise', 'sages'. It is the equivalent of the Irish *fili* and the Norse *thulr*. Every hymn in the Rgveda is attributed to a seer, to whom it was believed to have been revealed. Sometimes these seers are deities or supernatural beings. In many cases the seer's name or family is recorded. There is evidence for ancient families with mantic powers, like the Greek *Iamidae*. The *Mahābhārata* and the *Purānas* are said to have been composed by ancient seers, Vyāsa and others. In the *Mahābhārata* itself the place of inspiration is taken by yoga, the essential feature of which is the concentration of thought on some object or idea (elsewhere commonly associated with mantic activity) involving magical power (*G.L.* II, 582, 607, 624). The Brahmins or *rishis* of ancient India bear a close resemblance to the druids and seers of ancient Gaul as described by Caesar, in their educational system, the nature of their speculations, their secluded forest life, and their attention to traditional oral literature (*Poetry and Prophecy*, p. 12). Here, too, the transition from the seer (brahmin) to the philosopher can be traced; for the philosophy of the Upanishads is of mantic origin (*G.L.* III, 891).

The Upanishads contain pronouncements or debates on abstract subjects which interested the intellectual people of India, princes and brahmins, from the eighth to the fifth centuries B.C. The sages are chiefly occupied with the conception of *brahma*, a self-existent power which pervades and comprehends the world. But the word *brahma* originally meant spell, prayer, and then spiritual power, often contrasted with *ksatra*, the temporal power of the prince. The underlying idea is that the seer's power, in the abstract, is the dominant force in the world. The impersonal *brahma* finally becomes the personal Brahma (masc.), a new supreme deity or creator. The seer is in a twofold way the intermediary between man and deity: in the Hymn he addresses deity on man's behalf, though he is inspired by deity; as the revealer of wisdom, he conveys messages from deity to man (*G.L.* III, 848 ff.). It is precisely in such terms that Diotima describes the functions of the prophet and the priest (*Symp.* 202 E).

Roughly contemporary with the philosophy of the Upanishads are the Hebrew prophets whose works have been preserved, from Amos in the first half of the eighth century onwards, and the early didactic poetry of Greece. It is pointed out[1] that all these are manifestations of parallel phases of culture, in the early post-heroic times when writing is beginning to be used for literary purposes. The parallel is curiously close between Amos and Hesiod. Both were shepherds, who were feeding their flocks when the inspiration came to them. 'I was no prophet', said Amos to Amaziah, 'neither was I a prophet's son; but I was an herdman, and a gatherer of sycomore fruit: and the Lord took me as I followed the flock, and the Lord said unto me, Go, prophesy unto my people Israel.' Neither Amos nor Hesiod, however, was ignorant: they were versed in antiquarian lore. There is a close resemblance, moreover, in the economic and social evils which (unlike the Indian philosophers) they are concerned to denounce. This is no accident. It is suggested that the opening or re-opening of the Mediterranean lands to commercial enterprise and the consequent rise in the standard of living had occasioned simultaneously in Greece and Palestine those conditions which led to revolutions, dictatorships, and the cancellation of debts in seventh-century Greece. Hesiod and Amos alike bitterly condemn the violence, injustice, and corruption of the richer classes; both associate justice with the deity and are convinced that injustice will lead to disaster. There is, of course, a wide difference between them in respect of their attitude towards their work. Amos speaks as the direct mouthpiece of the Lord, who at other times appears to him in visions. The mantic origin of Hesiod's wisdom is more remote; but there is no reason to doubt that his description of the call which first came to him from the Muses while he was tending his sheep under Helicon

[1] In *G.L.* II, 722 ff.

99

represents a real experience. It has been compared to Caedmon's dream recorded by Bede. Caedmon had never been taught to sing; he could not take his turn with the harp until he had received the gift of poetry in a dream. Thereafter, by going over in his mind and 'ruminating' upon all that he had learnt by listening to the monks, he was able to turn this knowledge into sweet song.[1] Hesiod, similarly, had a memory stored with myths of the origin of the world, the birth of the gods, the battle with the Titans, as well as with gnomic wisdom distilled from popular experience and with peasant lore of works and days. As he ruminated upon all this knowledge during those long days spent in solitude on the hills which have made so many shepherds into musicians, poets, or prophets, there came a moment when the daughters of Memory, the Muses, impelled him to pour his thoughts into the mould already provided by the epic poetry of the minstrels, who by grace of the Muses and Apollo had sung to the lyre the glories of the men of old (*Theog.* 94).

We are here reminded of the minstrels in Homer. Phemius, like Caedmon, had never been taught, but was inspired by the god who had put into his heart all the modes of song. Demodocus, instructed by the Muse or even by Apollo, could tell all that the Achaeans had done and suffered at Troy 'as if he had been present or heard the story from another'. For us these phrases describing inspiration have become so trite and conventional that they have lost all their vital meaning. But there are minstrels now living who make precisely the same claims as Caedmon or Demodocus or Hesiod, and go to work in the same way. Radlov has given the following account of a Kirghiz minstrel:[2]

The procedure of the improvising minstrel is exactly like that of the pianist. As the latter puts together into a harmonious form different runs which are known to him, transitions and motifs according to the inspiration of the moment, and thus makes up the new from the old which is familiar to him, so also does the minstrel of epic poems.

[1] Bede, *Eccles. Hist.* IV, 24: cuncta quae audiendo discere poterat rememorando secum et quasi mundum animal ruminando in carmen dulcissimum convertebat (*cit.* G.L. I, 635 ff.).

[2] *Proben der Volkslitteratur der Türkischen Stämme*, v, 16 ff., quoted by Chadwick, *G.L.* III, 182.

Through an extensive practice in production, he has whole series of 'elements of production', if I may so express it, in readiness, which he puts together in suitable manner according to the course of the narrative. Such 'elements of production' consist of pictures of certain occurrences and situations, such as the birth of a hero, the growing up of the hero, the glories of weapons, preparations for battle...characteristics of persons and of horses.... The art of the singer consists only in arranging all these static component parts of pictures with one another as circumstances require, and in connecting them with lines invented for the occasion....The amount of the formative elements and the skill in putting them together is the measure of the skill of the minstrel.... When I asked one of the most accomplished minstrels whom I had learnt to know if he could sing this or that song, he answered me: 'I can sing any song whatever; for God has implanted this gift of song in my heart. He gives me the word on my tongue, without my having to seek it. I have learnt none of my songs. All springs from my inner self.' And the man was right. The improvising minstrel sings without reflection, simply from his inner being, that which is known to him, as soon as the incentive to singing comes to him from without, just as the words flow from the tongue of a speaker without his producing intentionally and consciously the articulations necessary to produce them, as soon as the course of his thoughts requires this or that word. The accomplished minstrel can sing a day, or a week, or a month, just as he can speak, and narrate all the time.

The power of this Kirghiz minstrel to 'sing any song whatever' is exactly that power which Demodocus exercises when Odysseus asks him to 'shift' (μετάβηθι) to the story of the Trojan horse, and promises that, if the minstrel can duly recount it, he will tell all men how the god has endowed him with inspired song (θέσπιν ἀοιδήν). Thus challenged, Demodocus 'impelled by the god began and showed forth the song, taking it up where it tells how...etc.'.[1] Either the Muse or Apollo himself has taught him the 'paths' of song (οἴμας), including Radlov's 'elements of production', and he can take up the narrative at any point and continue it 'in due order' (κατὰ κόσμον, 489; κατὰ μοῖραν καταλέξης, 496), the god giving him the word on his tongue without his having to seek it. Princes

[1] *Od.* VIII, 492 ff.: ὁ δ' ὁρμηθεὶς θεοῦ ἤρχετο, φαῖνε δ' ἀοιδήν, ἔνθεν ἑλὼν ὡς....

also, according to Hesiod, owe their eloquence to the Muses, who shed sweet dew on their tongues, so that honeyed words flow from their lips and they can easily reconcile a dispute with soft persuasive speech (*Theog.* 80 ff.). 'It is an old saying that whenever a poet is seated on the Muses' tripod, he is not in his senses but is like a fountain giving free course to the water which keeps flowing on' (Plato, *Laws*, 719 c).

Radlov's description teaches us more about the meaning of 'rhapsody' than can be learnt from notes on ῥάπτειν ἀοιδήν by scholars who think of Homer at his desk sub-editing lays with scissors and paste. We can also see from it that there are no sharp lines to be drawn between the original creative poet, the minstrel who improvises on traditional themes, and the reciter like Ion. They form, as Socrates says, a chain transmitting the magnetic force of inspired imagination from its farthest source to the audience moved in sympathy with the rhapsode's transports.

The evidence produced in this chapter has sufficiently lighted up the background behind the minstrelsy of Homer and the didactic poetry of Hesiod, which, so long as attention was confined to the surviving documents of Greek literature, might well seem like miraculous and unaccountable phenomena. The distinctions between the prophet, the poet, and the sage disappear in the complex figure of Castrén's *shaman*, 'who knows the future, the past, and everything which is taking place in the present, both above and below the earth'. Past, present, and future are revealed equally to the seer Calchas and to the didactic poet inspired by Hesiod's Muses.[1] If prophetic inspiration can reveal the past and present as well as the future, and poetic inspiration can reveal the present and future as well as the past, prophecy and poetry must be the outcome of a single form of experience, characterized by Plato as divine or inspired 'madness'. The experience can be conceived in two ways. The patient may feel that a supernatural power has entered and taken possession of him: he has become ἔνθεος, like

---

[1] *Il.* I, 69; Κάλχας Θεστορίδης, οἰωνοπόλων ὄχ' ἄριστος, ὃς ᾔδη τά τ' ἐόντα τά τ' ἐσσόμενα πρό τ' ἐόντα. Hesiod, *Theog.* 31, 38 ἐνέπνευσαν δέ μ' ἀοιδὴν θέσπιν, ἵνα κλείοιμι τά τ' ἐσσόμενα πρό τ' ἐόντα... εἰρεῦσαι τά τ' ἐόντα τά τ' ἐσσόμενα πρό τ' ἐόντα.

the Pythian priestess or the Sibyl. Or he may feel that his own soul has left his body in ecstatic trance and visited the world of spirits. The mimetic ritual performance of the *shaman* is designed to symbolize and bring home to the audience this journey to the other world. If the methods seem crude to us, that is no reason for dismissing the whole performance as a calculated imposture, though it might sink to that level if the prophet should lose faith in his own powers. Where such faith is still living, we must recognize the fact of a spiritual experience comparable to that of medieval and contemporary mystics. The comparison is drawn by Mrs Chadwick, and she adds some wise remarks on the possibilities of misunderstanding.

One of the greatest difficulties which one has to try to overcome in reading the writings of St Theresa and of the other medieval mystics is that of really understanding what she is talking about. The vocabulary is our own, the diction is familiar, but the mould, the literary formulae, are alien to the traditional mould in which modern secular thought is cast. The familiar words and formulae are symbols for unfamiliar ideas. How much more must this be so when we seek to interpret the utterances of a Chuckchee *shaman* ! How little qualified are we to know the traditional, as distinct from the lexicographical value of word and phrase, to interpret the traditional figurative diction—to know when a *shaman* does not intend us to place a literal interpretation on his words !... For instances we may turn to certain books of incantation current among the Mussulman *bakshas* which make mention of Turkish saints who mount on lions, dragons etc., while similar feats are attributed to many notable characters of the ancient Mussulman world. But it is clear from the oral literature current among the Tatars of Central Asia today that identical feats are there attributed to the heroes and heroines in a manner which shows that they are to be understood as among, not the actual, but the spiritual experiences of these people. As a typical instance of the literal interpretation of ritual symbolism by those ignorant of its true significance we may refer to the statement made of a great Mongol *shaman* of the time of Jenghiz Khan who is said to have counted among his other 'prodigies' (*prodigues*) that of having ascended to heaven on his horse—clearly a typical piece of *shamanist* ritual, such as that performed symbolically by the Buryat *shaman* on his *ongon*, or 'hobby-horse'. (*Poetry and Prophecy*, p. 70.)

These considerations should put us on our guard against dismissing as mere wonder-working charlatans or magicians such figures as Abaris, flying through the air on his arrow, Aristeas, travelling in spirit far from his body, Salmoxis, Melampus, and others. Nor should we allow the cloud of legendary marvels surrounding Orpheus, Epimenides, or Pythagoras to detract from their serious significance for the history of religion and philosophy. If it had so chanced that the only record left of Parmenides was the opening lines of his poem, he would be set aside as a magician who boasted of having travelled in the Sun's chariot beyond the gates of day and night, or as a mythical doublet of Phaethon.

Hesiod's Muses announce that 'while they know how to tell many fictions that are like the truth, they can also, when they will, declare the truth'. It is generally agreed that this preface means that the contents of the theogony are claimed to be a revelation of truth about the remotest past, not plausible figments of the poet's invention. But the further assumption that 'fictions like the truth' is intended to describe the epic literature of entertainment is questionable. It may well be doubted[1] whether the stories of the Homeric poems were regarded as fictitious (ψεύδεα) in Hesiod's day. As late as the fourth century we find Plato quoting the *Odyssey* for the domestic economy of the Cyclopes and the *Iliad* for the rise of the third variety of constitution. In the latter passage Plato adds that the lines he quotes 'are as true to nature as they are inspired. Poets, indeed, singing as they do under the divine afflatus, are among the inspired and so, by the help of their Graces and Muses, they often grasp the truth of what has really happened.'[2] Plato would, no doubt, have allowed a larger scope to Homer's imagination (as we call it) than Hesiod would have done; but his words definitely state that historic truth about the distant past is revealed to poets by inspiration, not merely handed on to them by

---

[1] As by Chadwick, *G.L.* I, 635 ff.

[2] *Laws*, 682 A: λέγει γὰρ δὴ ταῦτα τὰ ἔπη (*Il.* XX, 216 ff.) καὶ ἐκεῖνα ἃ περὶ τῶν Κυκλώπων εἴρηκε (*Od.* IX, 112 ff.) κατὰ θεόν πως εἰρημένα καὶ κατὰ φύσιν. θεῶν γὰρ οὖν δὴ καὶ τὸ ποιητικὸν ἐνθεαστικὸν ὂν γένος ὑμνῳδοῦν πολλῶν τῶν κατ᾽ ἀλήθειαν γιγνομένων ξύν τισι Χάρισι καὶ Μούσαις ἐφάπτεται ἑκάστοτε. Hermias, *in Phaedrum*, p. 88. 17 (Couvreur), citing this passage, read ἐνθεαστικόν, which some editors of the *Laws* bracket.

human tradition. It is significant that Hesiod's phrase 'fictions like the truth'[1] is borrowed from the *Odyssey*, where it describes the avowedly false tale in which Odysseus tells Penelope that he is a son of Deucalion and has entertained her husband in Crete. Hesiod's second line, moreover, 'we know how to declare the truth when we will', is based on another verse in the *Odyssey* where Eumaeus speaks of the false tales of vagrant beggars who 'will not speak the truth'. The epic poet, inserting such falsehoods where they form part of his whole narrative, is still under the inspiration of the Muse, and, after all, it is true that men tell lies. Homer might well have said of his Muse precisely what Hesiod says, and meant thereby that, though his story includes some false tales told by his characters, the story itself is 'the truth of what really happened' grasped by intuitive revelation.

However it may be with Homer, we need not doubt that the poets who composed the theogonies and cosmogonies of the post-heroic age—those 'theologians' in whom Aristotle recognized the precursors of the natural philosophers—would all have claimed, with Hesiod, that they were uttering revealed truth. They would have understood what Amos meant when he announced his prophecies as 'the words of Amos, who was among the herdmen of Tekoa, which he *saw* concerning Israel'.[2]

In the earliest extant literature of Greece, the differentiation of poetry into species has already begun. In Homer the literature of entertainment has already advanced from improvised minstrelsy to the full epic form. The literature of instruction, as represented by Hesiod, still combines elements which later took their several ways. There is the gnomic element, continued by Theognis and in the political poetry of Solon and Tyrtaeus, and the agricultural and astronomical information, elaborated in later Georgics. Poetry of this kind is obviously based on ordinary experience and worldly

[1] Hes. *Theog.* 27: ἴδμεν ψεύδεα πολλὰ λέγειν ἐτυμοῖσιν ὁμοῖα, ἴδμεν δ', εὖτ' ἐθέλωμεν ἀληθέα γηρύσασθαι (*v.l.* μυθήσασθαι). *Od.* XIX, 203: ἴσκε ψεύδεα πολλὰ λέγων ἐτυμοῖσιν ὁμοῖα; XIV, 124, ἄνδρες ἀλῆται ψεύδοντ', οὐδ' ἐθέλουσιν ἀληθέα μυθήσασθαι.
[2] Compare the opening words of Obadiah: 'The *vision* of Obadiah: Thus saith the Lord'; and of Micah: 'The word of the Lord that came to Micah... which he *saw* concerning Samaria.'

wisdom, although the instruction is conveyed in a tone of superior authority. The cosmogony and theogony stand on a different footing. It is no less obvious that these elements are not the outcome of immediate observation. They enshrine myths of great antiquity, whose origin was unknown to the poet who transmitted them. They retained the sacred character of religious revelation. From the sixth century onwards they were assailed by Ionian rationalism on moral grounds; but, like the unedifying parts of other revelations, they were not abandoned, but defended by the expedient of allegorical interpretation. A deeply religious poet like Aeschylus could discover a profoundly moral significance even in the 'violent deeds' of Cronos and Zeus and in the amours of the Father of gods and men. Plato himself, where he condemns these myths as unfit to be told to thoughtless young people who would take them literally, admits that they might be capable of an allegorical meaning, such as could be revealed in a mystery (*Rep.* 377–8). Aeschylus and Plato were right in their instinctive feeling that cosmogonical myths are not to be taken at their face value, as if they professed to be records of historical events on the human plane. Even the Milesian philosophers had learnt these myths at their mother's knee. It is not unreasonable to suppose that, however enlightened they might become in later life, they could never entirely throw off the weight of authority invested in the magnificient language of the greatest among poets.

CHAPTER VII

THE PHILOSOPHER AS SUCCESSOR OF THE SEER-POET

IN Plato's *Protagoras*, when Socrates and his young friend visit the great sophist at the house of his rich host, and inquire into his methods of instruction, Protagoras acknowledges that he is a sophist and educates men, adding that he makes no attempt to conceal his superior wisdom for fear of unpopularity. In earlier times, he says, the possessors of such wisdom thought it prudent to assume various disguises: poetry in the case of Homer, Hesiod, Simonides; rituals of initiation and the delivery of oracles, as in the case of Orpheus and Musaeus; gymnastic, like Iccus of Tarentum and Herodicus in his own day; or music, like the Athenian Agathocles and many others. Here once more, in a somewhat unexpected context, we find the association of poetry and music, prophecy, and ritual and physical purification which we noted in the derivations of Apollo in the *Cratylus*,[1] while Protagoras' own manner of educating men by imparting wisdom corresponds to the derivation of 'Muse' from μῶσθαι meaning 'inquiry and philosophy'. The implication in both passages is that the wise man, whether called by his older title *sophistes* or by the more modest term 'lover of wisdom', was still recognized in the fifth and fourth centuries as one of the differentiated types which had emerged from the complex prophet-poet-sage, studied in the last chapter. His affinities have been ignored by modern historians of philosophy whose minds have been obsessed by the nineteenth-century 'conflict of religion and science'. They have assumed that enlightened rationalism is necessarily in opposition to the superstitious beliefs and practices of a now obsolete religion, or that a philosopher whose religious interests cannot be overlooked must have kept his religion and science in compartments, separated by a bulkhead strong enough to prevent their getting together and quarrelling.

[1] Above, p. 88. Cf. Aristophanes, *Frogs*, 1030 ff.

But, once they are seen against the background we have tried to fill in, some at least of the early philosophers show clearly enough a consciousness of their position as the successors of the composite *shaman* type. As such we shall consider them in this chapter, before turning, in the next, to the complementary aspect of the philosopher as the rival of the other two, now distinct, figures, the seer and the poet.

There is little need to dwell at length on the character of Pythagoras. He belonged to that small class of 'divine' men whose figures become legendary as soon as, or even before, they are dead. Quite apart from the later neo-Pythagorean legend, Aristotle already records miracles ascribed to him.[1] Owing to this transfiguration, among great historical characters we know least, by way of historical fact, about these divine men, of whom we should desire to know most. The important point is that, in highly civilized communities, legends of this sort do not gather round insignificant people or mere charlatans; or, if they do, charlatans do not win the respect of men like Aristotle and Plato. The epithet 'divine' (θεῖος) has a wide range of meaning. It could be taken literally, as when Pythagoras or Plato was supposed to be the son of a god.[2] In the context of the belief in metempsychosis, it could denote the condition of a soul which had achieved purification and was destined to escape further reincarnation and to join the company of the gods. This may be what is meant by the saying that 'among rational creatures there are gods and men and beings like Pythagoras' (Aristotle, *frag.* 192). At the least, 'divine' signified 'divinely inspired' and was so applied to the seer and the poet. At bottom, the word recognizes the existence of a class of men whose wisdom is not derived from ordinary experience in the light of common day but from access to a world of gods and spirits or a timeless reality however conceived. In considering the system of a 'divine' philosopher it is idle to speak of sciences 'taking over' doctrines from religion or of religion as 'grafting

[1] Aristotle, *frag.* 191 (*Vors.⁵* I, p. 96), appears to have spoken of Pythagoras as the successor of Epimenides, Aristeas, Hermotimus, Abaris and Pherekydes.

[2] According to Aristotle, *loc. cit.*, the Crotoniates actually called Pythagoras the Hyperborean Apollo.

doctrines' on philosophy. The great pre-Socratic thinkers of this type have not, each of them, two distinct visions of the universe—a religious one for Sundays and a scientific one for weekdays. Each has a single, unitary vision, embracing all that he believes about reality, all that he would call wisdom. In the Italian tradition the fundamental impulse is religious and moral, not mere intellectual curiosity which might lead to the acceptance of any type of conclusion about the real nature of the world. If you study Nature for the good of your soul, and to help you on the Way of Life, your system of Nature must be of a kind that will help you, not one which will defeat your deepest hopes by a materialistic atheism denying the very existence of an immortal soul.

We have here to overcome a difficulty that confronts the modern mind in seeing the connexion between departments of thought which have come to be completely dissociated. To our thinking mathematics—arithmetic, geometry, astronomy, music—has nothing to do with religion and morals. We do not expect a pure mathematician to be conspicuously moral or religious: instances to the contrary may occur to one's mind. But the connexion was obvious to Pythagoras, and after him to Plato, in whose scheme of education the path to wisdom lies through the study of pure mathematics and ends in the vision of the good, the knowledge that is virtue. It is true that in the generations after Pythagoras the two aspects of his philosophy soon began to drift apart. The stricter communities adhered to the Pythagorean way of life, to be followed by observing rules of conduct, certain kinds of abstinence, and so on. Others revered the founder of mathematical science, to be pursued for its own sake. A further step was taken when mathematics was divorced from physics. The 'numbers' which constitute reality were no longer confused with collections of tangible things, or the figures of geometry with the coloured surfaces of material bodies.

Numbers and figures became what we call 'abstract', and by Plato's time it was realized that the pure mathematical sciences are systems of eternal truths, containing no reference to physical bodies in time and space, which might be blotted out of existence without affecting their validity. When this point is reached, it becomes hard to understand how numbers could be the 'nature' or real being of physical things. In the materialistic system of Leucippus and Democritus, they are replaced by particles of solid impenetrable body and so lose all connexion with religious and moral ideas. So these divergent currents of thought drifted apart; but it is not impossible to trace them back to their common source in the original system of Pythagoras.

We know that the Pythagorean school was no mere succession of master and pupils, such as we find in the Ionian tradition, but a fraternity with something of the character of a monastic order. It was, moreover, modelled on the mystical cult-society, into which admission was gained, not by right of birth into a family, clan, or state, but by initiation, a privilege sought by personal choice because it answered to some need personally felt. In the process of initiation there were two stages: a preliminary purification, which might be merely ceremonial, fitting the candidate to proceed to the second stage, the revelation of symbolic cult-objects and ritual dramas. To witness these was to assure oneself of a 'better lot' in the other world. The revelation was accompanied by some instruction in the meaning of the sacred things seen and enacted. 'Blessed is he who has seen these things; the uninitiate shall never have a like portion after death' (*Hymn to Demeter*, 480).

The entire procedure rests on the belief that there is another world, an invisible world of gods and spirits, where the individual soul will have its place after death. Revelation is the only means of access to knowledge of this world; the initiates claimed to be 'those who know' (οἱ εἰδότες) or 'the wise' (σοφοί). In the Pythagorean organization there was a noviciate, a probationary stage before full admission. The common life of the order was governed by rules, including abstinence from certain kinds of food and dress. And, as in the mystery cults, there was a rule of secrecy, and a tradition that all discoveries were to be attributed to the Founder, presumably because they were conceived as developments of his original revelation of truth.

In the early part of the *Phaedo*, and in many other places, Plato has developed the deeper significance attached by the Pythagoreans to the idea of purification followed by revelation. It is the deliverance of the soul, by origin and nature divine, from the prison-house of the mortal body, a partial deliverance during this life to be completed after death. The knowledge, whereby it is delivered, is the contemplation of truth—intellectual truth manifested through the divine order of the heaven or cosmos. Thus Pythagoreanism was a philosophy as well as a religion. Philosophically, the truth contemplated is the ultimate nature of things; religiously, it is the knowledge which enables man to advance to spiritual perfection, by assimilating his own nature to the unseen order of the world.

A man whose thoughts are fixed on true reality has no leisure to look downwards on the affairs of men, to take part in their quarrels, and to catch the infection of their jealousies and hates. He contemplates a world of unchanging and harmonious order, where reason governs and nothing can do or suffer wrong; and, like one who imitates an admired companion, he cannot fail to fashion himself in its likeness. So the philosopher, in constant companionship with the divine order of the world, will reproduce that order in his soul and, so far as man may, become godlike. (*Rep.* 500.)

Some critics have seen no connexion between this conception of knowledge and the doctrine of reincarnation, which was undoubtedly taught by Pythagoras. But, as we have already seen, the Platonic theory of *Anamnesis* provides the link; and it now seems more probable that this theory was rooted in the older Pythagorean tradition. Pythagoras was regarded as a prophet of the mantic Apollo and the hierophant of a sacred revelation. The content of the revelation is the intellectual truths of mathematics, apprehended by the reason, not given in everyday sensible experience. The rational soul (τὸ λόγον ἔχον), in this dualistic system, is the divine, immortal element in our nature, opposed to the passions and senses of the body. The knowledge gained in contemplation comes from that other world of gods and spirits which the soul visits when detached from the body in concentrated thought, and still more when it is set free by death. The fallen soul thus regains its divinity: man becomes godlike by assimilating his moral nature to the harmonious order the intellect reveals. Here the mathematical and the religious aspects of this philosophy meet in the central idea of harmony. The harmony of the musical scale was first reduced to mathematical ratios by Pythagoras. The discovery prompted the intuition that 'the whole Heaven (or visible universe) is harmony and number'—an intuition destined, it seems, to be verified by the whole trend of modern physics in a manner of which Pythagoras could have no conception. Philosophy, 'the highest form of music', is both the discovery of mathematical truth and the way of life which brings the soul into tune with the beauty and goodness implied in the term 'cosmos'.

Heracleitus was a man of very different temperament from Pythagoras, but his claim to be, in his own way, a prophet is equally unmistakable.

He was of a proud and high spirit beyond all other men and one who looked down on all others, as appears from his treatise where he says: 'Much learning does not teach insight; else it would have taught Hesiod and Pythagoras, Xenophanes and Hecataeus.'...He said that when young he knew nothing, but when full-grown he had come to know everything. He was no man's pupil, but asserted that he had 'searched himself' and learnt everything from himself. (*D.L.* IX, 1 and 5.)

He was accordingly the one philosopher of note whom the later compilers of 'successions' could not affiliate to any predecessor. The surviving fragments justify his claim to originality; and their oracular style partly explains why no one could understand him. It was even said that he did not wish to be understood by the multitude: 'he dedicated his book in the temple of Artemis, and according to some he deliberately made it the more obscure in order that only those who were capable should have access to it and that familiarity should not breed contempt....Theophrastus put it down to his melancholy temperament (or genius) that some parts are half finished, others make a strange medley.'[1]

---

[1] D.L. IX, 6. The master's style was no doubt imitated by those followers described by Theodorus in *Theaet.* 180A as 'plucking from their quiver little oracular aphorisms to let fly at you'.

Heracleitus' attitude towards the contents of his treatise is expressed in the opening fragments:

Listening not to me but to the *logos*, it is wisdom to confess that all things are one.

But though this *logos* stands for ever, men prove as unable to understand it both before hearing it and when they have heard it for the first time. For, while all things come to pass in accordance with this *logos*, men seem unacquainted with them when they make acquaintance with such words and things as I set forth, explaining each thing according to its nature and telling how it is.

Men are 'unacquainted with such words'—the phrase recurs in Aristophanes, where the chorus of mystics, after invoking Iacchos, warn off the profane: 'Let everyone be silent and keep apart from our band, who is unacquainted with such words as these and is not pure in heart.'[1] Aristophanes is paraphrasing the proclamation of the Eleusinian hierophant warning the assembly that they must 'understand the language' (φωνὴν συνετοί) and be pure in hand and soul. Heracleitus sets forth how things are in his *logos*; but men cannot read its meaning, as the uninitiate cannot read the meaning of mystic symbols and ritual language. Their souls are 'barbarian'; they cannot even understand the language of their own eyes and ears (*frag.* 107 = 4 Byw.). Heracleitus seems to mean that men might become acquainted with the truth, either by using their eyes to study Nature, or their ears to listen to Heracleitus' *logos*; but they remain blind and deaf to both.

When he tells his readers to listen, not to him, but to the *logos*, it is obvious that 'the *logos*' means something more than '*my* discourse': it means rather 'the truth' which the discourse expresses—a truth which 'stands for ever' as an objective reality, governing everything that happens. The *logos* is indeed something more concrete than our modern terms suggest: all human thought and intelligence is a portion of the thought (γνώμη) which guides all things, and this thought itself can be spoken of as 'fire'—a

---

[1] Heracl. *frag.* 1 (2 Bywater); γινομένων γὰρ πάντων κατὰ τὸν λόγον τόνδε ἀπείροισι ἐοίκασι πειρώμενοι καὶ ἔπεων καὶ ἔργων τοιούτων.... Ar. *Frogs*, 355: ὅστις ἄπειρος τοιῶνδε λόγων καὶ γνώμη μὴ καθαρεύει. I take ἔργα to mean 'things' (as in Plato, *Phaedo* 100A), not 'actions'.

moving, ever living, and conscious thing.[1] The thought or truth is uttered in Nature, but 'Nature loves to hide herself...with a good sort of incredibility, whereby she escapes being known'.[2] Men could discern it with their eyes and ears, if their souls could understand the language of the senses; but, as it is, they cannot understand 'the things they meet with' or recognize them when they are explained, for 'men of no understanding are like the deaf' (frags. 3–5 Byw. = 34, 4, 17). The fault lies, not in the senses, but in the lack of intelligence to interpret their message. Heracleitus also speaks cryptically, like Nature and like 'the King whose oracle is at Delphi, who neither speaks out nor conceals his meaning, but indicates it' (frag. 11 Byw. = 93) and, as Sophocles says, 'hints to the wise deep-meaning oracles, but to fools teaches only something trivial'.[3] Several fragments point to Heracleitus' deliberate intention to baffle the donkeys who prefer straw to gold; but probably he also felt that the truth was really enigmatic, consisting of what to the logic of his time were contradictions. These he reproduced faithfully in his discourse, so that later he was supposed to have denied the maxim of contradiction.

Heracleitus thus claimed to be the prophet of a wisdom or insight which he found within himself and which expressed the one truth about the world. Self-taught, he attacked all his predecessors and contemporaries—poets and philosophers alike—for 'the learning of many things' (πολυμαθίη).

Much learning does not teach insight; else it would have taught Hesiod and Pythagoras, Xenophanes and Hecataeus (frag. 40 = 16 Byw.).

People think that Hesiod knew very many things, when he did not know day and night; for they are one (frag. 57 = 35 Byw.).[4]

---

[1] Compare frag. 41 (19 Byw.): ἐν τὸ σοφόν, ἐπίστασθαι γνώμην ᾗ κυβερνᾶται πάντα διὰ πάντων; and 64 (28 Byw.): τὰ δὲ πάντα οἰακίζει κεραυνός. Cleanthes imitates both fragments in his Hymn to Zeus 10: πυρόεντα ἀειζώοντα κεραυνόν...ᾧ σὺ κατευθύνεις κοινὸν λόγον, ὃς διὰ πάντων φοιτᾷ and 34: δὸς δὲ κυρῆσαι γνώμης, ᾗ πισυνὸς σὺ Δίκης μέτα πάντα κυβερνᾷς.

[2] Frags. 10 and 116 Byw. (123 and 86), combined by H. Gomperz.

[3] Soph. frag. 771 (Pearson): σοφοῖς μὲν αἰνικτῆρα θεσφάτων ἀεί, σκαιοῖς δὲ φαῦλον κἂν βραχεῖ διδάσκαλον.

[4] In the Theogonies, darkness exists before light or day appears. Heracleitus denies that any opposite can exist without its opposite.

'Lovers of wisdom' must know many things indeed! (*frag.*
34 = 49 Byw.). In this last fragment Bywater and Diels must be
right in regarding the word 'philosophers' as part of the quotation,
which has no point without it. In its general sense, it could describe
the curiosity which led a Solon or a Hecataeus to travel and see
the world (Herod. 1, 30). Or Burnet may be right in accepting
the statement that the Pythagoreans were the first to call themselves 'lovers of wisdom', instead of claiming to be wise. In either
case the fragment must be a condemnation of those who run about
the world picking up information of all sorts and mistake that for
the pursuit of wisdom, for a 'knowledge of many things' is always
opposed by Heracleitus to the knowledge of the one thing which is
the wisdom he possessed himself. Pythagoras, at any rate, came
within this condemnation: he 'practised inquiry (ἱστορίη) above
all men', but the 'wisdom' he concocted out of other men's
writings was only 'a knowledge of many things, an imposture'
(πολυμαθίην, κακοτεχνίην, *frag.* 129 = 17 Byw.). The concluding
words suggest an allusion to a line in the Homeric *Margites*, describing a slave 'who knew many crafts and knew them all badly'.
The line is quoted in [Plato] *Alcib.* II, 147A of one 'who possesses
what is called a knowledge of many things, a jack of all trades' (τὴν
καλουμένην πολυμαθίαν τε καὶ πολυτεχνίαν), but lacks the one
piece of knowledge which constitutes wisdom. Socrates explains
that Homer wrote 'enigmatically' and by 'knew them all badly'
really meant that it was 'bad for him to know many things' (κακὸν
τὸ πολλὰ εἰδέναι). The same contrast appears in another line attributed to the *Margites*: 'the fox knows many things, but the hedge-
hog one thing of much importance'.[1] In all these places the
'knowledge of many things' has a bad sense. In condemning it,
Heracleitus condemns all ἱστορίη, a term which covered the speculations of the physical philosophers as well as the information
collected by travellers and historians. Of the poets, Homer,
Hesiod, Archilochus and Xenophanes are rebuked by name; and
mankind are declared to lack insight and intelligence, when they
follow the poets and take the crowd for their teacher, not knowing

---

[1] Archilochus, *frag.* 118 (103 Diehl): πόλλ' οἶδ' ἀλώπηξ, ἀλλ' ἐχῖνος ἓν
μέγα. Cf. Aesch. *frag.* 390N[2]: ὁ χρήσιμ' εἰδώς, οὐχ ὁ πόλλ' εἰδὼς σοφός.

that the bad are many, the good few (*frag.* 104=111 Byw.).
Fragment 14 Byw. (*Vors.*⁵ 1, p. 149, l. 36) preserved in Polybius
speaks of those who 'bring untrustworthy witnesses to confirm
doubtful things', and the context refers to poets and mythographers.
'Eyes are better witnesses than ears' (*frag.* 101*a*=15 Byw.).
Heracleitus claimed to have used his own senses and intelligence,
instead of following the poetical theogonies and cosmogonies or
listening to men who mistook the 'much learning' of others for
wisdom. His own wisdom came from within himself. It is inspired wisdom like Pindar's: 'I have many arrows in my quiver;
they have a voice that speaks to men who can understand (φωνᾶντα
συνετοῖσι), but for the crowd they need interpreters. Wise is he
who knows much by inborn genius (φυᾷ); those who have learnt
from others are like ravens chattering in vain against the divine
bird of Zeus.' (*Ol.* II, 83.) It is the same claim that was made by the
minstrel Phemius: 'I am self-taught; a god has planted (ἐνέφυσεν)
in my heart all the modes of song.' So Heracleitus found wisdom
by 'searching himself'; but, on the other hand, this wisdom is not
the private opinions of Heracleitus, but 'common to all'. 'We
must follow that which is common (τῷ ξυνῷ=τὸ ξὺν νόῳ), yet,
though the *logos* is common, the many live as if they had a private
wisdom of their own' (*frag.* 2=92 Byw.). Other fragments to
the same effect teach that the one wisdom would be accessible to
all, if only they could awake from the private world of the
dreamer and stop listening to the pretended wisdom of poets and
philosophers. Let them look at Nature with eyes opened by
understanding and they will find it there; and let them look into
their own nature; they will find it there also. Heracleitus himself
is wise; he has seen the truth and reproduced it in his *logos*. But
this *logos*, like the truth itself, is cryptic, only to be expressed in
apparent contradictions which will baffle fools. It is in this sense
that Heracleitus claims a unique inspiration, superseding all the
poets, prophets, and sages of the past or of his own day.[1] Hera-

---

[1] Many have tried to make out that Heracleitus was a mystic in the religious
sense, and influenced by, or sympathetic with, the Orphic and Pythagorean
doctrine of immortality and all that it implied. Later adherents of this doctrine
tried to find in Heracleitus statements in support of this assumption; but when

cleitus wrote in prose, though his language was highly poetical. He would have scorned to figure as the successor of Hesiod and other authors of poetical theogonies and cosmogonies. Moreover, the narrative form would not fit the truth he had to declare. The world is an 'ever-living (and ever-dying) fire', everlastingly in process of transformation. There is no such thing as cosmogony, no history of a cosmos arising out of a simpler primitive condition.

If Heracleitus was the prophet of a *logos* which could only be expressed in seeming contradictions, his great contemporary Parmenides was the prophet of a logic which would tolerate no resemblance of contradiction. Each claims to utter the truth by direct inspiration; but whereas Heracleitus found his truth exemplified everywhere in the visible world of change with its unending warfare of opposite powers, Parmenides dismissed the witness of the senses as a delusion. The intelligence (νόος), in which he put all his trust, was the faculty of reason, arguing from point to point and deducing sure conclusions from unquestionable axioms. He is said to have been taught by Pythagoreans, and, although he broke away from their school, its influence survived; for the method of reasoning he imported into philosophy is the method of geometry. He is the first philosopher to offer rigid logical proof instead of making dogmatic announcements. His premisses are not derived from observation, for the natural world is shot

we examine the very little they could find it either contradicts their thesis or proves nothing either way. His whole system of thought contradicts the notion of the individual soul as an indestructible persistent substance; there is no such thing in Nature. The Pythagorean view of opposites as one a good, the other an evil, and of harmony as ending strife in peace, is denied over and over again: you cannot have the one opposite without the other, and harmony *is* a strife of opposite tensions. Plato sees the difference between Heracleitus' harmony and the Pythagorean, where he makes Eryximachus blandly suggest that the Pythagorean reconciliation of opposites in peace and love was 'perhaps what Heracleitus meant to express, though what he actually says is not satisfactory'. He says that the One 'being at variance with itself is drawn together', like the *harmonia* of the bow or the lyre. But it is very illogical to say that a harmony *is* at variance. He must have meant that things which were at first at variance afterwards came together in agreement and concord (*Symp.* 187). But as Plato knew very well, that is just what Heracleitus did *not* mean. His whole temperament, proud and contemptuous, is the opposite of the humility of the religious mystic. One might as well try to prove that Nietzsche was at heart a Quaker.

through with false appearances. His thought is metaphysical, at work on the abstract concepts of being and unity. The procedure is *a priori*, and the conclusions contradict all sensible experience. At the same time, he believes he is revealing the only being that actually exists, a reality occupying space.

What is specially of interest to us is Parmenides' open confession that the whole content of his poem is a revelation accorded to him by a goddess. However the tradition may have come to him, his journey to, or round, the heavens recalls the heaven-journey of the *shaman's* ritual drama. He travels on a chariot, attended by the daughters of the Sun, on the way of the divinity,[1] which conducts the man who knows (εἰδότα φῶτα) 'as far as his heart desires' and 'far from the beaten track of men'. Beyond the gates of Day and Night (which may symbolize the primary pair of opposites in the misleading world of appearances), he meets the goddess who promises to instruct him in all things—both in 'the unshaken heart of rounded truth' and in 'what seems to mortals, in which there is no true belief'. The whole of the rest of the poem contains the revelation dictated by the goddess. There is a significant contrast, in respect both of form and content, between the two parts of the poem.

The Way of Truth is metaphysical. Parmenides is told not to trust eye or ear, but to judge by reasoning (λόγῳ) and keep his thought (νόημα) from the way of inquiry which assumes the reality of becoming and perishing and change. He is to see with his intelligence (νόῳ) things which are surely present to it, though afar off (from the senses).[2] These things are the necessary properties of a One Being, formally deduced in a series of highly compressed demonstrations from the abstract conceptions of Being and Unity. The method, as we have already remarked, is obviously derived from geometry, the only science in existence which could be said

---

[1] δαίμονος (masc.) was read by Sextus as his context proves, and clearly means the Sun. The alteration δαίμονες is gratuitous. I cannot believe in the reading κατὰ πάντ' ἄστη. Bergk's κατὰ πᾶν πάντῃ, 'everywhere over everything' or 'over the All', will account for the MS. corruptions. Misread κατὰ πάντ' ἄντη, it would give rise to πάντ' ἄτη and πάντα τῆ. Cf. *frag.* 1, line 32, διὰ πάντὸς πάντα περῶντα, and 4, line 3, πάντῃ πάντως κατὰ κόσμον.

[2] *Frag.* 4: λεῦσσε δ' ὅμως ἀπεόντα νόῳ παρεόντα βεβαίως.

to have evolved a method; and the properties deduced are geometrical. The One Being is a geometrical solid, occupying the whole of space, having the perfect shape of the sphere, and filled with continuous, uniform, and homogeneous 'being'.[1]

The second part, the Way of Seeming, abandons the method of logical deduction: the goddess here 'puts an end to the trustworthy reasoning and thought (πιστὸν λόγον ἠδὲ νόημα) about the truth' (8.50). The 'deceitful cosmos of words', describing what seems to mortals, is a cosmogony in the traditional style of dogmatic narrative. The first part has provided a rational account of the ultimate reality which in any other system would serve as the initial state of things (ἀρχή) or starting-point for the becoming of the ordered world as our senses perceive it. The first step is to fill the geometrical sphere with the (Pythagorean) opposites, Light and Night, just as in the mythical cosmogonies creation begins with the appearance of light in darkness. If this step could legitimately be taken, we should here pass from the 'being' constructed by pure thought to the world of sensible experience, and the whole process of cosmogony could follow smoothly on the traditional lines. But with astonishing candour and insight, Parmenides declares that the step is illegitimate. The strife of opposite powers in the order of time, involving plurality and motion, change and becoming, contradicts the attributes of the One Being; for what *is* cannot become, and what is one cannot be many. The 'immortal and imperishable' being which earlier philosophy had ascribed to the original substance of the world is now seen to be a timeless being: 'it never was, nor will be, but is now all at once.' No further being could come out of it at some moment of time —why 'sooner rather than later'? Cosmogony can only be a deceitful story, a myth. Parmenides' Muse at this point lays aside her power of 'declaring the truth' and begins to exercise her other power of telling 'false tales that are plausible'.[2] This announcement carries with it the condemnation of all cosmogony—poetic or philosophic.

[1] The contents of the Way of Truth are discussed in F. M. Cornford, *Plato and Parmenides*, ch. II.

[2] 8.60: τόν σοι ἐγὼ διάκοσμον ἐοικότα πάντα φατίζω. Cf. Xenoph. 35: ταῦτα δεδοξάσθω μὲν ἐοικότα τοῖς ἐτύμοισιν; Hes. *Theog.* 27 (Muses): ἴδμεν ψεύδεα πολλὰ λέγειν ἐτύμοισιν ὁμοῖα.

Who is this goddess who delivers her revelation to Parmenides? Proclus seems to imply that he called her 'the nymph Hypsipyle', in allusion, no doubt, to the high gates of Day and Night, beyond which she meets him.[1] But in essence she is unquestionably the goddess of Reason, a projection of that faculty which is exercised in mathematical reasoning, deducing certain conclusions from self-evident principles. Parmenides, we are told, was taught by Pythagoreans, who must have been the immediate pupils and associates of Pythagoras himself. He formulates an implication already present in Pythagoras' view of the world and of human nature: the immortal soul, which can exist apart from the body and visit the other world, is the rational soul ($\lambda \acute{o} \gamma o \nu \, \check{\epsilon} \chi o \nu$), as opposed to the senses and passions residing in the perishable body; and the reality it discerns when it leaves the senses behind is the world of number and figure, the objects and truths of mathematics. Parmenides' originality lies in his perception that there is a gulf, which cannot be bridged, between that realm of timeless, metaphysical truth and the welter of changing qualities which the senses, and the opinions of mortals founded on the senses, falsely mistake for realities. Henceforth the immortal and divine element in man is no longer merely the spirit which, when it leaves the sleeping body, communes with gods in prophetic dreams and visions and discerns the course of past, present, and future time; it has become the faculty which thinks and gives a rational account of metaphysical reality beyond the boundaries of time and change. Parmenides, however, remains a prophet, since his entire discourse is revealed to him by its inspiration. In other words, he has this much in common with Heracleitus, that he feels his discourse to be, not merely what he says and believes, but the truth.

Parmenides wrote in verse. In doing so, he was following the tradition that poetry is the language of prophetic revelation. The quality of his verse does not suggest that he would have thought himself a poet in any other sense, or that he expected his extremely condensed and abstract arguments to appeal to a wide public. It is more likely that he wished to record the truth in a compendious

[1] Procl. *Parm.* 640, 38. It is hard to believe that Proclus could have concocted this name simply from the word $\pi \acute{u} \lambda \alpha \iota$ in 1.11.

form which could be easily committed to memory. It is otherwise with Empedocles, who invokes his Sicilian Muse to speed his chariot from the Abode of Holiness and prays that his 'tongue may be turned aside from the madness' of the Eleatics.[1] From the context it seems that this madness consisted in Parmenides' arrogant claim to have gained 'the heights of wisdom', from which the whole living world revealed by the senses could be dismissed as an illusion. Nor did Empedocles share Heracleitus' no less arrogant contempt for the 'learning of many things'. His nature was as rich and vital and many-sided as Goethe's, eagerly welcoming every form of experience and bent upon 'apprehending everything in the way it is manifest', whether to the senses or to thought.

More than any other of the Presocratics, he has suffered from criticism obsessed by the nineteenth-century 'conflict of religion and science'. Burnet, for instance, writes that in his religious poem, the *Purifications*,

there are certain points of contact with the cosmology....But these points are not fundamental, and the cosmological system of Empedocles leaves no room for an immortal soul, which is presupposed by the *Purifications*. All through this period, there seems to have been a gulf between men's religious beliefs, if they had any, and their cosmological views. The few points of contact we have mentioned may have been enough to hide this from Empedocles himself.[2]

Other critics have done their best to keep the two poems apart by assigning them to different periods of his life: he is said to have been scientific in youth and religious in old age, or vice versa. The first condition for an understanding of Empedocles is to banish the notion of a gulf between religious beliefs and scientific views. His work is a whole, in which religion, poetry, and philosophy are indissolubly united. His imagination is constructive, gathering elements from every available quarter—Hesiodic and Ionian

---

[1] *Frag.* 4.
[2] *Early Greek Philosophy*[3], 250. I protested against this view in *From Religion to Philosophy*, 1911. Since then the appearance of Bignone's *Empédocle*, 1916, an admirable study inspired by a sympathetic insight into the poet's mind, should have made further protest superfluous.

cosmogony, Parmenidean rationalism, Orphic mysticism, poetic legend, the experience of a physician, a poet's sensuous response to the sights and sounds of nature, and the fears and hopes of a spirit exiled from heaven for 'a brief span of life that is no life'— but building all these elements together into a unitary vision of the life of the world and the destiny of the human soul, bound, like the macrocosm, upon the wheel of birth and death. As a poet, he earned the unbounded admiration of Lucretius:

> Carmina quin etiam divini pectoris eius
> vociferantur et exponunt praeclara reperta,
> ut vix humana videatur stirpe creatus   (I, 731).

As physician, he is the successor of Alcmaeon and a principal figure in the western school of medicine. He is also a physician of the soul preaching the way of purification. Here he claims to be speaking from his own experience. He is one of those fallen spirits exiled from heaven by decree of Necessity, and doomed to be 'born in all manner of mortal forms, changing one for another of the painful paths of life'. 'I have been ere now a boy and a girl, a bush and a bird, and a dumb fish of the sea.' His claim to have been reincarnated in each of the four elements[1] has astonishingly close parallels in Celtic literature. In the Irish story of Mongan (an Ulster King who, according to the annals, died in A.D. 625) and the *fili* Forgoll the possession of mantic powers is associated with metempsychosis. Mongan's father, the god Manannan, foretells the life and death of his son: 'He will be in the shape of every beast... a wolf...a stag...a spotted salmon in a full pool...a seal...a swan, etc.' (*The Voyage of Bran*, seventh or early eighth century). The catalogue here contains only the names of animals, birds, and fishes. In the Welsh *Book of Taliesin* there are catalogues with the word *bum* ('I have been'), e.g. 'I have been a journey (?), I have been an eagle, I have been a sea coracle...I have been a sword in the hand, I have been a shield in battle, I have been a string in a harp.' 'These catalogues...include the names of various animals, birds, reptiles, etc. which may point to some belief in either trans-

---

[1] Cf. Empedocles, *frag.* 115, 9 ff.

migration or transformation; but they also contain the names of inanimate and even incorporeal things.'[1]

It is difficult in these cases to decide whether transmigration or metamorphosis is meant. The Tatar *shamans*, the Brahman seers, the mantic god Othin, claimed the power of transforming themselves into birds, beasts, and even inanimate things; and this power is associated with supernatural knowledge, as in the Greek instances of Proteus and Thetis. But the difference between metamorphosis and metempsychosis is, after all, not great: both beliefs imply that the human soul can be detached from its own body and enter that of another creature. The unity of all life, the kinship of all living things, is the fundamental principle; and we cannot dismiss the notion that it is based on some genuine psychological experience, merely because we do not believe in transmigration and are not poets. Books on psychology have mostly been written by philosophers and men of science whose habits of thought are uncongenial to that poetic imagination (as we call it) which can 'see into the life of things' and lose the sense of separate existence in a communion of feeling with the whole of Nature, as if the daughters of Memory could free the soul from the limitations of space as well as from those of time. It is not wise, or even genuinely scientific, to brush aside as idle fancy or outworn superstition the experience of the greatest poets, because it is beyond the reach of the ordinary man and cannot be translated into terms of what he would call an 'explanation'. The philosophy of Empedocles, whether we like it or not, is animated and illuminated from within by this prophetic and poetic gift of insight, though, here as elsewhere, the Muses may sometimes be telling a false tale that is only like the truth.

Empedocles, as Bignone remarks,[2] although a contemporary of Pericles, Euripides and Sophocles, seems to belong to another world. His spiritual affinities are rather with Epimenides, Pherekydes, Onomacritus, Pythagoras; and yet he has the complexity and inquietude of one who stands between an age of decadence and a renaissance, the spiritual ambitions and mysticism of medieval man combined with modern man's curiosity and intellectual

[1] Chadwick, *Growth of Literature*, I, 459, 465, 468; III, 848 ff.
[2] *Empédocle*, 5.

daring. He reproduces with singular completeness every form of Plato's divine madness, every corresponding aspect of his god Apollo and his prototype Orpheus, and sums up in his own person all the characters which he describes as typifying the final, highest incarnation before the return to divine bliss: seer, minstrel, physician and leader of men.[1]

Meanwhile at Athens Socrates, a singularly unpoetical figure, was exhorting his fellow citizens to 'care for their souls'. From Plato's *Apology* and early dialogues it appears that this 'soul' is a man's true self, which possesses an eye capable of discerning the genuine value or worthlessness of all the ends we set before us in life. It was Socrates' characteristic conviction that all men wish for true happiness, if only they could be brought to see in what happiness consists; once they did see it, they could not fail to follow their wish in action. No man can see with perfect clearness where his own good lies and then prefer other ends which he now knows to be valueless. Socrates' method was cathartic. He would examine men and induce them to examine themselves, in order to clear away the mists of prejudice and false belief and set free their own inmost desire.

Socrates was a product of the Periclean age, a man of this world, convinced by his own experience that, if happiness can be found at all, it can be found here and now in the pursuit of human perfection. So much seemed to him to be certain truth and man's paramount concern. No doubt in his youth he had sought the company of all men who were reputed to be wise—the poets, the sophists, and the representatives of the Ionian natural philosophy at Athens. But as the skies grew darker with the oncoming of war and revolution, the dispute whether material bodies are ultimately composed of air or water or the four elements became less and less significant, especially to one who could so clearly distinguish what can from what cannot be known. Socrates had no physical or metaphysical doctrines to impart, and he could truthfully say that he had never taught anyone anything; for the nature of goodness and happiness is not a matter of belief that can be handed about, but something that every man must see for himself, or fail to see.

[1] *Frag.* 146.

We must, accordingly, not be misled by the story of the oracle declaring that no one was wiser than Socrates into supposing that Socrates felt himself to be the prophet of the Delphic god. Among the wise men of all ages he is perhaps unique in his firm repudiation of the idea that he had any revelation to offer. Plato has faithfully recorded this attitude in the *Apology*. The Socrates there portrayed declares that he is telling the truth about himself, and we have no ground for doubting that he is the real Socrates as seen by the only friend capable of understanding him. Nothing inconsistent with that portrait can be accepted from Aristophanes' irresponsible travesty in the *Clouds* or from the simple-minded self-portraiture of Xenophon.

It is only in Plato's middle dialogues that Socrates first takes on, in addition to his real character, the poetical or prophetic traits needed for the full disclosure of the Platonic revelation.[1] The recognized convention of the imaginary conversation, an offshoot of the prose mime, gave legitimate scope for such a development without misleading the reader. We have already described this transfiguration of Socrates, and pointed out that Plato himself has sufficiently indicated that he was aware what he was doing. The Socrates of the *Phaedo*, the *Republic* and the *Phaedrus* has a message to deliver; and he delivers it partly in the form of discourses where the method of question and answer is becoming a mere form, partly in the symbolic imagery of poetical myths.

Socrates in the *Crito* (56 B) describes himself as the sort of person who will not be won over to obey any motive other than the reason (λόγος) which, upon reflexion, seems to him to be the best. The 'true self', to which Socrates listened, becomes in the *Phaedo* the separable immortal soul of the Pythagorean tradition. It is there called by the inclusive name 'psyche', but it is opposed to the senses and passions connected with its bodily associate, and in

---

[1] We may well suppose that it is to this Platonic Socrates that the words of Alcibiades refer, when he describes in the *Symposium* the extraordinary effect of Socrates' conversation: ὅταν γὰρ ἀκούω, πολύ μοι μᾶλλον ἢ τῶν κορυβαντιώντων ἥ τε καρδία πηδᾷ, καὶ δάκρυα ἐκχεῖται ὑπὸ τῶν λόγων τῶν τούτου· ὁρῶ δὲ καὶ ἄλλους παμπόλλους τὰ αὐτὰ πάσχοντας. (*Symp.* 215 D, E.) The passage comes appropriately in a dialogue devoted to the Platonic doctrine of Eros.

the *Republic* it appears as the 'reflective part' (λογιστικόν). As such, it corresponds to that intelligence (νόος) which, in Parmenides' poem, leaves the senses and the sense-world behind and penetrates the region of eternal metaphysical truth and mathematical reasoning. But it is not a faculty of purely passionless thought and intuition; it has its own characteristic desire in the passion for wisdom, philosophy, and its own pleasure in the enjoyment of truth (*Rep.* 580).

As we have seen, the religious belief in immortality carried Plato beyond the rational agnosticism of Socrates, truthfully reproduced in the *Apology*. As a consequence, in the middle dialogues from the *Gorgias* onwards, poetical myth appears as a distinct element alongside of the dialectical argument inherited from Socrates. In both elements it is the highest part of the soul that is at work. In the myth it exercises the old mantic power of prophetic vision, formerly attributed to the soul when it leaves the body in sleep, 'free to reach out, in its pure and independent condition, to perceive some new knowledge of things past, present, or to come' (*Rep.* 572A). Thus Plato the philosopher resumes the role of prophet and poet which Socrates had disclaimed, although, by keeping dialectic and myth apart, Plato acknowledged his master's distinction between truth that can be established as knowledge by rational argument and truth that can only be divined and must remain a matter for belief and persuasion.

In this chapter we have dwelt upon the aspect of the philosopher as the conscious inheritor of a past in which the exceptional wisdom of the sage had been attributed to divine inspiration and expressed in poetry. But there is another side to the picture. As Plato himself says,[1] there was a quarrel between philosophy and poetry already of long standing, dating indeed from the days when the natural philosopher appeared as a distinct figure who had definitely laid aside the prophet's mantle and the poet's lyre.

[1] *Rep.* 607B.

CHAPTER VIII

THE QUARREL OF THE SEER AND THE PHILOSOPHER

WE have now to consider the differentiation of our three figures and the consequent clash between them. First, a word may be said about the divergence of the seer and the poet.

We have adopted the view that poetry is the language of prophecy in the wide sense of that term. Poetry, throughout its history, has resisted every effort to bring it down to the level of everyday speech. Poetry cannot dispense with a more or less exalted language, because it must express a more or less exalted mood. The exaltation is what the ancient poet meant by the inspiration of the Muses, and recognized as akin to, or identical with, the enthusiasm of the prophet.

The identity, or common quality, of the two kinds of inspiration has been overlooked by scholars who confine their attention to Greek literature and consequently think of ancient poetry as beginning with Homer, and continued somewhat later by Hesiod, forgetting that Homer stands already at the end of a long tradition. For in Homer, and in the heroic age which he professes to depict, the seer and the minstrel are already distinct. The minstrel's business is to entertain, by improvising on the glories of the men of old or of his own day. The seer's business is to interpret the intentions of the gods, and foresee the future by augury like Calchas, or like Theoclymenus he may be entranced in intuitive visions of oncoming doom. Here one consequence of the differentiation already appears. The seer's inspiration has come to be more concerned with the future than with the past; he is becoming a prophet in the narrow sense, valued and consulted for his foreknowledge of coming events. The poet, on the other hand, is occupied with his imaginative vision of the past.[1]

[1] Cf. Schol. on Hesiod, *Theog.* 32: ἵνα κλείοιμι τά τ᾽ ἐσσόμενα, πρό τ᾽ ἐόντα· παρὰ τῶν Μουσῶν φησιν ἀκούων μανθάνω τά τε ἐσσόμενα καὶ τὰ ὄντα καὶ

We may recall the profession of Castrén's *shaman*: 'God has appointed that I must wander both beneath and upon the earth.... I am a *shaman*, who knows the future, the past, and everything which is taking place in the present, both above and below the earth.'[1]

We need not dwell long on the seer's knowledge of the hidden present. The faculty of intuitive divination, which Theoclymenus had inherited from a line of seers descended from Melampus, enabled him to see the heads and faces of the laughing wooers shrouded in night, the walls and roof sprinkled with their blood, and the courtyard filled with their ghosts hurrying to Hades.[2] The same faculty could transcend the limits of space as well as those of time.

Samuel told Saul that his asses had been found; Elisha reported to the King of Israel the words spoken by the King of Syria in his chamber.[3] Much didactic literature takes the form of contests in which two seers or sages or poets challenge one another to a display of their knowledge or powers of divination. In the *Melampodia* attributed to Hesiod Mopsus is asked by Calchas how many figs there are on a certain tree. When Mopsus gave the number correctly, Calchas died of his defeat. The *Mahābhārata* similarly tells how a king (not a brahman) numbered the leaves and fruits on a tree which he was passing in his chariot.[4] Apollo, feigning to seek the advice of the wise Centaur, is told that he knows not only that which is to be and when it will come, but the number of the leaves that earth puts forth in spring and the number of the sands in the sea and the rivers.[5] The contest of Homer and Hesiod, though late in its present shape, belongs to this traditional form, which also lies behind the competition of the dead tragedians in Aristophanes' *Frogs*, and perhaps also the musical and poetical competitions at the great festivals.

In the main, however, the more practical duty of the seer was to foresee the future, or, if he could not foresee it intuitively, to infer

προγεγονότα, ἵνα δείξῃ ὅτι ὅμοιόν τί ἐστιν ἡ ποίησις τῇ μαντείᾳ· τὸ κυριώτερον κεῖται ἐπὶ μάντεως, οὐκ ἐπὶ ποιητοῦ, τὰ ἐσσόμενα μὴ δυναμένου λέγειν τοῦ ποιητοῦ.

[1] Above, p. 96.
[2] *Od.* xv. 225 ff., xx, 351 ff.
[3] I Sam. ix. 6; II Kings vi. 11.
[4] *Mahābh.* III, 72, *cit. G.L.* II, 591.
[5] Pind. *Pyth.* IX, 44.

the intentions of the gods by the interpretation of their signs and omens. This is that pseudo-science of augury which Plato, and the ancients in general, clearly distinguished from intuitive or inspired divination. It was regarded as a rational procedure of inference or conjecture, comparable to the deciphering of a message in code.[1] Natural philosophy was bound to come into conflict with the pretensions of the seer.

It will be convenient to consider first the more profound and philosophic problem of destiny, which emerged clearly only at a late stage. If future events can be predicted, they must be already determined, either by the providential will and purpose of the gods or by inexorable necessity. And if they are so determined, man seems to be left with no free choice of his own actions in the future; however horrible the doom foretold by prophecy, he can do nothing to avert it. Already in Homer the contradiction is obscurely felt. The freedom of the gods themselves, though they are sometimes said to be all-powerful, is limited by Fate. We can hardly expect to find in Homer the solution of a problem which still vexes our contemporary philosophers.

In later antiquity the Stoics tried to cut the knot by identifying Fate with the will of Zeus, and by this time Fate had already come to be identified with the necessity supposed to be inherent in the chain of physical causes and effects.[2] The sequence could have been determined by Providence, and its future course is theoretically capable of being foreseen by divination. What has to be sacrificed is the freedom of man's will as commonly conceived. Man can only endeavour to identify his will with the will of Zeus and accept his destiny whatever it may be. Even so, a persistent critic could argue that his acceptance or non-acceptance must itself have been determined before he was born.

Epicurus, as we have seen, tried to break out of the network of inexorable necessity by the desperate expedient of endowing atoms with a minimum degree of freedom to swerve, for no reason, from

[1] Cf. p. 73 above.
[2] Cicero, de Div. 1, 121: 'Fieri igitur omnia fato ratio cogit fateri. Fatum autem id appello quod Graeci εἱμαρμένην, id est, ordinem seriemque causarum, cum causae causa nexa rem ex se gignat', etc.

the straight line of their fall through endless space. In so doing he was evading the logical consequence of his materialism. Democritus appears to have been made of sterner stuff, unless it is true that he kept his ethical doctrines on the different level of moral exhortation, unsupported by his physics. In the material world of atoms and void he is said to have left no room for Providence or for freedom. The infinite universe was not a work of design; events had no first cause; all that 'has been and is and will be' is predetermined from infinite time by necessity.[1] Democritus, accordingly, could accept and attempt to explain precognition of the future.

Epicurus, on the contrary, in order to protect his freedom, denied this determinism and with it the possibility of divination. The gods, moreover, were not to intervene in anything that happens inside the world we live in. Man is to shake off the terrors which had beset his primitive ancestors, when they imagined that 'what goes on in the sky and under the earth'—thunder, lightning, comets, eclipses, earthquakes—were portents of divine anger. As we have seen, the desire to exclude any divine significance here led Epicurus to devote much attention to the second department of his system, meteorology, and to assert in this field the extraordinary principle that, since this class of phenomena lies beyond the range of the close view, we must accept *every* natural explanation as true, if not in our world, then in some other.

It is instructive to observe the amount of space given by Lucretius to the several topics of meteorology. In Book v, 273 lines are occupied with the formation and motions of the heavenly bodies, their eclipses and so forth. In Book vi atmospheric and subterranean phenomena occupy 606 lines; and of these more than half are concerned with thunder and lightning, 102 with waterspouts, clouds, and rain, and 167 with subterranean things, earthquakes, volcanoes, the sources of the sea. All minor matters, such as snow, winds, hail, frost, ice, are dismissed in eight lines, as easily explicable by anyone who has grasped the principles of Atomism. It is obvious that neither Lucretius nor his master was interested in any science of astronomy or meteorology. Their interest was

---

[1] [Plut.] *Strom.* 7= *Vors.*⁵ 68 [55] A 39 (vol. II, p. 94). The words τὰ γεγονότα καὶ ἐόντα καὶ ἐσόμενα are evidently a quotation.

focused on those phenomena above and below the earth which had been, and still were, associated with divine agency. The list of phenomena under this head was inherited from the earlier Ionian systems; hence the natural philosophers were frequently called 'meteorologists', as if their concern had been solely with the things in the sky and beneath the earth. We noted how Hippocrates regarded this as the proper domain for the 'empty assumptions' of the philosopher, and anticipated Epicurus' view that such objects were too far removed from sensible experience for the truth of his dogmatic assertions to be submitted to any test. It seems obvious that, from the time of the Milesians onwards, attention had been fixed on just this set of natural phenomena because of their religious significance. Man's very existence depended on the alternation, in due measure, of rain and drought, cloud and sunshine, in the seasonal round of the year. Zeus the cloud-gatherer could grant or withhold the life-giving rain; and eclipses, comets, meteors, thunder and lightning, earthquakes, volcanic eruptions were signs of divine displeasure. Sooner or later the philosopher who interpreted all these phenomena in terms of purely natural changes was bound to come into conflict with the priest, whose office was to secure the gifts of the gods in return for sacrifice, and still more with the seer, who interpreted their signs and omens.

We do not know whether the Milesian meteorology had to encounter any opposition from religious quarters. It may not have been obvious at the outset that religion was in any danger. The divinity of the sun or of the stars was not impaired by the theory that they were nourished by exhalations from earth and sea; and if the formation of clouds and rain involved the condensation of air and water, the rain might none the less be sent by Zeus. To this day the science of meteorology exists side by side with a church whose bishops sanction prayers for rain or drought, and it never occurs to the Meteorological Survey to compile statistics correlating the observed rainfall with the number of prayers offered in a given district. In the ancient state the worship of the gods and human conduct were regulated by ancestral custom and law. Against all this the natural philosopher had nothing to say. Even in the matter of omens the natural explanation could be reconciled with the supernatural, as may be seen from Plutarch's comment on a famous anecdote.

We are told, there was brought to Pericles from one of his farms a ram's head, with only one horn; and Lampo the soothsayer, observing that the horn grew strong and firm out of the middle of the forehead, declared that the two parties in the state, namely those of Thucydides and Pericles, would unite and invest the whole power in him with whom the prodigy was found; but Anaxagoras, having dissected the head, showed that the brain did not fill the whole cavity, but had contracted itself into an oval form, and pointed directly to that part of the skull whence the horn took its rise. This procured Anaxagoras great honour with the spectators; and Lampo was no less honoured for his prediction, when, soon after, upon the fall of Thucydides, the administration was put entirely into the hands of Pericles.

But, in my opinion, the philosopher and the diviner may well enough be reconciled, and both be right; the one discovering the cause and the other the end. It was the business of the former to account for the appearance, and to consider how it came about; and of the latter to show why it was so formed and what it portended. Those who say that, when the cause is found out, the prodigy ceases, do not consider that if they reject such signs as are preternatural they must also deny that artificial signs are of any use: the clattering of brass quoits, the light of beacons, and the shadow of a sundial, have all of them their proper natural causes, and yet each has another signification.   (*Pericles* vi trans. Langhorn.)

Later in the career of Pericles, however, his enemies took advantage of his growing unpopularity to attack him through his friends. Among these was Anaxagoras, who had declared that the moon was made of earth and the sun was an incandescent rock, somewhat larger than the Peloponnese. He had also discovered the true causes of solar and lunar eclipses. Long ago Thales had learnt in the East that eclipses occurred in cycles, and he had successfully predicted one visible in Asia Minor in 585 B.C. It was becoming increasingly difficult for educated men to regard them as portending terrestrial disasters, although the defeat of the Athenian army at Syracuse was due to the respect paid by its general to the seers' interpretation of an eclipse of the moon. In the public mind the astronomers and natural philosophers were lumped together with other 'sophists', some of whom were credited with unorthodox speculations about the nature of the gods or, like Protagoras, with questioning whether we could know anything about them. The seers and the priests began to be alarmed. It was a seer, Diopeithes, who carried a decree authorizing the indictment of 'those who disbelieve in divine things or teach theories about what goes on in the sky'.[1]

Nilsson has pointed out that the belief in oracles and omens played a much larger part in Greek life than we commonly recognize. The public, he thinks, were not much affected by the intellectual discussions of the sophists.

The real clash took place between that part of religion which interfered most in practical life and with which everyone came in contact every day, namely, the art of foretelling the future, and the attempts of natural philosophy to give physical explanations of celestial and atmospheric phenomena, of portents, and of other events. Such explanations undermined the belief in the art of the seers and made it superfluous. For if these phenomena were to be explained in a natural way, the art of the seers came to naught. Belief in the oracles also was weakened.... Naturally the seers and interpreters of oracles and omens defended their art, and since their art was implied in the old religion, the defence of the old religion also fell to their lot....The trials for atheism were useless. They were not able to check the increasing disbelief, and they ceased in the course of time. They are no honour to Athens, but we should try to understand the situation from which they arose. This situation was created by the interference of religion in practical life and politics, and it explains why men who were at the same time politicians and seers thought it possible to dispel the danger by means of laws and courts. They were supported by the Athenian people, for the people disliked the attacks on the gods who had given glory and power to their city and in emergencies they feared the wrath of these gods.[2]

In the most famous of the trials for impiety, the indictment of Socrates was drawn, with great ingenuity, in carefully chosen

[1] Plut. *Per.* XXXII: εἰσαγγέλλεσθαι τοὺς τὰ θεῖα μὴ νομίζοντας ἢ λόγους περὶ τῶν μεταρσίων διδάσκοντας.

[2] M. P. Nilsson, *Greek Popular Religion*, 1940, pp. 135 ff. The whole chapter on seers and oracles is illuminating. A concise expression of the popular reaction to 'meteorology' occurs in Euripides, *frag.* 913 N²: τίς τάδε λεύσσων θεὸν οὐχὶ νοεῖ | μετεωρολόγων δ' ἑκὰς ἔρριψεν | σκολιὰς ἀπάτας, ὧν ἀτηρὰ | γλῶσσ' εἰκοβολεῖ περὶ τῶν ἀφανῶν | οὐδὲν γνώμης μετέχουσα;

terms. The decree of Diopeithes had attacked the teachers of theories about what goes on in the sky for not believing in 'divine things' (τὰ θεῖα). This might mean no more than what the seers in particular most objected to, namely the natural explanations of meteoric phenomena, casting doubt on their significance as omens sent by the gods. Or 'divine things' might mean religion in general; the philosophers were suspected of not believing that gods existed. Socrates, however, was not charged in the indictment with teaching meteorology or with atheism; he was accused of 'not recognizing (*or* "not believing in") the gods recognized by the state, but introducing other new divinities'.[1] For the negative count it is not apparent whether any testimony was produced, either by the prosecution to prove that Socrates by any overt act had shown his disbelief in the gods, or by Socrates to prove that he had taken part in the public worship. It is probable that, as the Platonic *Apology* suggests, Meletus and his friends relied on the confusion, in the public mind, of Socrates with the natural philosophers, Anaxagoras, Archelaus and Diogenes. This confusion had been fostered by the comic poets. The members of the jury had been taught to believe that 'there is a certain Socrates, a wise man, who has studied what goes on in the sky and investigated everything under the earth'; and people supposed that men who studied such things 'did not believe in gods' (*Apol.* 18B). Anyone, in fact, who took seriously the picture of Socrates' school in the early part of the *Clouds*, would have believed that he set his pupils to study 'the things in the sky and beneath the earth' and initiated them into a secret cult of Air, Ether and Clouds as the only true divinities (*Clouds*, 365). In these mysteries Strepsiades is taught that Zeus does not exist. His reign is over, and his throne has passed (not to Dionysus, 'the son of Zeus', but) to Dinos. Rain,

---

[1] I here follow Mr Coleman Phillipson (*The Trial of Socrates*, 1928, ch. XIII), who has brought the acumen of a trained lawyer to bear on the problems of the trial. He sees no reason to doubt the authenticity of the document which Favorinus said was extant in his own time (D.L. II, 5, 40). This reads: ἀδικεῖ Σωκράτης οὓς μὲν ἡ πόλις νομίζει θεοὺς οὐ νομίζων, ἕτερα δὲ καινὰ δαιμόνια εἰσηγούμενος. . . . Mr Phillipson and others have sufficiently disposed of the theory that Socrates was accused of devotion to a heterodox religious cult, not approved by the State, but an unlicensed importation from abroad.

thunder and lightning are not sent by the sky-god, but are due to rather unseemly disturbances in the clouds. Besides the denial of omens, we note here the insinuation that the cosmic gods of the Ionian philosophers were to supersede Zeus himself. Since Zeus Polieus, associated with Athena Polias, was very much a 'god of the city', the *Clouds* does represent Socrates as 'not believing in the gods recognized by the city, but setting up other strange divinities'—air and the clouds. Moreover, these novel 'gods' and their behaviour were described in obviously physical terms, which would justify, in the popular mind, the accusation of sheer atheism. In his cross-examination of Meletus, Socrates provokes his accuser to make this charge, and thereby to contradict the terms of the indictment itself; for one who 'introduces new divinities' cannot be an atheist. Meletus, he says, has confused him with Anaxagoras (*Apol.* 26 c ff.). For the rest Socrates roundly denies that there is a word of truth in Aristophanes' picture of his alleged school; he has no concern whatever with meteorology,[1] and he has never taught anyone in secret (*Apol.* 19 c).

But the phrase in the indictment, 'novel divinities' (δαιμόνια), had been cunningly chosen to make the charge appear relevant to Socrates. There is not the least reason to doubt the evidence of Plato and Xenophon that the reference was to the 'divine sign', that θεῖόν τι καὶ δαιμόνιον which Socrates expressly says is 'what Meletus is holding up to ridicule in the terms of his indictment' (*Apol.* 31 c). This statement is confirmed by the *Euthyphro* (3 B ff.), where the seer immediately interprets the phrase as meaning the divine sign, and by Xenophon's whole treatment of this count in the accusation. There should be no further need to labour this point.[2] Mr Phillipson writes:

The accusers found in the daemonium of Socrates what they considered sufficient ground for an accusation of impiety; and, no doubt,

---

[1] If we may believe Xenophon, Socrates' attitude towards 'meteorology' was like that of Hippocrates and Epicurus, in so far as both these thought that such matters were beyond the reach of knowledge which could be brought to the test of experience (above, p. 32).

[2] Mr Coleman Phillipson (*op. cit.* p. 281) has reviewed the evidence and the recent literature.

they reasoned more or less in this way. This daemonium of Socrates was of an internal, indeterminate character, and could not be related to the authorized deities. It was of a peculiar, indeed unparalleled, nature, for Socrates was the only man who claimed to have intercourse with it. By means of it Socrates declared that he had the power of immediate communion with the god, and that therefore he could dispense—and probably he did dispense—with the usually recognized means of ascertaining the divine will. This singularity was an undesirable anomaly in such a city as Athens, where the State and the national religion were indissolubly united. Moreover, it was also a dangerous anomaly. Socrates' devotion to his life-long mission was stimulated and fostered by it; he rejected the obligations inseparably bound up with citizenship; he made mock of those who fulfilled such obligations, he showed an anti-democratic bent, and inculcated anti-democratic doctrines in others—so that this daemonium of his was not only an unauthorized religious innovation, but also a menace to the State. If every citizen were allowed to have recourse to such private and new-fangled oracles, discord would inevitably result, the national religion would be completely overthrown, and the treasured Athenian democracy, with its liberty and equality, would cease to exist. Hence—as Anytus and his colleagues must have reasoned—the daemonium was, from every point of view, an object deserving attack; that the only way to attack it was in a charge of irreligion; and that in such a charge a majority of the votes of the judges might confidently be counted on.

Accordingly, as Socrates openly admitted, his daemonium (τὸ δαιμόνιον)—which for him was a divine sign, a voice, that is a manifestation of the God, but not a god—was an obvious target: it was very easy to give a slight twist to his expression and turn it into δαιμόνια, divinities —indeed, καινὰ δαιμόνια, new divinities—notwithstanding the fact that he never used the word as a substantive nor in the plural, meaning a divine being or beings. Thus, the very formulation of the charge was *ab initio* a sophistical proceeding on the part of the accusers.

The accusers had, in fact, skilfully availed themselves of the opportunity of associating this novel 'divine thing' with those other novel divinities—Air, Ether, Clouds—who were to oust Zeus, and with Anaxagoras' blasphemous doctrine that 'the sun is a stone and the moon earth' (*Apol.* 26D). What is of special concern to our argument is that both the false and the true elements in the indictment are connected with the belief in divination. The alleged atheism of the Ionians and Socrates' belief in his divine sign both threatened the vested interests of the seers who interpreted oracles and the signs of divine grace or displeasure in the gift of rain and the manifestations of thunder and lightning, eclipse and earthquake.

The *Apology* is a forensic speech. Socrates was confronted with a vaguely worded accusation, unsupported, so far as we know, by any testimony which he could refute, and relying on a long-standing confusion and prejudice in the minds of the court. In such a situation it was perfectly legitimate for him to defend himself by entrapping his accuser into a confession of what was really in his mind—the charge of complete atheism—and convicting him of contradicting his own indictment. It remained for Plato to analyse Socrates' real attitude towards the pretensions of those seers and priests whose interests, apart from political motives, had prompted the trials for impiety. He undertook this delicate task in an imaginary conversation between Socrates and a well-known soothsayer, Euthyphro.

Socrates and the seer meet at a moment when both are involved in legal proceedings based on charges of impiety. Socrates explains that Meletus is attacking him for 'making new gods and not believing in the old ones'. Euthyphro replies: 'I see, Socrates: no doubt this is because you speak of that divine thing which often comes to you.' The indictment treats this as an innovation in religion; and Meletus knows that it is easy to raise popular prejudice against such claims. Euthyphro himself has been laughed down as a madman when he has addressed the Assembly with predictions of the future, though his predictions always come true. He is now engaged in prosecuting his own father for a murder which, whether justified or not, taints the whole household with impurity. He feels a religious obligation to cleanse himself from this stain, although his friends regard it as an impiety that a son should charge a father with murder. They do not understand the religious significance of piety and impiety. Socrates begs Euthyphro to enlighten him on the meaning of piety or holiness or righteousness (none of these words quite covers the sense of τὸ ὅσιον). As usual, he asks for a definition.

The discussion which follows seems to reach no positive conclusion, and many interpreters have been puzzled where to look for one. Here, as in several other early dialogues, Plato has remained faithful to Socrates' method in refusing to 'teach' his readers and leaving them to think out the matter for themselves. But he has, I believe, sufficiently indicated where they should seek for an answer to the question which the *Euthyphro* must be designed to raise: What was Socrates' real attitude towards religion?

The two main divisions of the conversation correspond to the two recognized departments of official religion: prophecy and priestcraft. In the *Politicus* (290), for example, religious officials fall into two classes. The prophets (μάντεις) who possess 'a sort of knowledge by divination' are regarded as interpreters and go-betweens from the gods to mankind. (The prophet, that is to say, interprets the will of the gods, either by augury or by direct inspiration.) The priest claims no inspiration. His art is to carry out the ritual, the cult of the gods (θεῶν θεραπεία as the *Euthyphro* calls it). He 'knows how, by means of sacrifice, to present the gods with gifts agreeable to them, and by prayers to ask from the gods good things which we may enjoy'. The two definitions of piety in the *Euthyphro* correspond to these two departments. The essential character of a pious act is first defined as 'what is pleasing to the gods' or in accordance with their will. This is the will or pleasure which seers like Euthyphro know how to interpret. When this definition has been dismissed Socrates turns to the sphere of priestcraft, a species of traffic in which we give the gods their due need of sacrifice and receive benefits in return.

This second aspect of religion is briefly disposed of. If all blessings come from the gods, what good can we do them in return? We can offer homage and thanks, but we must first be sure that such a return is pleasing to them and thus an act of piety. So we are back again at the first definition: 'what pleases the gods'. And, since that has been dismissed, we seem to have failed altogether to find out what makes an act pious. So we end with apparent failure; but the backward reference invites us to look again at the conclusion of the first part of the argument.

There, Socrates had asked Euthyphro whether the gods take

pleasure in what is righteous because it is righteous, or what is righteous is righteous because it pleases the gods. Arguing from analogy, he gets Euthyphro to admit that the gods are pleased with righteous conduct because it is righteous; it is not their approval that makes it so. This admission is fatal to the definition, because it makes the character, 'pleasing to the gods', a mere accidental attribute of righteous conduct. So the definition fails, and we turn to priestcraft. But the admission itself contains a positive conclusion of great practical importance and one intimately related to the problems raised in the whole dialogue. It implies, moreover, the Socratic doctrine which we should expect to find in an early dialogue attempting to define one of the great virtues. All virtue is one, and it consists in the knowledge of good and evil or right and wrong—a knowledge immediately accessible to the eye of every human soul, when its vision is cleared of prejudice and false conceit. Euthyphro has claimed to be guided, in his own action against his father, by the intuitive power of the seer to know what the gods approve. But he cannot explain how he knows; and it is quite obvious that Socrates does not believe that he, or any other prophet, can tell what the gods think one ought to do. In the *Cratylus* (400 D) Plato makes Socrates speak of the gods almost in the same terms as Protagoras: we should do best of all to recognize that 'we know nothing about the gods—neither about the gods themselves, nor about the names by which they call one another'— those names which Euthyphro interpreted. The conclusion is that in all matters of human conduct—those matters to which Socrates devoted his attention—we must be guided, not by what anyone tells us the gods approve, but by our own direct insight, the 'knowledge of good and evil'. If we see plainly, we shall act accordingly, and we may then believe (though we cannot know) that our action is approved by heaven.

If this interpretation is correct, the *Euthyphro* illustrates the opposition between the seer and the philosopher as envisaged by Socrates. We gain fresh light on the way in which the Socratic doctrine was obscurely felt by the prophets and priests as threatening their own position. Socrates believed in the insight of the 'true self' or intelligence which can know and will the good. He also spoke of the guidance of a divine sign or voice, received from without. In both respects he seemed to be setting up his private illumination against the authority of the State and its accredited religion. His case presents a curious parallel to that of Joan of Arc, whom the Church first condemned as a heretic and afterwards discovered to be a saint.

Reviewing the whole case of Socrates we reach the following conclusions. (1) The prosecution relied on the confusion, in the public mind, of Socrates with the 'sophists' in general and in particular with the Ionian physicists whose meteorological doctrines were incompatible with the art of augury and perhaps even with the existence of Zeus. This confusion was groundless. Socrates was not concerned with physical questions, but may have thought, like Hippocrates, that man has no means of checking by experience assertions about 'what goes on in the sky and under the earth'. In any case such speculations had no bearing on Socrates' problem: how men ought to live if they would be happy.

(2) In the sphere of intuitive divination, Socrates was not entirely sceptical. We have Plato's authority for the attention he paid to warning dreams and to the voice of his divine sign. It is impossible to reconcile Plato's evidence with Xenophon's. According to Plato,

the premonitory sign was of momentary duration. It emanated from a divine original, but was not ascribed to any particular deity. It was not a divine being itself (θεὸς or δαίμων); ... Meletus, in his accusation, wrested it into the sense of a divine being. It was only prohibitory or inhibitory in its operation: that is, it was only an injunction to abstain from doing a given thing, not a command requiring something to be done or a suggestion prompting to a given course of action. It was manifested frequently to Socrates, and from his early age; it warned him against all kinds of things and fortuitous events, and even against seemingly trivial things. The ground of the warning was purely practical, namely, that to do such things would be, not of necessity morally right or wrong, but rather unsafe, unwise, or inexpedient. Socrates believed that the sign was almost peculiar to him. It came to him unsolicitedly; and Socrates' belief in it was serious and sincere.[1]

[1] I borrow this convenient summary from Mr Coleman Phillipson, *op. cit.* p. 91.

Most scholars now prefer to accept Plato's careful limitation of the scope of the divine sign, rather than Xenophon's account, according to which it sometimes gave positive advice, not for Socrates' guidance only but for his friends, and included questions of right and wrong. Whatever its scope, Socrates unquestionably accepted 'divination' (as he called it) in this form. He was not prepared, like some nineteenth-century agnostics, to dismiss as superstitious nonsense anything he could not understand and account for 'scientifically'. It is probable that, in the light of his own experience, he would accept the possibility of inspired prophecy in the case of the Pythian priestess and other oracles, although, like other men of his time, he must have been aware that the priests who put the prophecies into shape and interpreted them might use their power for political or self-interested ends.

(3) On the other hand, if Plato is right, this private oracle, coming apparently from some divine source outside, was not a positive guide to conduct. It did not relieve Socrates of any responsibility for his actions. As he says in the *Crito*, in deciding what he ought to do, he would not listen to anything but the reason (λόγος) which seemed to him, on reflexion, to be the best. This agrees with the conclusion we found in the *Euthyphro*: that man must use his own inward faculty of insight to distinguish good and evil, and not be guided by others who tell him that some action is right on the ground that they know it to be pleasing to the gods. This faculty was not, like the divine sign, peculiar to Socrates; it exists in every human soul.

In Platonism, with its doctrine of immortality and the recollection of the Ideas, this faculty, as we have seen, is identified with the divine reason in the soul which apprehends the eternal realities. In mythical terms it is man's guardian genius or daemon. It is connected with divination by dreams in the *Timaeus*. Their warning or soothing visions are sent by the reason to the irrational part of the soul, which cannot understand rational discourse. Inspired divination comes only when the power of understanding is fettered in sleep or by some disorder or by divine possession. The visions must be interpreted by sober reflexion afterwards. It will be seen that here significant dreams are not ascribed to any outside source. A passing reference to divination by inspection of the liver of sacrificial victims seems to dismiss such methods of augury. Aristotle similarly ignores the interpretation of omens, but acknowledges that the evidence for prophetic dreams is too strong to be dismissed.

It thus appears that, down to the time of Aristotle, the principal clash between the philosopher and the seer arose over the physical explanation of 'the things in the sky and under the earth'. The old belief that these were signs of divine counsel or displeasure which augury had the skill to interpret is rejected both by the Ionian natural philosophers and by the Socratics. But the seers did not lose their occupation, for the popular credulity was not shaken by speculations which could easily be represented as impious or atheistical. The Stoics, moreover, with their faith in a benevolent Providence, sought to justify both kinds of divination, including omens of every sort. Hence it was necessary for Epicurus to devote so much attention to the department of 'meteorology', so as to exclude the supernatural from this province. Excess of zeal led him to announce the extravagant principle that *every* natural explanation is to be accepted in this field. With his denial of immortality, the divinity of the human reason of course disappears.

CHAPTER IX

THE QUARREL OF PHILOSOPHY AND POETRY

THE very existence of a quarrel between poetry and philosophy is evidence that there was a common field which both parties claimed for their own. The main purpose of the foregoing chapters has been to dispel the current illusion that this common field was originally occupied by the poets, and then, in the sixth century, suddenly invaded by the prosaic rationalism of a science of nature, having a quite independent origin in the direct observation of phenomena. I have tried to show that the conflict arose rather from the differentiation of the three types, poet, prophet and sage, out of the single figure still extant in the *shaman*. The original assumption was that all knowledge which lies beyond the reach of the senses in everyday experience is knowledge revealed to persons with exceptional intellectual and artistic gifts, who have undergone a special training and mastered a special technique.

Such persons have access to the unseen world. They have direct communion with gods and spirits, whose will they can interpret. Also they can survey the whole course of temporal events, the past, the hidden present, and the future. This power is claimed in identical terms for the prophet, inspired by Apollo, and for the poet, inspired by the Muses. With these forms of 'divine madness' Plato ranks the madness of the philosopher, rapt by the passion for truth into the region above the visible heavens. Behind Plato's myth lies the heaven-journey of Parmenides, who first declared that the truth revealed to him was not the past and future, but a timeless and unchanging reality. Nevertheless, he stands in the succession of those earlier prophets and poets who had visited the other world in search of mysteries.

When poet and seer become distinct, the seer's concern, as we have remarked, is to foresee the future, while the poet is occupied with his imaginative vision of the past. This vision extended backwards to the very beginning of things. The epic covered an era best described as legendary, in which the elements later distinguished as myth and history were still blended. The gods moved freely on the same stage with heroes, who were in some cases their immediate descendants. Behind this era lay the mythical epoch of Hesiod's *Theogony*, the generations of the gods before man existed, the succession of the divine dynasties, the war of Olympians and Titans; and beyond that again, cosmogony, the original formation of an ordered world. So long as this entire field was occupied by the poets, no clear line could be drawn anywhere between fact and fiction, poetry and history. The warm and living humanity which Homer's heroes share with the gods who move among them still produces even on the modern mind an overwhelming sense of reality, such as Virgil, Dante and Milton can convey only in certain episodes. The genius of Homer thus secured for the poets who succeeded him an authority which in most other civilized societies has been vested in the priesthood. In Greece the priests were officials in charge of the offering of sacrifice and worship which the gods expected in exchange for the benefits thy could grant or withhold. The seers were occupied with the interpretation of omens signifying the divine intentions. But the nature of the gods and the origin of the world remained within the province of the poets; and it was here that the philosophers first came into competition with them.

Whatever may have been the historical causes of this situation, it meant that in Greek society speculative theology was, to an exceptional degree, independent of cult, and consequently of any vested interests of the priesthood. In Greece the temple was not, as it was in Babylon or Egypt, the central citadel of culture; and, on the other hand, the writings of Homer and Hesiod, although prophetic in the sense we have defined, were not sacred or shielded by taboo against criticism. As social changes were accompanied by revised ideals of human character and conduct, the poets themselves could modify and amend or expurgate the Homeric and Hesiodic theology, thus perpetuating their own prophetic function. This process went on alongside the development of the philosophic conception of divinity, and there was considerable interaction between the two.

On the whole it was the philosophers who influenced the poets, for it was they who were bringing rational criticism to bear upon a theology for which the earliest poets were held responsible. The poets' attitude was necessarily more conservative, because poetry cannot dispense with the imagery of myth and its emotional appeal. The Zeus of Aeschylus has withdrawn to heights far removed from the summit of the Homeric Olympus; but he has not lost all his human character, and even his mythical adventures are retained, though they may be read in terms of symbolism and allegory. The philosopher's business is to dispel the veil of myth and penetrate to the 'nature of things', a reality satisfying the requirements of abstract thought. Our present concern is to trace the progress of this effort, as affecting the concept of the divine.

If the Homeric poems had not survived and been canonized as an indispensable element in Greek education and culture, the sharply defined individual gods of his Olympian pantheon might have faded away or been transformed by the profound changes in social and political conditions. As it was, the sixth century saw the rise of a mystery religion of a quite different type, answering to the needs of a class to which the aristocratic ideals of the heroic age made little appeal. At the same time the Ionian philosophers asserted the divinity of Nature, a single living substance whose life was immanent in the world. But Nature was not set up as a religious object. No one offered prayers or sacrifices to this impersonal divinity, which at first appeared in no way to threaten the cults of organized polytheism. The city states, so long as they lasted, maintained the worship of their local civic deities of the Homeric tradition. Pantheism, if it becomes a religion at all, can only be a universal religion, and it could not come into its own until the city state had broken down. After Alexander it re-emerges as the philosophic religion of the Stoic.

Xenophanes' attacks on the anthropomorphic gods of Homer and Hesiod are well known; but it is hard to be sure whether he meant to deny their existence or was merely exercising the poet's right to modify a theology which the earlier poets were believed to have formulated. It should be remembered that Plato, though he repeated Xenophanes' criticisms, never proposed to abolish the State cults, or to institute a worship of the World Soul or of the Demiurge of the *Timaeus*.

'Xenophanes declared that it is as impious to say that the gods were born as to say that they die: in either case it follows that there is some time when they do not exist' (Aristotle, *Rhet.* 1399 b 6). This verdict disposes of all theogonies, including Hesiod's, and of the Olympian family as such: if the gods are immortal, they must be eternal. But it sounds more like an assertion than a denial of their existence. Xenophanes also complained that Homer and Hesiod attributed to the gods actions which even men regard as shameful; and he objected to their being represented in human form by the painter and sculptor. He denied, too, that the arts of civilization had been bestowed on man from the first by the gods; mankind had, in the long course of time, sought and found better ways of living. There is nothing in all this that necessarily implies an intention to abolish the traditional gods, still less to substitute for them a worship of the divine universe.

When we turn from the negative to the positive side of Xenophanes' teaching, the evidence is still not decisively clear. Scholars of the first rank have held that he completely rejected polytheism and asserted that the living world is the only god. What concerns us, however, is not the abolition or amendment of the Olympians, but the philosophic concept of divinity, set up in contrast to those too human figures whom Homer himself had already seemed to regard with a tinge of scepticism and even humour. In the *Iliad* and *Odyssey* it is the heroes, not the gods, that embody ideals of human 'virtue'. The question remains whether, if we take Xenophanes as meaning to abolish the Homeric pantheon, he can be said to have any religion at all to offer in exchange.

What are the attributes of the one god who is the divine universe? 'Xenophanes says that the god is eternal, one, everywhere alike, limited, spherical in shape, and capable of perception in every part.'[1] The round world is a living creature endowed with consciousness or, in ordinary language, a body animated by a soul

[1] Hippol. *Ref.* 1, 14, 2 (*Dox.* 565).

co-extensive with it. Its body is finite[1] and spherical. The god is eternal, for gods are universally held to be 'immortal and imperishable', and this, as we have seen, implies that they have no beginning of existence. Accordingly, since this god is the world, there is no cosmogony, whereas Anaximander had endowed his 'boundless' with the divine attributes, and then generated out of it a perishable world. There is no such divine substance extending beyond the world and enveloping it, or breathed in by it, as the Pythagoreans supposed. The divine epithets belong to the world itself.

'He always remains in the same place, altogether unmoved; nor does it beseem him to go from place to place' (*frag.* 26). This is not a denial of any change inside the world. It probably means that, unlike other animals, which must move about to seek their food, the world, needing no sustenance, stays where it is.[2]

Though it does not require limbs or special sense organs, the world 'sees, hears, and thinks as a whole'. This god is conscious, and 'without effort sways all things by the thought of his mind'. The word 'sways' (κραδαίνει) need mean no more than 'moves'; it does not suggest a designing intelligence planning the order of the world or providentially controlling events. There is no justification for speaking of this god as a 'person in the fullest sense of the word',[3] if 'person' suggests someone with whom man can establish some sort of religious relation. Nor can it be argued that because Xenophanes attacks the Homeric gods for immorality, he 'implicitly affirms the morality and truthfulness of God'. This god is no more a moral being than is the divine world-stuff of the Milesians; and he has no opportunity for being truthful, having

[1] *Frag.* 28, stating that the underside of the earth reaches down 'indefinitely' (ἐς ἄπειρον), can be explained as denying that the earth floats on water (*Thales*) or on air (*Anaximenes*), or that there is any hollow Tartarus beneath it. The earth extends downwards, unlimited *by anything else*, to the bottom of the sphere (Gilbert, *Meteor. Theor.* 280, 671). The sun, according to Xenophanes, moves in a straight line εἰς ἄπειρον, 'indefinitely', not 'to infinity'; it burns out in a short time (Zeller, I⁷, 669).

[2] Cf. *Timaeus* 33 B–34 A, where Plato's description of the world's body closely follows Xenophanes (F. M. Cornford, *Plato's Cosmology*, p. 55); Aet. II, 5, I (*Dox.* 332 f., from Aristotle): the world needs no nourishment; hence it is eternal.

[3] As Adam does, *Religious Teachers of Greece*, p. 210.

no means of communication with mankind; for Xenophanes, we are told, denied all kinds of divination.[1] It must once more be emphasized that this god of the Ionian philosophers is not a religious object, and there is no question of any cult. The world is alive, and life, as Aristotle points out, normally implied some kind of consciousness or awareness and an inherent power of motion. Beyond that we cannot go.

When Xenophanes condemned the myths of the battles of Titans, Giants and Centaurs as 'fictions of the men of old' (*frag.* 1, 21), he was rejecting the claim of Hesiod's Muses to be revealing the truth about the remote past, and setting up his own claim to prophetic insight in opposition to theirs.

Heracleitus' insight into the nature of things and into his own nature led him to a very different conclusion; but he resembles Xenophanes in claiming for himself a prophetic knowledge which the poets (and the philosophers as well, including Xenophanes) had not attained. His god also may be described as the life of the world, the fire which is 'ever-living', and therefore also ever-dying, in the ceaseless transformation of the elements. His quarrel with Homer and Hesiod is not on the grounds of anthropomorphism and immorality. 'Homer was wrong in saying: Would that strife might perish from among gods and men.' He did not see that he was praying for the destruction of the universe, for 'War is the father of all'. 'Hesiod is most men's teacher. Men are sure he knew very many things, a man who did not know day and night; for they are one.'[2] Both poets were blind to the one truth, that no one opposite can exist without the other, and that the only harmony consists in the unending tension between them. There can be no peace without war, no day without night, no rest without motion, no harmony without discord. There must surely be an allusion here to pious dreams of a better world of endless day, perpetual spring, and peace in some Elysium or Islands of the Blest. In Heracleitus' universe there is no room for such an existence; nor yet for a god who '*transcends*' all opposites and puts

---

[1] Cicero, *de Div.* 1, 5, 'divinationem funditus sustulit'.

[2] Heracleitus, A22; B53 and 57=*frags.* 44, 35 Byw. (*Vors.*⁵ vol. II, pp. 149, 162, 163).

an end to their strife in a final static harmony, such as the Pythagoreans conceived. 'God is day *and night*, summer *and winter*,
peace *and war*, satiety *and hunger*.' Man may long for perpetual
day and summer and peace and satiety, and condemn their opposites
as evil, which he hopes to be rid of. But 'to God all things are fair
and good and right, though men consider some things wrong and
others right'.[1] The life which animates the world is indifferent to
our human values; these are no more absolutely valid than our
distaste for sea water, which fishes find healthy, or for mud, which
pigs prefer to wash in.

Heracleitus' claim to be a prophet with unique insight rests on
the conviction that the Logos, the thought which steers all things,
was to be discovered within himself as well as in Nature. It was
not a private wisdom accumulated by 'learning many things'
from others, but a wisdom which is 'common to all', if men only
had souls to understand it. The Logos, moreover, has a physical
existence. It is the fire in the world outside us, and a portion of it

[1] Adam's comment (*Relig. Teachers*, p. 233): 'In his *Intellectual System of the
Universe* Cudworth speaks of God as "reconciling all the Variety and Con-
trariety of things in the Universe into One most Admirable and Lovely
Harmony". This is precisely what is involved in Heracleitus' view of the Godhead', confuses Heracleitus' view with Platonism. See above, p. 116, n. 1. Burnet
(E.G.P.[3] 167) is also wide of the mark: 'In it' (God, the 'one wise', pure Fire)
'the opposition and relativity universal in the world disappear.' As for right
and wrong, it is impossible, without the context, to determine the meaning of
frag. 113, 114 (=91 Byw.) with its reference to human laws or customs (νόμοι):
'Thought is common (ξυνὸν) to all. Those who speak with understanding (ξὺν
νόῳ) must strengthen themselves with what is common to all, as a city with its
law and much more strongly. For all human laws are nourished by the one
divine; for this rules as much as it will and suffices for all and prevails (over all).'
It is at any rate certain that the mass of mankind do not 'speak with understanding' or grasp the one divine thought. Their customs and enactments are
not likely to accord with it. Cf. Cleanthes, *Hymn to Zeus*, 24: οὔτ' ἐσορῶσι θεοῦ
κοινὸν νόμον οὔτε κλύουσιν, ᾧ κεν πειθόμενοι σὺν νῷ βίον ἐσθλὸν ἔχοιεν. And
we should take account of the Heracleitean passage in Hippocr. *de Victu* I, 11:
'Custom (νόμος) and nature, by means of which we accomplish all things, do
not agree though they do agree. For custom was settled by men for themselves
without their knowing those things about which they settled the custom; but
the nature of all things was arranged by the gods. Now that which men arranged
never remains constant, whether right or wrong; but whatsoever things were
arranged by the gods always remain right. So great is the difference between
the right and the wrong' (trans. W. H. S. Jones).

is within us. Here we encounter a notion which reappears in many other philosophic systems: our intelligence is a portion of the divine intelligence, and therefore capable of understanding the 'thought' which governs Nature. In popular belief and in the Orphic-Pythagorean tradition, this divine faculty was supposed to receive revelations of truth in dreams, when the soul was set free from the body. 'It sleeps when the limbs (organs) are active, but, to the sleeper, in many dreams it reveals a judgement of weal or woe drawing nigh' (Pindar, *frag.* 131).[1] Aristotle, in an early work, similarly declared that 'the soul in sleep, being alone by herself, recovers her proper (heavenly) nature and divines and prophesies the future' (*frag.* 12). Heracleitus dissents from this view. The sleeper is shut up with his private fancies; he 'turns aside into a world of his own'. When the channels of sense are closed, the mind is cut off from contact with the mind outside, preserving only, in respiration, a sort of root. It becomes rational again only when we wake and look out through the windows of sense.[2] The idea that truth is revealed in dreams is thus denied; but the important conception of the human mind as akin to the divine mind is preserved. It guarantees the truth of Heracleitus' *logos* and is the basis of his claim to be a prophet. We have here the philosophic counterpart of the poet's claim to be inspired by the Muses, and the seer's claim to be possessed by Apollo. The philosopher is *entheos* in a prosaic and literal sense: his mind is a detached part of the divine mind in Nature. This mind, moreover, is the rational part of him, not the irrational.

The intransigent logic of Parmenides robbed the philosopher's One Being of every attribute of life: it is neither conscious nor capable of any motion. It could not, accordingly, be called a god. The only divine quality it retains is imperishability, for Being can neither come out of not-being nor cease to be. The whole of cosmogony and theogony is relegated to the second part of Parmenides' poem, as matter of mortal opinion, 'in which there is no true belief'. Here Parmenides gave, in the traditional form

[1] Cf. Aesch. *Eum.* 104: εὔδουσα γὰρ φρὴν ὄμμασιν λαμπρύνεται, ἐν ἡμέρᾳ δὲ μοῖρ' ἀπρόσκοπος βροτῶν.

[2] Aenesidemus, *ap.* Sext. Math. VII, 129.

of poetic narrative, his own amended version of the world's story; but it is recognized as a fiction which can, at the best, be only somewhat more like the truth than Hesiod's or Anaximander's. The truth revealed in the first part leaves no room for religion of any sort. Since it also left no room for natural philosophy, the philosophers of the next generation had to seek a way out and restore the reality of motion and consciousness in Nature.

Here the ways begin to part. One road leads to the materialism of atomistic physics. The One Being is pulverized into an infinite plurality of atoms, each of which retains its imperishable nature but is equally devoid of any possibility of life. The assertion of an infinite void gives the atoms room to move about and combine in complex structures. But the motion is merely mechanical locomotion, and it is postulated as a given fact, of which no explanation is offered by Leucippus and Democritus. Atoms and void are declared to be the sole ultimate realities, with the consequence that Atomism, though it can describe the rearrangement of material bodies which happens sometimes to produce an ordered world, cannot plausibly account for the existence of life and consciousness, and ought, strictly speaking, to deny their existence altogether. The Atomists stopped short of atheism only because they shrank from the parallel conclusion that they themselves possessed nothing recognizable as life and thought. They had not heard of behaviourism.

In the other direction, Empedocles and Anaxagoras, while admitting that their material elements were indestructible and unchanging, saw the necessity of providing a moving cause. The result is that the divine life of Nature begins to become distinct from material bodies. It is deposited in separate substances, still extended in space, but invisible and intangible and endowed with the soul attributes of self-motion and consciousness. The Love and Strife of Empedocles and the Mind of Anaxagoras are cosmic powers, and they may be called philosophic gods, though once more there is no suggestion that they should be worshipped or should oust the popular divinities. Empedocles tells us that, as the bodily elements in our sense organs enable us to see and feel earth, air, water and fire, so we perceive Love by love and Strife by strife. But Love and Strife are invisible. Of Love he writes: 'Contemplate her with thy thought, and sit not bemused by thine eyes. Her, whom even mortals recognize as implanted in their members, whereby they have thoughts of love and accomplish the works of union, calling her by the names of Joy and Aphrodite—her no mortal man has yet discerned moving round among these (bodily elements).'[1] In other words, Empedocles is the first to reveal the truth that the invisible power we call love in ourselves is the same as the power which works in all Nature; and this is true also of Strife. The exhortation to contemplate Love, not with the senses, but with thought (νόῳ), echoes Parmenides: 'Look at things which, though far off (from the senses), are surely present to thought (νόῳ).' The divine, says Empedocles, cannot be seen with the eyes or touched by the hands. He repeats Xenophanes' protest against anthropomorphism; the divinity (Love?) is described as a 'sacred and superhuman mind (or soul, φρήν), rushing through all the world with swift thoughts',[2] like the god of Xenophanes, who 'sways all things by the thought of his mind' (νόου φρενί). It is easy to exaggerate the significance of these expressions and to invest them with a religious meaning borrowed from Jewish or Christian scriptures. But they need mean no more than the identification of the conscious and moving force animating our own bodies with the force which moves the cosmos. The philosopher's intuitive knowledge of this power is guaranteed by the principle that like knows like.

The Mind of Anaxagoras is the corresponding factor in his physical system. It is the thinnest and purest of substances, self-moving and setting all other things in motion by virtue of its 'knowledge' of them. Its function is to produce order out of an original state in which 'all things were together'. A portion of it resides in all living creatures. It is not called 'God', and it has no moral attributes. This Mind was hailed later by the Socratics as furnishing a suggestion of the designing intelligence of the artist

---

[1] *Frag.* 17, 21 ff. The antecedent of ἥτις in l. 22 is τήν in l. 25. καὶ θνητοῖσι may be taken (as above) with νομίζεται or with ἄρθροις: 'her who is recognized as implanted even(?) in mortal members'.

[2] *Frag.* 134, assigned by Bignone to the physical poem.

who brings order into unordered material with a purpose in view. Body could no longer move itself. Either it must move at random, as in Atomism, and then the existence of an order such as the world exhibits is a product of chance that may well seem incredible; or it must be rearranged by a distinct intelligence capable of foreseeing and desiring the result. But this development still lay in the future.

Later in the fifth century Diogenes of Apollonia revived the doctrine of Anaximenes, once more identifying the primary substance and living soul of the world with Air. Like the Mind of Anaxagoras, it has power, by virtue of its knowledge of all things, to direct their motion and dispose all things in the best possible order. These properties entitle this 'eternal and undying body' to be called a god; and small portions of it constitute the souls of all living things, 'namely, air warmer than that outside us and in which we are, but much colder than that near the sun' (*frag.* 5).

With Diogenes and the Atomists we have reached the end of the Pre-Socratic natural philosophy. Looking back over the 'quarrel' between philosophers and poets, we see that it turned chiefly on the rationalist's objections to the anthropomorphism of the myths. The poets could not altogether dispense with the Olympian personalities, though they might amend their moral character, like Aeschylus and Pindar, or even, like Euripides, represent their immorality as casting doubt on their existence. The philosopher is free to ignore the mythical adventures of humanized gods, and he has no concern with the cults of organized religion. His God is at first the immortal and imperishable power of motion and consciousness animating the whole body of the world—a conception in no way alien to Greek religion, which had long since deified Heaven and Earth. It might even be maintained that philosophy had reverted to the much earlier conception of superhuman power diffused throughout Nature, from which a plurality of daemons and finally of fully personal gods had taken shape.[1] This God, as we have seen, is not a person or an object of worship. His important characteristic is unity. This went with the assumption, made by the early monistic systems, that the nature of things (φύσις) or source (ἀρχή) of the ordered world is a single substance. After

---

[1] Cf. Nilsson, *History of Greek Religion*, ch. IV.

Parmenides it became necessary to substitute a plurality of material elements, but simultaneously the divine moving power acquires a separate existence and so can retain its unity. Philosophy thus laid one of the foundations for a monotheistic and universal religion, in which the Logos of Heracleitus and the Mind of Anaxagoras could be fused with a spiritualized Zeus.

On the other side of the subject, I have tried to show how the philosopher retains his prophetic character. He relies for his vision of divinity and of the real nature of things on the assumed identity of his own reason with a portion of the cosmic consciousness. The power of thought immediately discerns a reality akin to itself, which is hidden from the senses. The intuitive reason (νοῦς) replaces that supernormal faculty which had formerly been active in dreams and prophetic visions; the supernatural becomes the metaphysical. All philosophy is based on the postulate that the world must be an intelligible order, not a mere welter of sights and sounds flowing in upon our senses from moment to moment. The perception of this order is not derived from sense-experience and observation, followed by cautious generalization and hypothetical inference. The philosopher's intelligence goes out to meet it, confident in its unaided power of insight and reasoning.

The natural philosopher is in competition with the didactic poet in so far as they cover the same field of cosmogony and theogony. The Muses had revealed to the inspired poet the history of the world back to the farthest bounds of the inaccessible past. Their tale was a tissue of myths of every sort, drawn from many different sources and from every stage of civilization. Such was the whole inherited stock of wisdom; and it was invested with all the prestige due to its association with established religion. It would have been a miracle if the wise men of the sixth century, who sought to obtain wisdom of the same order from Egypt and Babylon, should have swept their minds clean of all mythical preconceptions and looked out on Nature with eyes as innocent as Adam's on the day of his creation. Was it not more natural that they should continue the rationalizing process which had already been long at work in expurgating the grosser elements of myth as these became incredible?

From the point of view now gained we can return to our preliminary survey of the system of Epicurus. One of his three departments contained things wholly imperceptible by the senses (ἄδηλα) and accessible only to thought. These are the gods and the ultimate material realities, atoms and void. The gods were to be banished from our world. For their existence Epicurus fell back upon the old evidence of dreams. But in order to ensure the veracity of these visions, he had to invoke a power of the mind to project its thought into the unseen. This power, which is completely inexplicable on his materialist assumptions, is also to be exercised in gaining a 'mental apprehension' of atoms and void. The result is an intuition of self-evident facts, which claims to be infallible. It is easy for us now to recognize here the prophetic reason of the philosopher, sallying forth to apprehend its self-evident premisses and reasoning from them with unshakable dogmatism. For all his exaltation of the senses as the criterion of truth, Epicurus' procedure in this field of the imperceptible is essentially similar to the despised Plato's.

PART II

PHILOSOPHICAL COSMOGONY
AND ITS ORIGINS
IN MYTH AND RITUAL

CHAPTER X

ANAXIMANDER'S SYSTEM

IN the first part of this book we started from Epicurus' system to examine the common belief that this final expression of Ionian natural philosophy was pre-eminently scientific. We found that it was not in fact anything of the kind, but a dogmatic structure based on *a priori* premises. These premises were ideas and principles which seemed perfectly clear and self-evident to the reason. We have now seen how the reason itself, in which the philosopher trusted, had inherited its claim to immediate and certain apprehension of truth from the prophetic faculty of the inspired sage. The example of medieval scholasticism is sufficient to show how a philosophy may be eminently rational, and yet take its premises from revelation and deduce a whole system of the universe without feeling the need to check its conclusions by any close study of observable facts.

We may now turn back from the end of the Ionian philosophy to its beginning at Miletus in the sixth century. We shall take Anaximander's system and reconstruct it so far as the trustworthy evidence will carry us. Afterwards we shall consider how it is related to the mythical and poetical tradition of cosmogony that lies behind it.

Misled by Aristotle's habit of regarding his predecessors as more or less imperfectly anticipating one or more of his own four causes (material, formal, moving and final), the older historians of philosophy accepted his view that the early Ionians were concerned only with 'principles of a material kind', such as water or air. Accordingly they were represented as putting to themselves the question: What is the one (material) substance of which all things consist? But if we look at the systems themselves, the question they answer is a different one: How did a manifold and ordered world arise out of the primitive state of things?

The world-order to be accounted for is a static arrangement of the great elemental masses in four concentric regions—the heavenly fires at the circumference, earth in the centre, water and air (or mist and cloud) in the interval between sky and earth. Cosmogony then proceeds to describe the formation of sun, moon, and stars, and to explain those 'meteorological' phenomena which bulked so large in Lucretius. Finally it describes the origin of living creatures.[1] Later Ionian systems essayed to continue the story with the early history of mankind and the rise of civilization.

One assumption of all cosmogony is that the world-order as we now see it is not everlasting, but had a beginning in time, and that the starting-point or initial state of things (for which Anaximander probably used the word ἀρχή) was a simpler condition in which the parts of the ordered world were not yet distinct. This initial state of things Anaximander called 'the Boundless'—in what sense we shall consider later. Here we may note that the Boundless is said to be immortal and imperishable, in contrast with the world-order which arises out of it. Being imperishable, it is also the permanent stuff or 'nature of things' (φύσις) of which all things at all times are ultimately composed. Under this aspect Aristotle has some justification in calling it a principle of a material kind. It will be convenient to postpone further discussion of its nature and attributes until after we have traced the process by which a world is formed out of it.

The process leading from the initial state to the ordered condition is described as the 'separating out of opposites', such as the hot and cold, from the indiscriminate mass. Aristotle[2] divides the physical philosophers in general into two classes according to their conceptions of the process whereby a manifold world is got out of a

---

[1] For this table of contents cf. Aristotle, de Part. Anim. 640b5: οἱ μὲν οὖν ἀρχαῖοι καὶ πρῶτοι φιλοσοφήσαντες περὶ φύσεως (1) περὶ τῆς ὑλικῆς ἀρχῆς καὶ τῆς τοιαύτης ἀρχῆς ἐσκόπουν, τίς καὶ ποία τις, καὶ (2) πῶς ἐκ ταύτης γίνεται τὸ ὅλον, καὶ τίνος κινοῦντος...οὕτως γὰρ τὸν κόσμον γεννῶσιν. (3) ὁμοίως δὲ καὶ περὶ τὴν τῶν ζῴων καὶ τῶν φυτῶν λέγουσιν. Eur. frag. 910: ὄλβιος ὅστις τῆς ἱστορίας ἔσχε μάθησιν...ἀθανάτου καθορᾶν φύσεως κόσμον ἀγήρων, πῇ τε συνέστη καὶ †ὅπῃ† καὶ ὅπως.

[2] Phys. Α, IV, 187a12.

unity. Some regard reality as a single underlying body, from which all other things arise by thickening and thinning. This correctly describes Anaximenes, in whose theory the notion of permanent substance superficially modified is uppermost. Anaximander's original stuff is rather the initial state—not one of the familiar special forms of body, but a primitive fusion. Hence Theophrastus[1] says: 'He speaks of his principle as being not water or any other of the so-called elements, but a different nature, which is unlimited (or indeterminate).' Hence Aristotle assigns Anaximander to the second class, 'who say that, out of their unity, the Opposites contained in it are "separated out" as Anaximander says (φησι)'. This class also contains the pluralists who came later, such as Empedocles and Anaxagoras. These start with a plurality of distinct things in a single mixture, in which they were 'all together' and from which they were 'separated out'. Aristotle's language would naturally imply that 'separated out' (ἐκκρίνεσθαι) was Anaximander's own term. The commoner expression 'separated off' (ἀποκρίνεσθαι) is used by Simplicius (loc. cit.), following Theophrastus, in the same sense. Theophrastus thus confirms Aristotle's description. The evidence is as good as any that we have for Anaximander's views. The Opposites, then, were at first contained in the original unity and subsequently emerged into distinctness. If there is assumed to be no absolute beginning of existence, the Opposites must have been in the unity before they could come out of it.[2] What were these Opposites? Simplicius

---

[1] Phys. Op. 2 ap. Simpl. Phys. 24, 13.

[2] Burnet (Early Greek Philosophy[3], p. 57, note 1) writes: 'Theophrastos (ap. Simpl. Phys. 150, 22) says ἐνούσας γὰρ τὰς ἐναντιότητας ἐν τῷ ὑποκειμένῳ... ἐκκρίνεσθαι. I do not believe these words are even a paraphrase of anything Anaximander said. They are merely an attempt to "accommodate" his views to Peripatetic ideas and ἐνούσας is as unhistorical as the ὑποκείμενον.' But Simplicius is quoting, not Theophrastus, but the text of Ar. Phys. 187a20 on which he is commenting: οἱ δὲ ἐκ τοῦ ἑνὸς ἐνούσας τὰς ἐναντιότητας ἐκκρίνεσθαι ὥσπερ Ἀναξίμανδρός φησι. Aristotle quotes Anaximander's word ἐκκρίνεσθαι and his statement is consistent with that of Theophrastus, Phys. Op. 2 (Dox. 476, 3): οὐκ ἀλλοιουμένου τοῦ στοιχείου τὴν γένεσιν ποιεῖ, ἀλλ' ἀποκριναμένων τῶν ἐναντίων διὰ τῆς ἀϊδίου κινήσεως. If we are to reject the testimony of the only authorities who had read Anaximander's book, we had better admit that we know nothing about him.

specifies 'hot, cold, moist, dry, and the rest'. The important point about them is that they are not qualities, but things. 'The hot' was not warmth, considered as an adjectival property of some substance which is warm. It is a substantive thing, and 'the cold', its contrary, is another thing. Hence it was possible to think of the hot and the cold as two opposed things which might be fused together in an indistinct condition, like a mixture of wine and water. Just as the water and the wine could, in imagination, be separated out again, so the hot could draw apart from the cold.

The initial state of things (ἀρχή), we are told, was called by Anaximander 'the Boundless'. He did not identify it with any one of the four things—fire, air, water and earth—which were commonly recognized as occupying their distinct regions in the world-order. It was some sort of indistinct unity, out of which all these four could emerge to take up their appointed stations. Aristotle has preserved Anaximander's reason for not identifying his original unity with any one of the four: the elements (as they were later called) 'are opposed to one another; air, for example, is cold, water moist, fire hot; and if any one of these were boundless (unlimited), the others would have been destroyed by this time'.[1] This argument reveals two interesting points. First, that the initial state of things must be something 'boundless' or unlimited is laid down as an ultimate premiss, from which it can be inferred that it cannot be identified with any one of the hostile elements. What 'boundless' meant is a question to which we shall return later. The second point is the hostility or 'opposition' of the elements, which, when they have become distinct, are engaged in perpetual warfare, preying on one another and 'paying to one another the penalty of their injustice according to the order of time' (frag. 1). Air (or mist) is cold; fire hot; water is 'moist, earth dry. These two pairs of opposites may be called (in later language) the essential properties of the elements, or, as the early philosophers said, their 'powers', in virtue of which they act upon one another and are acted upon in their characteristic behaviour. This opposition

[1] *Phys.* 204 b 27.

provides the clue to the process whereby an ordered world comes into being out of the boundless unity. To this process we will now turn.

This separating process began in consequence of 'the eternal motion', whose nature must be considered later. In the first stage the opposite things have not yet become the visible elements. The hot is not yet flame or fire; the cold includes what will later be differentiated into air, water, earth. The beginning of the process is described by Theophrastus in archaic terms evidently echoing Anaximander's own words: 'He says that that which could generate hot and cold out of the eternal (i.e. the Boundless) was separated off at the coming into being of this world.'[1]

The word translated 'that which could generate' (γόνιμον) is used of the fertilized egg as opposed to the 'wind-egg' (ἀνεμιαῖον). In Aristophanes' parody of the Orphic Cosmogony, the World-egg laid in primaeval Night is called 'wind-born' (ὑπηνέμιον); but the germ of Anaximander's world is not infertile. It seems to be a nuclear portion of the indistinct stuff, somehow separated off from the rest by the eternal motion, and pregnant with the opposites which are to be further separated out of it in the birth of the world. The primary opposites here named are the Hot and the Cold. At this stage the Cold may be identified with 'the Moist' or 'the primary moisture'—not yet water, but what will become air (mist, cloud), water, and earth. Theophrastus continues: 'And out of this (the nucleus) a sort of sphere of flame[2] grew round the air (or moist) encompassing the earth, like bark on a tree.' The Hot moves out to the circumference and becomes incandescent, forming a spherical sheath of visible fire, enclosing the cold moist core of the nucleus. In place of 'the Cold' we now hear of 'the *air* (mist)

---

[1] Ps. Plut. *Strom.* 2 (*Dox.* 579, 13; Ritter and Preller, 19).

[2] It is arbitrary to dismiss the word 'sphere' as an 'inaccuracy' because 'the comparison to the bark of a tree distinctly suggests something annular' (Burnet, *Early Greek Philosophy*[3], p. 63, following Heidel). Theophrastus is evidently following Anaximander's text closely. 'Bark' does not imply any shape. We can speak of the 'crust' of the earth without implying that the earth is rectangular like a loaf, or flat like a pie, or spherical like an apple-dumpling. Besides, the first living creatures 'enclosed in a prickly bark' cannot have been 'something annular', but more like sea-urchins.

encompassing the earth'. Presumably the core is still humid throughout—a dark cold mist enveloping a somewhat denser watery mass at the centre.

The process then goes on as follows: as the cold core differentiates further, the second pair of primary opposites, Wet and Dry, become distinct.[1] The watery mass of earth is partly dried by the heavenly fire. Dry land becomes distinct from water, and the seas shrink into their beds. At this point the Hot, already differentiated into fire, acts as cause, evaporating some of the moisture and drying the earth. So, finally, the four popular elements have come to fill their appointed regions. The next stage is the formation of the heavenly bodies.

When this (sphere of flame) was torn off and enclosed in certain rings, the sun, moon, and stars came into existence.

The heavenly bodies came into being as (each) a ring of fire, separated off from the fire in the world and enclosed by mist ('air'). There are breathing-holes, like the holes in a flute, at which the heavenly bodies are seen. Hence eclipses occur when these breathing-holes are blocked; and the moon appears now to wax and now to wane according as the passages are open or blocked.[2]

The ring of the sun is 27 (or 28) times, the ring of the Moon 18 (or 19)[3] times, the size of the earth. The sun is outermost, next to it the Moon, and lowest the rings of the fixed stars and the planets.[4]

These figures can be explained as follows. We are told that the earth is a cylindrical drum, whose diameter is 3 times its height. The distances from the earth of the Sun ring and the Moon ring are 27 and 18 times the diameter of the earth. This suggests the missing figure 9 for the distance of the stars and planets. However

[1] R.P. 20a, Vors.[5] A 27 (1, p. 88).

[2] R.P. 19, 20, Vors.[5] A 10, 11.

[3] The variants 28 for the sun and 19 for the moon have been explained by the supposition that each ring is one earth-diameter in thickness, so that the figure would be 18 or 19 according as measurements were made to the inside or the outside of the ring.

[4] The text of the last paragraph was restored by Diels. Cf. Boll, s.v. Hebdomas, Pauly-Wiss. VII, 2565. According to Diod. II, 30, 6 the Chaldaeans put the fixed stars below the planets. For a similar view among the Persians, see R. Eisler, Weltenmantel, i. 90.

the figures may be explained, it is obvious that they are *a priori* and cannot be based on any kind of observation. No scientific method of measuring the distance of the Sun could result in its being placed so far beyond the fixed stars.

Each heavenly body is a ring of fire enclosed in a tube of dark mist ('air'), dense enough to hide the fire from our sight except at a single 'breathing hole, like the nozzle of a pair of bellows'.[1] It is probably meant that all the rings of the fixed stars and perhaps also those of the planets (excluding Sun and Moon) are at the same distance from the earth. The view consistent with our authorities would be that all these rings lie on the circumference of an imaginary sphere, and all revolve together, as if they formed a solid sphere, in the daily revolution of the heavens. It may be conjectured that this sphere, broken into rings, represents the original 'sphere of flame' which sheathed the nascent world. This would account for all the stars being at the same distance from the earth, as was currently assumed.[2] It is not explained how the Moon and Sun rings came to be formed farther out.

At the centre is the earth, 'freely suspended and not held in its place by anything, but staying there because of its equal distance from everything'.[3] This statement is very remarkable. Anaximander has abolished the solid firmament (like the shell of the world-egg) which could sustain the water on which Thales had made the earth float. His fiery firmament has burst into rings. Apparently he argued that the earth needed no support, but stayed where it was, in the centre, because there was no reason why it should move in any one direction rather than another. Later Ionians reverted to the notion that the earth needed support; they made it a flat disk floating on the air. We may note further that Anaximander has not the Epicurean conception of infinite space through which all bodies must fall 'downwards'. He seems rather

[1] R.P. 19a, *Vors.*[5] A21.
[2] Some historians understand that there is only a single ring of stars, which they identify with the Zodiac or the Milky Way. But this leaves all the other stars unaccounted for. Burnet's theory (*Early Greek Philosophy*[3], p. 69) contradicts all the testimonies.
[3] R.P. 20, *Vors.*[5] A11.

⟩ate the Platonic doctrine of a finite spherical universe, in
⟩wnwards' only means 'towards the centre'.[1]
⟨, the earth is 'rounded, circular, like the drum of a
ωοlumn.[2] We stand on one of its surfaces, the other is opposite'
(R.P. 20). 'The earth is cylindrical in shape, with its depth a third
part of its breadth' (R.P. 20a). In these last words we again
encounter a dogmatic statement which cannot be based on
observation.

'The sea is what remains of the original moisture, most of which
was dried up by the fire, while the rest was turned salt by the
burning up' (R.P. 20a).

Besides his explanation of eclipses, Anaximander explained
thunder and lightning, thunderbolts, waterspouts and whirlwinds
as all due to the blast of the wind. The wind itself was a current of
air due to the action of the sun on its finest and moistest particles.
Anaximenes added accounts of hail, snow, the rainbow, and
earthquakes.

The world-order is now complete: Earth, with its dry land and
seas, at the centre; the heavenly bodies revolving round it.
A cosmos has been evolved out of the initial undifferentiated state
of things by the separating out of the opposites, hot and cold,
moist and dry.

We may turn next to the initial state of things from which the
world-order arose. Since this is negatively described, as that which
is *not* limited, its nature is best approached from a consideration of
the limited world-order with which it is contrasted.

As we have seen, the cosmogonical process is essentially a
'separating out' of opposite powers. There are four of them, each

---

[1] Cf. also *Phaedo* 190A: The earth needs no air to keep it from falling but the
uniformity of the heaven in all directions is sufficient to hold it still.

[2] The text of Hippolytus is corrupt. γυρόν (a correction of ὑγρόν) may be
Anaximander's own word, στρογγύλον a gloss (Roeper). Cf. Hesych. γυρόν· . . .
κυρτόν (convex), στρογγύλον, κυκλοειδῆ. Suidas: γυρόν· κυρτόν, στρογγύλον,
citing Homer, *Od.* xIX, 246, γυρὸς ἐν ὤμοισιν. κυρτόν = convex: there is no
evidence that γυρόν can mean 'concave' (κοῖλον). If γυρόν does not mean
simply 'circular', it seems as if it must mean 'convex' or 'vaulted' with respect
to its upper (and lower ?) surface.

of which takes up its station in its appointed region: the hot becomes the heavenly fires in opposition to the primary moisture, which further differentiates into the cold air (mist, cloud), the wet seas, and the dry earth. Later, in Empedocles' system, fire, air, water, earth become the four elementary bodies of which all other bodies are compounded, and they retain a corresponding position in Plato and Aristotle.

Thus in the order of space we have, at the two extremes, the fires of heaven at the circumference of the round world, and earth at its centre. Between them is moisture in all its forms, cloud, mist, vapour, rain, the water of the seas. The heat of the heavenly fires acts on this moisture, evaporating it and feeding upon it. There is also the contrary process of condensation. The inter-mediate element, which Thales called 'water' and Anaximenes called 'air (mist)', travels up and down between heaven and earth. As Aristotle remarks, 'no physicist made fire or earth his unlimited unity, but either water or air or what is intermediate between them, because fire and earth have each its determined place, whereas water and air oscillate undecidedly up and down'.[1] Anaximenes saw in these processes of rarefaction and condensation the explana-tion of the cosmic arrangement:

The form of air is as follows. When it is most even, it is invisible, but heat and cold, moisture, and motion make it visible. It is always in motion; otherwise it would not change so much as it does. As it is condensed or rarefied it assumes a different appearance. When dilated, so as to be rarer, it becomes fire; whereas winds are condensed air, cloud is formed from air by felting, and further condensation produces water, then earth, and finally stones. Thus heat and cold are the opposites which are most of all responsible for becoming.[2]

This intermediate element is identified by Anaximenes with Anaximander's boundless body, which extends beyond the limited world. 'Just as our soul, being air, holds us together, so do breath and air encompass the whole world.' This boundless breath figures also in the earliest Pythagorean cosmogony, in which the world grows, as a living creature, by breathing it in. The finished cosmos

---

[1] *Phys.* III, 5, 205 a 25.
[2] Hippol. *Ref.* 1.7, R.P. 28, *Vors.*[5] Anaximenes A 7.

thus presents the picture, in the order of space, of four concentric provinces occupied by the opposed powers, and surrounded by the Boundless.

Still more illuminating are the occurrence and behaviour of the same four powers in the order of time. This phrase is Anaximander's own: 'things pay to one another the penalty of their injustice in the order of time' (*frag.* 1). This representation is derived from the alternating conflict of heat and cold, drought and moisture, in the cycle of the year. The comparatively abstract expressions 'the hot', 'the cold' etc. are appropriate to the familiar notion of the four powers dominating the seasons. The circle of the year is not homogeneous, but divided into parts, not necessarily equal in length, each marked by the prevalence of some opposite. In the main division of summer and winter (still used by Thucydides), the two primary powers, hot and cold, prevail alternately. The other two, dry and moist, drought and rain, come to be equated with spring and autumn. Thus Alexander Polyhistor, describing Pythagorean doctrine, says: 'Light and Darkness, Hot and Cold, Dry and Moist, are things that have equal portions in the cosmos. Of these the prevalence of the Hot gives summer; of the Cold, winter; of the Dry, spring; of the Wet, autumn.'[1]

Each power in turn advances, in 'unjust' aggression, at the expense of its contrary, and then pays the penalty, retreating before the counter-aggression of its antagonist. Thus in the whole cycle the balance of justice is maintained.

This conception of the behaviour of the seasonal powers in the cycle of time is applied by Empedocles to the strife of his four elements in the order of space: 'For all these are equal and coeval; but each has a different prerogative (τιμή) and its own character and ways [ἦθος can mean 'haunts', 'character', 'habits'], and they prevail in turn in the revolution of time.'[2] Thus the traffic and interchange of the elements, travelling up and down between the extremes of fire and earth, is, as it were, another form of the strife of seasonal powers. In each case we find a cycle of Becoming. Aristotle uses the spatial form to illustrate a logical point: 'We

---

[1] *Ap.* Diog. L. VIII, 24, *Vors.*[5] 1, p. 449.
[2] *Frag.* 17, 27. The last line recurs in *frag.* 26 with κύκλοιο for χρόνοιο.

observe in Nature a certain kind of circular process of coming-to-be (κύκλῳ τις γένεσις)....When the earth had been moistened an exhalation was bound to rise, and when an exhalation had risen cloud was bound to form, and from the formation of cloud rain necessarily resulted, and by the fall of rain the earth was necessarily moistened: but this was the starting-point, so that a circle is completed.'[1] And again:

The cause of this perpetuity of coming-to-be...is circular motion: for that is the only motion which is continuous. That, too, is why all the other things—the things, I mean, which are reciprocally transformed in virtue of their 'passions' and their 'powers of action', e.g. the 'simple' bodies—imitate circular motion. For when Water is transformed into Air, Air into Fire, and the Fire back into Water, we say the coming-to-be 'has completed the circle', because it reverts again to the beginning. Hence it is by imitating circular motion that rectilinear motion too is continuous.[2]

It is in circular movement, therefore, and in cyclical coming-to-be that the 'absolutely necessary' is to be found....The result we have reached is logically concordant with the eternity of circular motion, i.e. the eternity of the revolution of the heavens...since precisely those movements which belong to, and depend upon, this eternal revolution 'come-to-be' of necessity, and of necessity 'will be'. For since the revolving body is always setting something else in motion, the movement of the things it moves must also be circular. Thus, from the being of the 'upper revolution' it follows that the sun revolves in this determinate manner; and since the sun revolves *thus*, the seasons come-to-be in a cycle, i.e. return upon themselves; and since they come-to-be cyclically, so in their turn do the things whose coming-to-be the seasons initiate.[3]

From these and many other passages that might be quoted from Greek literature we can trace the persistence in philosophy of the primitive circularity of time. The sun's annual revolution through the signs of the Zodiac governs the cycle of the seasons, the advance

[1] *Post. Anal.* B 12, 95b38, Oxford trans.
[2] *De Gen. et Corr.* B 10, 336b34, Oxford trans. The rectilinear motion of the four simple bodies, up and down, is oscillatory and so 'imitates' the perpetual recurrence of the circular movement of the heavenly bodies.
[3] *Ibid.* B 11, 338a15, Oxford trans.

and retreat of the opposed powers, heat and cold, drought and moisture, and the consequent birth and death of vegetation.

In the light of these representations of the spatial and temporal order, it will now seem natural enough that the origin of life, within the ordered world, should be attributed by Anaximander to the interaction of the opposite powers. 'Living things arose from the moisture as it was evaporated by the sun' (*R.P. 22a*). Living creatures were not made: there is no trace in the Milesian systems of a divine artist or creator. They must, therefore, have been born: and this coming-to-be (*genesis*) results from the fundamental cosmic process. Born in the slime warmed by the sun's heat, the first living things must have had a suitable form. Here observation is called in. 'The first animals were produced in the moisture, each enclosed in a prickly bark' (like the sea-urchin). When they grew older they took to the dry land, the 'bark' split off them, and they 'survived for a short time'. Man cannot have been born originally as he is now, because 'while other animals quickly find food for themselves, man alone requires a long period of suckling. Hence, had he been originally as he is now, he would never have survived' (*R.P. 22*). He must then have been nursed inside his parent, after the manner of the *galeus*, a fish which is said by Plutarch to lay its egg and then nurse its young inside its own body, giving them 'as it were a second birth' when they have grown large enough to fend for themselves. These speculations should not be represented as anticipating Darwinian generalizations about adaptation to environment and the survival of the fittest, or even as hypothesis *based* upon the observation of a fish with peculiar habits.[1] They are deductions from the assumption that animal life had a natural origin in the action of the sun's heat on moisture. Given that doctrine, which may well have come from Egypt, it is not a long

[1] As A. Mieli remarks (*I Pre-aristotelici*, 1, 57), to say that man was generated and nursed *inside* a fish (as Plut. *Quaestt. Conv.* VIII, 8, 4 puts it) is very different from saying that the human species was *evolved from* a species of fish. Censorinus (*Vors.*5 1, p. 88) understood that men were formed inside 'fishes or fish-like animals' and nursed there till puberty, when they broke out as men and women, able to find their own food.

step to infer that the first animals must have been of a type which could live in warm slime, and that human beings cannot have originally been born as helpless infants. The *galeus* is then invoked to illustrate the way in which a fish-like creature can nourish its young to maturity.

We are now in a position to consider two points about which we have very little direct information: the nature of the Boundless, which enveloped the limited world, and the 'eternal motion'. Our information is so scanty that it is impossible to reach even a probable conclusion, if Anaximander's system is treated as a purely rational construction, having no relation to earlier modes of thought.

Our previous discussion has left us with two images: (1) the revolving circle of time, derived from the circle of the year, in which the four seasonal powers prevail in turn over their opposites and 'pay the penalty of their injustice'; (2) the revolving sphere of the world in space, the sphere of change, becoming and perishing, in which the same four powers occupy their appointed stations as the four great elemental masses, carry on the same warfare, and by their consequent interaction give birth to individual living things. Outside the limited world, in which these cycles of change revolve, there is the Boundless which is described as 'ageless and deathless'. The Boundless is the source (ἀρχή) from which the world arose, and it remains outside the world as the 'eternal' background of the cycle of change and becoming.

It may well be that here Anaximander's thought is not altogether clear, as judged by the standards of later science. We may falsify our account if we proceed to confront him with clear-cut alternatives which seem to us logically distinct. We should not assume that 'boundless' means either 'spatially unlimited', or 'qualitatively indeterminate', or both (as Theophrastus supposed). Perhaps neither sense, if taken strictly, is applicable. In the sixth and fifth centuries the word had several meanings, all to be derived from the absence of limit or of beginning and end.

In *Physics*, III, 4–8, Aristotle opens his essay on 'the Unlimited' with a review of this concept in early speculation. He distinguishes between the Ionian monists (with whom we are now concerned), who believed in a single unlimited body—'water or air or what is intermediate between them'—and the later pluralists, Anaxagoras and Democritus, who started with an unlimited aggregate of elementary particles. He then makes some general remarks. The physicists, he says, are right in regarding the Unlimited as a principle or source (ἀρχή); for it must have some function, and the only function it can have is that of a principle or 'beginning'. This is supported by an argument which has an archaic ring.

For everything must either *be* a beginning or *have* a beginning; and the Unlimited has no beginning, for then it would have a limit.

Also, as being a beginning, it is both ungenerated and imperishable; for that which comes into being must come to an end, and all passing away must have a term.

Hence, as we have said, this principle *has* no beginning, but is held to be the beginning of all other things, and to 'encompass all things' and 'guide all things', as all those assert who do not recognize, over and above the Unlimited, other (moving) causes such as Intelligence (Anaxagoras) or Love (Empedocles). And they identify it with 'the divine'; for it is 'immortal and indestructible', as Anaximander says, with the majority of the physicists.

On this passage Simplicius refers to the proof in Plato's *Phaedrus* (245 D) that soul must be immortal, as being the sole source of motion and self-moved:

A beginning (source, ἀρχή) is ungenerated. For all that comes into being must come from a beginning; but a beginning cannot itself come out of anything, since, if it came out of something, it would no longer be a beginning. And, being ungenerated, it must also be imperishable.

The common source of these passages in Plato and Aristotle may be Alcmaeon, who, according to Aristotle, said that the soul is immortal because it resembles the immortals in that it is always in motion; for all divine things—moon, sun, the stars, and the whole heaven—are always in continuous motion.[1] Alcmaeon also said that 'men perish because they cannot knit the end to the beginning': the body cannot reproduce the unending circular motion of the

[1] *Vors.*⁵ 1, p. 213 (Ar. *de Anim.* 405 a 29). Cf. Rostagni, *Verbo di Pitagora*, pp. 132 ff.

divine soul and the heavenly bodies. At any rate, Aristotle's remarks suggest various meanings of 'the Unlimited'.

(1) Unlimited may mean: 'having no beginning or source behind it, out of which it could come to be and into which it could perish'. The Unlimited has no beginning, but is itself the source from which all limited things come and into which they return: the initial and final state of things.

(2) As the source, it is endless in the sense of inexhaustible. Among the considerations leading to a belief in the Unlimited, Aristotle (*Phys.* 203 b 18) mentions the argument that 'if becoming and perishing are not to fail, that which comes to be must be drawn from an unlimited store'. This refers to Anaximander's own statement: 'he tells us why it is unlimited, namely in order that the existing process of becoming may not fail'.[1] The Unlimited, considered as a source, is never used up in the process of generating the limited things 'separated off' from it: there is always more in the reservoir. A strictly infinite quantity is, however, not required. When a world perishes, its materials return into the reservoir and go to form another, successive, world. A supply may be inexhaustible by the demands made on it, without being strictly infinite in quantity, as Aristotle pointed out (*Phys.* 208 a 8).

(3) The Unlimited has no beginning or end in time; it is called 'the eternal' (τὸ ἀΐδιον), in contrast with the contents of the limited world, where the distinct elements and all individual things are involved in the cycle of temporal becoming.

'This principle is eternal and ageless....Anaximander speaks of time as involving the distinction of coming-into-being (*genesis*), existence, and perishing.'[2] The Unlimited is exempt from these phases, immortal, imperishable, divine.

The contrast here is universal in Greek poetry and myth:

> Fair Aegeus' son, only to gods in heaven
> Comes no old age nor death of anything;
> All else is turmoiled by our master, Time.[3]

---

[1] *Plac.* 1.3.3 (*R.P.* 16a, *Vors.*⁵ A 14).
[2] Hippol. *Ref.* 1, 6 (*Vors.*⁵ A 11).
[3] Soph. *O.C.* 617, trans. Murray.

And in terms of space, mythology has the analogous contrast between an upper region—Olympus, the ether, Heaven—where the gods live untouched by change, and the lower earthly region where mortals are born and die. The Homeric Olympus is above the shifting changes of the elements.

'It is not shaken by winds, nor ever wet with rain, and the snow comes not nigh; but the clear air spreads without a cloud, and the white light floats over it.'[1]

Aristotle remarks that there is a mythical tradition of extreme antiquity, that the stars are gods and that 'the divine embraces the whole of nature' (*Met.* 1074b1). In his own system 'there is neither place, nor void, nor time outside the heaven (the circumference of the world). Hence whatever is there, is of such a nature as not to occupy any place, nor does time age it; nor is there any change in any of the things which lie beyond the outermost motion; they continue through their entire duration unalterable and unmodified, living the best and most self-sufficient of lives.' From this 'duration, immortal and divine, derive the being and life which other things, some more or less articulately but others feebly, enjoy' (*de Caelo*, A9). Democritus used the actual word Unlimited (ἄπειρον) to mean unlimited in time, eternal, when he said, 'The All is unlimited, because it was not created by anyone' (*Vors.*[5] II, p. 94 (A39)).[2]

Thus in one of its meanings 'Unlimited' is the abstract equivalent of 'immortal and imperishable' or 'divine'. And this exemption from the cycle of time, with its limits and distinctions of becoming, existence, and perishing, is associated with the spatial image of a supercelestial region outside the changing world. The popular imagination still confuses the ideas of an unchanging heaven in distant space and eternity beyond the reach of time.

(4) This leads to another statement about the Unlimited: that it 'encompasses all things and contains all things within itself'

---

[1] This description is cited by Galen in his commentary on the archaic cosmology in [Hippocr.] π. ἑβδομάδων 2, which calls the outermost sphere 'the Olympian world' (A. Mieli, *I Pre-aristotelici*, I, 108).

[2] Cf. also Melissus, *frag.* 2.

(*Phys.* 207a 18). As the circumambient, it extends beyond the limited world, in contrast with which it is unlimited, in the sense of not being itself encompassed by any further thing outside it. There are traces of an archaic argument implying that, if a thing is limited, it must be bounded by something else up to which it comes.[1] 'Unlimited' would then mean 'having nothing beyond to limit it'. Whether this means strict spatial infinity is, I believe, more than doubtful. It is arguable that the notion of strictly infinite extension was not grasped until later, when geometry was far enough advanced to force it upon mathematicians.[2] If the idea was familiar in the sixth century, how could Parmenides have held that beyond the limited sphere containing the whole of being there is neither something (for all being is inside) nor nothing, for empty space would be nothing, and 'nothing' cannot exist? So far as extension is concerned, 'Unlimited' may mean no more than 'not bounded by any other thing outside it'.

Aristotle, moreover, preserves an indication that, when Anaximander called his primary nature the Unlimited, he was thinking, not of the contrast between the abstract ideas of finite and infinite, but of the contrast between that primary nature and the elements which arise from it and limit one another in the world-order. He describes Anaximander as making the Unlimited, not a simple body like air or water, but something over and above the elements 'in order that the others may not be destroyed by the unlimited one. For the elements are in opposition to one another—air, cold; water, moist; fire, hot—and if one of them were unlimited, the rest would

---

[1] Cf. Ar. *Phys.* 203 b 20: the fourth argument for believing in an unlimited is that what is limited must always be so by coming up to *something else* which limits it. Simplic. (*Phys.* 467.3) calls this a 'more ancient' argument than those of the Epicureans. It may have been used by Anaximander himself. At 208 a 11 Aristotle replies that to be limited is not the same thing as to have contact with something else. Cf. [Ar.] *MXG.* 978 b 1 ff., where Xenophanes is attacked for arguing that many things can limit one another, but the One, having nothing else to limit it, must be unlimited.

[2] I have argued to this effect in 'The Invention of Space', *Essays in Honour of Gilbert Murray*, 1936, pp. 215 ff. Ar. (*loc. cit.*) mentions, as the fifth and most important cause of the belief in an infinite body (like Anaximander's) and innumerable worlds in an infinite void (the Atomists), that *number, mathematical magnitudes*, and what is outside the Heaven are supposed to be infinite, because they never give out in our *thought*.

have been destroyed by this time' (*Phys.* 204b 22). This looks like a criticism, on Anaximander's part, of Thales' identification of the primal nature of things with water, one of the limited opposites. In the warfare between the elements, the balance would be destroyed if any one were unlimited; the one would be able to encroach on its opposite indefinitely, without 'paying the penalty of its injustice'. In contrast with these mutually limited antagonists, the one source of them all is not limited by another thing on the same level with itself and fighting against it. The Unlimited is outside and above the warfare of limited powers in the world, an inexhaustible source from which they can arise and into which they perish; but there seems to be no reason why it should be strictly infinite in amount or in extent.

So long as 'the Unlimited' is an unlimited *something* (e.g. air) it is not conceived as strictly infinite. It only becomes so when it becomes either (1) the mathematical infinite, an abstraction, or (2) empty space, the physical infinite, which is '*nothing*', as in Atomism. This system has also an infinite number of *somethings*, viz. atoms. But Aristotle objected that there cannot actually exist an infinite *something* or an infinite plurality of *somethings*. He would not even allow that physical space can be infinite.

(5) If infinite extension is not implied, there is no objection to supposing that the immense mass was conceived as spherical in shape. So far from excluding the idea of shape, the Greek word is frequently applied to a circle or a sphere. Porphyry observes that the circumference of the circle and the surface of the sphere are uniform; and these are the only figures that can be called uniform in every respect. Hence the ancients with good reason described the circle and the sphere as 'unlimited'. Thus Aristophanes (*Danaids, frag.* 250) has the phrase 'wearing an unlimited bronze finger-ring'. As applied to a ring the word means that it has no juncture and shows no limit (πέρας) as beginning or end.[1] Rings which have a bezel with an inset gem are not unlimited, as not being uniform. So too Aeschylus (*frag.* 379) speaks of women standing round an altar as 'in an unlimited band', meaning the

[1] So also Aristotle, *Phys.* 207a2: rings without bezels are called unlimited (endless).

circular arrangement. Euripides also has 'an unlimited web' for the seamless tunic; and he calls the ether 'unlimited' because it is round and embraces the earth in its arms. This refers to the famous lines (*frag.* 941) which identify the unlimited sky above, encompassing the earth in its moist embraces, with Zeus and God. The parallel is very close to Anaximander's Unlimited, which 'encompasses all things' and, being immortal and imperishable, is 'divine'. Finally Empedocles uses 'unlimited' or 'boundless' and 'sphere' in the same breath: 'But he was equal every way and altogether boundless (ἄπειρων), a rounded Sphere' (*frag.* 28). This boundless sphere, moreover, actually has something enveloping it on the outside, namely Strife, which has been expelled from the spherical mass. Homer speaks of an island 'round which the sea forms an unlimited (unbroken) ring';[1] and the term 'unlimited' applied to the Stream of Ocean encircling the earth has the same meaning.

In view of all these passages, there is no objection to supposing that Anaximander thought of his Unlimited as an immense sphere. It is difficult to believe that any Greek would think of a divine being as of indefinite or strictly infinite extent.

Modern historians ascribe to Anaximander the belief, afterwards held by the Atomists, that there are at all times innumerable worlds, scattered throughout infinite space, and passing into and out of existence. I have argued elsewhere[2] that there is no satisfactory evidence for this startling doctrine before the time of the Atomists, when the conception of strictly infinite space had been established, and the 'Unlimited' was reduced to an endless void and an infinite number of atomic bodies. It belongs to the pluralist habit of mind, characteristic of the generation after Parmenides' attack on the monistic systems of the sixth century. There is nothing in the appearance of the natural world to suggest such a doctrine, if we remember that it was universally assumed that all the fixed stars were at the same distance from the earth and formed part of our world. The existence of unnumbered worlds which no one could ever see was deduced by the Atomists from the conviction that physical space, like the space of geometry, must be without any

[1] *Od.* x, 194, νῆσον, τὴν πέρι πόντος ἀπείριτος ἐστεφάνωται.
[2] *C.Q.* vol. XXVIII (1934), pp. 1 ff.

boundary, and from the dogma that there must be an infinite number of elementary material particles. Both these conceptions were, I believe, foreign to the minds and ways of thought of the sixth-century monists.

(6) As applied, then, to the circle and sphere, 'unlimited' means the absence of internal boundaries and distinctions, such as appear when the circle of the year is marked off into seasons, each with its prevailing power, or when the sphere of the world is divided into the provinces of the four elemental masses. The world was formed by the 'separating out' of the opposite powers, which thus became distinct and limited one another. Before this happened, and at all times in the circumambient stuff, the opposites, we are told, are present, but not distinct or limited. 'Unlimited' can thus mean 'indistinct', having no boundary where 'the Hot' ends and 'the Cold' begins.[1] This is not the same thing as 'qualitatively indeterminate', like Aristotle's ultimate matter, an abstraction considered as not yet endowed with the four primary qualities—hot, cold, wet and dry. Anaximander's opposites are not qualities, but things. These things were present in the Unlimited stuff, only not as distinct things in a mechanical mixture (like the mixture of four distinct elements in Empedocles' sphere): we must imagine them as fused, like wine and water, which are different, but not separate as water and oil are when you try to mix them.

The word 'Unlimited', then, has all these negative meanings without implying either 'infinite in extent' or 'qualitatively indeterminate'—the only alternatives proposed by later thinkers, like Theophrastus, to whom these conceptions had become familiar. But the Unlimited stuff has also positive properties which may throw some light on the nature of the 'eternal motion'.

It is not only 'ungenerated and imperishable'—which might be said of lifeless body—but 'immortal' and 'divine', terms which

---

[1] The contrary term πολύπειρον seems to mean 'having many boundaries' or internal divisions; it is applied to a people and to songs: Hom. *Hymn Dem.* 296, πολυπείρονα λαόν, Orph. *Arg.* 33, πολυπείρονας οἴμους, Emped. 17. 15, πείρατα μύθων, 'heads, divisions, of my discourse'. In Anaxagoras, *frag.* 12, ἄπειρον, applied to Νοῦς, may mean 'eternal' or possibly 'having no internal distinctions', not being a mixture of things limiting one another.

imply life. All the Milesians conceived their primary stuff as alive; hence they are called hylozoists. It does not correspond to the later conception of body or matter as opposed to, and excluding, life or soul. As Aristotle observes, where he reviews the early doctrines of soul, the essential characteristics of animate things are motion and some form of consciousness. The divine Unlimited, we are told, not only encompasses but 'guides all things (κυβερνᾷ πάντα), as all those affirm who do not recognize other (moving) causes such as Intelligence (Anaxagoras) or Love (Empedocles). And this is the divine; for it is immortal and imperishable, as Anaximander says' (*Phys.* 203 b 11). The term κυβερνᾶν, 'steer', 'govern', 'guide', clearly suggests not only motion but some conscious direction, as of the soul guiding and governing the body. Nor is this an anachronism. As we have seen, the one God of Xenophanes, who 'sees, thinks, and hears as a whole' (with no distinct sense organs), 'without effort sways all things by the thought of his mind'. The Logos of Heracleitus is both 'fire' and 'thought, by which all things are steered through all things'. The conception is perpetuated by Diogenes of Apollonia, whose Air, the substance of all things, has intelligence, whereby 'all things are governed (κυβερνᾶσθαι) and it controls all things. For this is god, which pervades all and disposes all and is contained in all' (*frag.* 5). What kind or degree of consciousness should be attributed to Anaximander's divine stuff, we cannot tell; but we may say that it contains implicitly the moving cause which emerges explicitly in Anaxagoras' Intelligence, a unique substance extended in space and yet knowing and controlling all things and capable of starting the cosmic revolution. Anaximander's successor, Anaximenes, expressly speaks of the divine Air as the life-breath (πνεῦμα) of the cosmos, 'embracing it, as our own soul, which is air, holds us together'. In his system the 'eternal motion' is the motion of the 'unlimited' Air, which accounts for the changes it undergoes; 'for it would not change so much as it does, if it were not in motion'.

If we would understand the sixth-century philosophers, we must disabuse our minds of the atomistic conception of dead matter in mechanical motion and of the Cartesian dualism of matter and mind. We must go back to the time when motion was an unquestioned symptom of life, and there was no need to look further for a 'moving cause'. Matter or body requires a distinct moving cause only when it has been deprived of its own inherent life. In support of his own contention that 'the world as a whole is unique and eternal, having no beginning or end of its whole life, containing infinite time and embracing it in itself', Aristotle says:

We may well feel assured that those ancient beliefs are true, which belong especially to our own native tradition, and according to which there exists something immortal and divine, in the class of things in motion, but whose motion is such that there is no limit to it. Rather it is itself the limit of all other motions; for a limit is a thing which embraces, and this motion,[1] being perfect, embraces those imperfect motions which have a limit and goal. Itself without beginning or end, unceasing throughout infinite time, it causes the beginning of some of the other movements, and receives the cessation of others. The ancients assigned heaven, the upper region, to the gods, in the belief that it alone was immortal; and our present argument testifies that it is indestructible and ungenerated. Further it suffers none of the ills of a mortal body and is, in addition, effortless, for it needs no constraining necessity to keep it to its path and prevent it from following a different motion which is natural to it (*de Caelo*, B I).

There are many echoes here of the description in the *Physics* of Anaximander's divine Unlimited. Aristotle recognizes the ancient association of divine and immortal life with eternal motion. All our authorities agree that Anaximander spoke of an eternal motion and attributed to it the separating out of the opposite powers and the consequent formation of a world-order. But they do not tell us the nature of this eternal motion, or how it could start the process of world-formation.

Motion becomes a problem for philosophy only when the mythical imagery of sex—the marriage of Father Heaven and Mother Earth and the genealogical scheme of cosmogony—has been abandoned. So long as the two meanings of *genesis*—'birth' and 'becoming'—were not distinguished, natural things came into

[1] ἡ κυκλοφορία is omitted by Stocks and Allan, with all MSS. but L. The 'imperfect motions' are the rectilinear motions of the four simple bodies, each of which moves towards its proper place and stops on reaching it.

existence by being born. A generative power in the 'nature' of things is implied in the very word 'nature' (φύσις); for φύειν means 'to give birth to'. But in Anaximander's system the language of sex has disappeared, having become incredible, and there is no suggestion of the alternative, an artist creator who makes things. Hence a gap opens in the scheme of cosmogony, demanding to be filled, sooner or later, by some mechanical account of motion. But the first philosophers were not conscious that the problem had arisen, as Aristotle complained: 'Those who at the very beginning set themselves to this kind of inquiry and maintained that the underlying substance was one (the Ionian Monists) did not trouble themselves' about the question of a cause of motion (*Met.* A III, 984a 27). The reason should now be plain. Motion was inherent in the divine stuff because it was alive, and eternal because that life was immortal.[1] So, too, Alcmaeon asserted as an obvious truth that the soul is immortal because like the immortals it is always moving; for all divine things—the heavenly bodies—are always moving continuously. The dogma persists in Aristotle himself: 'The activity of a god is immortality, i.e. eternal life; therefore, the divine must be in eternal motion. And since the heaven is of this nature, i.e. a divine body, that is why it has its circular body, which by nature moves for ever in a circle' (*de Caelo*, 286a9).

We cannot tell whether Anaximander himself used the phrase 'the eternal motion' (ἀίδιος κίνησις). When Theophrastus used it in describing his system, it had become practically a technical term for the revolution of a sphere and in particular of the heavenly spheres; and it is probable that this was what Theophrastus meant, rightly or wrongly. The effects of the eternal motion could be ascribed to the revolution of that part of the boundless mass which is involved in the formation of the world: these effects are the separating out of the opposite powers, and the 'coming into being of the heavens', i.e. of the rings which are the heavenly bodies. In Anaxagoras' system the same effects are expressly attributed to the revolution of the world-forming eddy, once this motion has been

---

[1] Simplic. *Phys.* 41, 17: ἄπειρόν τινα φύσιν...ἀρχὴν ἔθετο, ἧς τὴν ἀίδιον κίνησιν αἰτίαν εἶναι τῆς τῶν ὄντων γενέσεως λέγει. Note that here the eternal motion is said to be the motion of the Unlimited.

initiated by Intelligence. It seems likely that this is what Theophrastus meant. The aggregation of the elemental masses can be explained by the inherent hostility of the opposites forcing them apart and the complementary tendency of like things to come together.[1]

On the other hand, it is objected that, if the eternal motion is attributed to the boundless mass before the process of world-formation begins, an unlimited body cannot rotate. This objection has already been met by our argument that the term 'boundless' probably did not mean 'strictly unlimited' but was actually associated with spherical shape. It does not seem to have been obvious even to Aristotle's contemporaries that an unlimited body could not rotate; for he finds it necessary to prove this point by a series of geometrical demonstrations in the *de Caelo* (A 5). Even if this point is conceded, it remains obscure how an eternal revolution of the whole mass could at some moment start the formation of a particular world. I doubt whether Anaximander had any answer to this question: at any rate we hear of none. The solution may be that the nucleus or embryo of the world was still so near, in his imagination, to the world-egg of mythology that its becoming was not dissociated from birth and begetting sufficiently for him to feel the need of a mechanical type of motion. It is not surprising that a philosopher who was for the first time reaching out towards a mechanical explanation, in an age which had no conception of the laws of mechanical motion, should not have felt the need of filling a gap which is obvious to us. This may only be one more instance of our habit of demanding from the earliest thinkers answers to questions which never occurred to their minds. If so, it is idle to pursue the matter further in this direction.

It may, however, be possible to obtain some light from the consideration of a process which certainly figured in archaic thought. We are told that the sea was formed by the heat of the sun drying

---

[1] Even in Democritus' system, Aristotle (*frag.* 208 Rose) attributes the 'faction-fight' (στασιάζειν) of the atoms and their movement in the void to their 'unlikeness' (ἀνομοιότης) and other differences.

up the moist earth, and that the sea is still shrinking and at last it will all be dry.[1] This seems to imply that the process, which has been going on ever since the separating out of the opposites began, will end by destroying the order it created. The Hot is all the time gaining on its antagonist, the Cold moisture, which prevailed at the beginning. In the future it will destroy, by its 'injustice', the world and all it contains. But Justice must reassert itself: 'things pay to one another the penalty of their injustice in the order of time.' The principle of Justice can be saved only by supposing alternate destructions of the world by the Hot and by the Cold moisture. Our world will be destroyed by fire; its successor by water.

In the *Meteorologica* (A 14) Aristotle describes the rhythmical interchange of sea and dry land in various parts of the earth, following 'some order or cycle', but occupying immense periods of time. Such changes, he says, are local; and he criticizes 'men of narrow outlook who suppose the cause of such events to be change in the universe, in the sense of a coming-to-be of the world as a whole. Hence they say that the sea is being dried up and is growing less, because this is observed to have happened in more places now than formerly. But this is only partially true. It is true that many places are now dry, that formerly were covered with water. But the opposite is true too: for if they look they will find that there are many places where the sea has invaded the land. But we must not suppose that the cause of this is that the world is in process of becoming. For it is absurd to make the universe to be in process because of small and trifling changes, when the bulk and size of the earth are surely as nothing in comparison with the whole world.

Rather we must take the cause of all these changes to be that, just as winter occurs in the seasons of the year, so in determined periods there comes a great winter of a Great Year and with it excess of rain.[2] But this excess does not always occur in the same place. The deluge in the time of Deucalion, for instance, took place chiefly in the Greek world

[1] Ar. *Meteor.* B 1, 353 b 5 ff.
[2] Olympiodorus in his commentary (Ideler, Ar. *Met.* I, p. 257) explains that a 'great winter' occurs when all the planets are in a winter sign, e.g. Aquarius or Pisces; a great summer, when they are all in a summer sign, e.g. Lion or Crab.

and in it especially about ancient Hellas, the country about Dodona and the Achelous, a river which has often changed its course....Where such abundance of rain falls in the great winter it tends to make the moisture of those places almost everlasting. But as time goes on places of the latter type dry up more, while those of the former, moist type, do so less: until at last the beginning of the same cycle returns.'

In the next chapter comes the statement that Anaximander believed in the ultimate drying up of the sea. He was evidently one of those who regarded this as a cosmic process, destined to destroy the world it had formed.

The notion of alternate destruction of at least a great part of mankind by fire and flood was deeply rooted in Greek thought. In the *Timaeus*, the Egyptian priest tells Solon the reason why the Greeks have no very ancient traditions. There have been, and will again be, many destructions of mankind, 'the greatest by fire and water'. The myth of Phaethon, who could not drive the sun's chariot and so burnt up everything on the face of the earth, is based on the fact that deviations of the heavenly bodies cause, at long intervals, a great conflagration; and there have been many deluges, of which the Greeks remember only one, Deucalion's flood. Such destructions are said to occur regularly, 'after the usual period of years'. Plato himself starts his sketch of human pre-history from the assumption of a deluge in which only a few uncivilized mountain-dwellers survived.[1] In Empedocles, again, there appears the notion of a Great Year, in which worlds are generated and destroyed by two alternating and opposite processes. From Aristotle's remarks it seems probable that Anaximander accounted in this way for the formation and destruction of successive worlds. In our world fire is gaining on water, and the end will be a conflagration. The principle of Justice demands that the world which succeeds it will be formed by water gaining on fire and finally causing a deluge. Heracleitus was, perhaps, protesting against this scheme, when he maintained that there is only one 'everliving' world, in which the alternating process is going on perpetually. If there is anything in this conjecture, we may con-

[1] *Laws*, III, 677. Cf. Theophr. *Phys. frag.* 12 (*Dox.* 490, 30).

ceive the 'eternal motion' of Anaximander as the revolution of a Great Year, with its great summer and great winter, between which the balance sways as Heat and Cold prevail alternately. We cannot trace the cause of motion to anything more mechanical than the inherent repulsion of the hostile opposites.

The account of Anaximander's cosmogony—the birth of a world-order—is now complete. It describes in narrative form how, out of a simpler initial state, the main parts of the visible universe came to be disposed as we now see them. The order so produced, having come into being, will not endure for ever; the process, consisting in the mutual aggression of hostile powers, still continues, and will end by destroying the order it has generated. Only the ultimate 'nature of things', from which it came and to which it will return, is immortal and imperishable. From this inexhaustible and living source, when our world has perished, another will be born.

If we confine our attention to the three Milesians—Thales, Anaximander and Anaximenes—whose work covers the sixth century, we find that the rest of their physical speculation is concerned with what was later called 'meteorology', or, in simpler terms, 'what goes on in the sky and under the earth'. In Aristotle's more articulate system, these topics occupy a separate chapter, which he introduces as following upon those we have so far considered. His *Meteorologica* opens as follows:

We have now discussed the first causes of nature, and all natural motion, also the stars ordered in the motion of the heavens, and the physical elements—enumerating and specifying them and showing how they change into one another—and becoming and perishing in general.

There remains for consideration a part of this inquiry which all our predecessors called meteorology. It is concerned with events that are natural, though their order is less perfect than that of the first elements of bodies. They take place in the region nearest to the motion of the stars [i.e. just below the sphere of the moon]. Such are the milky way, and comets, and the movements of meteors. It studies also all the affections we may call common to air and water, and the kinds and parts of the earth and the affections of its parts. These throw light on the causes of winds and earthquakes....Further, the inquiry is concerned with the falling of thunderbolts and with whirlwinds (*typhoons*) and fire-winds (*presters*).

Following Aristotle's lead, the *Placita* devotes one book (II) to the cosmos and the order and movements of the heavenly bodies, and another (III) to τὰ μετάρσια, viz. what goes on in the region between the moon and the earth, and to the earth itself, the causes of earthquakes, and the sources of the sea. These topics complete the contents of the Milesian systems. They gave some account of wind, cloud, rain, hail, snow, the rainbow; typhoons and fire-winds; thunder, thunderbolts and lightning; earthquakes.

In accordance with our earlier argument about the medical origin of the empiricist theory of knowledge we may note in the Milesians the absence of any interest in the composition and working of the human body. The influence of medicine cannot be traced in the Milesians; medicine comes into contact with physical philosophy about the beginning of the fifth century. By that time the main pattern of cosmology was established. The later Ionian systems kept to the outline we have traced, whatever modifications and additions might be entailed by controversy and by the invasion of medical interests. These later developments we are not now concerned to follow. Our problem lies further back; we are seeking an explanation of the picture already drawn in this chapter. Is the Milesian cosmogony the work of rational inference based on observation and checked by at least rudimentary methods of experiment? Or are its features to be referred to an attitude of mind uncongenial to natural science as we understand it?

CHAPTER XI

PATTERN OF IONIAN COSMOGONY

HAVING now before us some picture of the earliest Ionian system, we can attempt to distinguish those elements in it which could be derived from immediate observation and those which must have been inherited from tradition.

Histories of philosophy and of natural science begin with this system, initiated by Thales, rounded out by Anaximander, and somewhat simplified by Anaximenes. Every reader is struck by the rationalism which distinguishes it from mythical cosmogonies. This characteristic must certainly not be underrated. The Milesians brought into the world of common experience much that had previously lain beyond that world. It is difficult for us to recover the attitude of mind of a Hesiod towards his vision of the past. As he looked back in time from his own age and the life he dealt with every day, past the earlier ages—the heroic, the bronze, the silver, the golden—to the dominion of Cronos, to the elder gods and to the birth of these gods themselves from the mysterious marriage of Heaven and Earth, it must have seemed that the world became less and less like the familiar scene. The events—the marriage and birth of gods, the war of Olympians and Titans, the Prometheus legend—were not events of the same order as what happened in Boeotia in Hesiod's day. We may get a similar impression by thinking of the Book of Genesis. As we follow the story from the Creation, through the series of mythical events which the Hebrews took over from Babylon, down to the call of Abraham, we seem to emerge gradually into the world we know, peopled with men like ourselves. So the past must have looked to everybody before the appearance of Ionian rationalism. It was an extraordinary feat to dissipate the haze of myth from the origins of the world and of life. The Milesian system pushed back to the very beginning of things the operation of processes as familiar and ordinary as a shower of rain. It made the formation of the world no longer a supernatural, but a natural event. Thanks to the Ionians, and to no one else, this has become the universal premiss of all modern science.

But there is something to be added on the other side. If we give up the idea that philosophy or science is a motherless Athena, an entirely new discipline breaking in from nowhere upon a culture hitherto dominated by poetical and mystical theologians, we shall see that the process of rationalization had been at work for some considerable time before Thales was born. We shall also take note of the re-emergence in the later systems of figures which our own science would dismiss as mythical—the Love and Strife of Empedocles and the ghost of a creator in the Nous of Anaxagoras. And when we look more closely at the Milesian scheme, it presents a number of features which cannot be attributed to rational inference based on an open-minded observation of facts.

In the first place the Milesians proceed on certain tacit assumptions which it never occurs to them even to state, because they are taken over from poetical cosmogony. As we have seen, the chief question they answer is: How did the present world-order, with the disposition of the great elemental masses and the heavenly bodies, come to exist as we now see it? Here at once it is assumed that the world had a beginning in time. The Ionians also asserted that it would some day come to an end, and be superseded by another world. Now there is nothing in the appearance of Nature to suggest that the world-order is not eternal, as we may see from the fact that Aristotle could declare that it was; not to mention Heracleitus and Parmenides, who, from their opposite standpoints, denied that any cosmogony was possible.

With this assumption goes the equally unfounded dogma that the order arose by differentiation out of a simple state of things, at first conceived as a single living substance, later, by the pluralists, as a primitive confusion in which 'all things', now separate, 'were together'.

Next, the differentiation is apparently attributed to the inherent hostility of certain primary 'opposites'—the Hot and the Cold, the Moist and the Dry—driving them apart. This hostility is personified by Heracleitus as War, the father of all things, and by Empedocles as the evil genius of Strife. In Anaximander the opposites prey upon one another and invade one another's provinces in 'unjust' aggression.

There is also a contrary principle of attraction between unlikes or opposites drawing them together into reconciliation and harmony—the Love of Empedocles. In Anaximander's scheme the hot and the cold, the moist and the dry, after they have been separated apart, interact and recombine. One of the consequences of this interaction is the birth of the first living creatures, when the heat of the sun warms the moist slime of earth.

If we now reduce these assumptions to a still more abstract scheme, we get the following:

(1) In the beginning there is a primal Unity, a state of indistinction or fusion in which factors that will later become distinct are merged together.

(2) Out of this Unity emerge, by separation, pairs of opposite things or 'powers'; the first being the hot and the cold, then the moist and the dry. This separating out finally leads to the disposition of the great elemental masses constituting the world-order, and the formation of the heavenly bodies.

(3) The Opposites interact or reunite, in meteoric phenomena and in the production of individual living things, plants and animals.

This formula, clothed in concrete terms, recurs in an Ionian system, evidently of the fifth century,[1] summarized by Diodorus (1, 7, 1). It opens with the words:

At the original formation of the universe heaven and earth had one form (μίαν ἔχειν ἰδέαν οὐρανόν τε καὶ γῆν), their nature being mingled.

After that, when their bodies had taken up their stations apart from one another (διαστάντων τῶν σωμάτων ἀπ᾽ ἀλλήλων), the world (κόσμος) embraced the whole order that is visible in it; the air was in continuous motion, and the fiery part of it ran together to the uppermost regions, its nature being buoyant because of its lightness. For this reason the sun

---

[1] Attributed to Democritus' Μικρὸς Διάκοσμος in Diels-Kranz, *Vors.*⁵ II, p. 134. It has been pointed out, however, that there is no trace of Atomism, and that consequently it is more likely to be a pre-Atomist system. See Bignone, *Empédocle*, p. 583.

and all the rest of the heavenly bodies were involved in the whole whirl; while the slimy and muddy part, together with the assembled moisture, established itself in one place by reason of its weight. The moisture was then collected to form the sea, and the more solid parts became soft muddy land.

The sun's heat then acted on the moisture and produced bubble-like membranes, such as may now be seen formed in marshy places. Life was generated in these, fed at first by the surrounding mist at night, and in the day time solidified by the heat. Out of these membranes, when they burst, all sorts of living creatures sprang: birds, the creeping things of earth, and the fishes. Later, when the earth had become more solid, it could no longer give birth to the larger creatures, but all living things were generated by the union of the sexes.

A sketch of the early history of mankind and the rise of civilization follows. Diodorus then points out that the formula is succinctly stated by Melanippe the Wise in Euripides:

The story is not mine—I had it from my mother—how (1) Heaven and Earth were once one form, and (2) when they were separated apart from one another, (3) they gave birth to all things and brought them to light, trees and winged creatures, fishes, and mortal men.[1]

In the group of closely related Orphic theogonies, Gruppe[2] saw one central doctrine, which may best be summed up in the words in which it is ascribed to Orpheus' pupil Musaios (Diog. L. prooem. 3): ἐξ ἑνὸς τὰ πάντα γίνεσθαι, καὶ εἰς ταὐτὸν ἀναλύεσθαι.

'Everything comes to be out of One and is resolved into One.' At one time Phanes, at another Zeus contained the seeds of all being within his own body, and from this state of mixture in the One has emerged the whole of our manifold world, and all nature animate or inanimate. This central thought, that everything existed at first together in a confused mass, and that the process of creation was one of separation and

---

[1] Eurip. Melanippe, frag. 484:

οὐκ ἐμὸς ὁ μῦθος ἀλλ' ἐμῆς μητρὸς πάρα,
ὡς Οὐρανός τε Γαῖά τ' ἦν μορφὴ μία,
ἐπεὶ δ' ἐχωρίσθησαν ἀλλήλων δίχα
τίκτουσι πάντα κἀνέδωκαν εἰς φάος,
δένδρη, πετεινά, θῆρας οὕς θ' ἅλμη τρέφει
γένος τε θνητῶν.

[2] I quote Mr W. K. C. Guthrie's summary of Gruppe's views in his Orpheus and Greek Religion, p. 74.

division, with the corollary that the end of our era will be a return to the primitive confusion, has been repeated with varying degrees of mythological colouring in many religions and religious philosophies.

In Apollonius' *Argonautica* (I, 496) Orpheus sings 'how (1) earth and heaven and sea were once joined together in one form, and (2) by deadly strife were separated each from the other'; how the heavenly bodies hold their fixed place in the sky, and the mountains and rivers were formed, and (3) 'all creeping things came into being'. Behind Apollonius is the tradition of the Orphic cosmogony parodied in the *Birds* of Aristophanes. There the primitive state of indistinction is called 'Chaos and Night, black Erebus and Tartarus', before earth, air and sky existed. Night is the first principle of the Orphic cosmogony recorded by Eudemus; it is not mere absence of light, but dark, cold, moist air. Aristotle compares the Night from which the theologians generate the world with the 'all things together' of the physical philosophers and the Chaos of Hesiod.[1] In the *Birds* Night produces the wind-born World-Egg from which is hatched out the winged Eros. (In Athenagoras' version of the myth the upper half of the egg forms the Heaven, the lower the Earth.) The function of Eros, who appears between them, is to reunite the sundered parents in marriage. 'There was no race of immortals till Eros united all in marriage.'[2] Then Heaven, Ocean and Earth were born—the three great departments of the world—and all the generations of the blessed gods.

We may now turn back to Hesiod's cosmogony, the one complete document of its kind which we can be certain was familiar to Anaximander.

First a word as to the type of poem to which Hesiod's *Theogony* belongs. It announces itself in the prelude as, in the first place, a hymn to the Muses: 'Let us begin our song with the Heliconian

---

[1] Ar. *Met.* 1071 b 26: εἰ ὡς λέγουσιν οἱ θεολόγοι οἱ ἐκ Νυκτὸς γεννῶντες, ἢ ὡς οἱ φυσικοὶ ἦν ὁμοῦ πάντα χρήματά φασι. 1072 a 7: οὐκ ἦν ἄπειρον χρόνοι χάος ἢ νύξ.

[2] *Birds*, 700: πρὶν Ἔρως ξυνέμειξεν ἅπαντα. | ξυμμιγνυμένων δ' ἑτέρων ἑτέροις γένετ' Οὐρανὸς Ὠκεανός τε | καὶ Γῆ πάντων τε θεῶν μακάρων γένος ἄφθιτον.

Muses, who hold the high and bold mount of Helicon.' It was they who came to Hesiod, as he tended his sheep, and breathed into him the inspired song, that he might celebrate what has been and shall be and, before all else, the Muses themselves. But the song which they inspire, namely the theogony which follows the prelude, is itself a hymn, sung by the Muses in praise of Zeus, the Lord of the aegis, and the other Olympians, and the elder gods, and Dawn and Helios, Earth, Ocean and Night and all the sacred race of the immortals.[1]

The hymn is one of the oldest forms of poetry.[2] In Greece the traditional metre is the hexameter, also appropriate to the oracle and to the epic. The hymn is in essence an incantation, inviting the presence of a god at the sacrifice and enhancing the efficiency of the ritual. Its effectiveness is increased by a recital of the history of the god and his exploits; hence it becomes biographical. Later, the use of the form is extended to heroes and to men; the famous deeds of the men of old are sung by the minstrel in the epic.[3] At every stage genealogies form a more or less important part. They are a didactic element, preserving what is believed to be the pre-history of the race, and, in some cases, the actual ancestry of important families, which serves as a basis for legal claims to property.[4] In Hesiod, the genealogies are designed to fit together into one pantheon a number of divinities, of very diverse origin, round the dominating figure of the European sky-god Zeus. The *Theogony* can thus be regarded as in the main a Hymn to Zeus, preceded by a short cosmogony. The Muses, 'uttering their immortal voice, celebrate with their song (1) first the awful race of the gods from the beginning, the children of Earth and the broad Heaven, and the gods born of these, the givers of good things (Cosmogony). Next (2) in turn, both in the beginning and in the end of their song, they hymn Zeus, Father of gods and men, how he is most excellent of the gods and greatest in power' (43 ff.).

[1] *Theog.* 11: (Μοῦσαι) ὑμνεῦσαι Δία τ' αἰγίοχον, κτλ. 36: Μουσάων ἀρχώ-μεθα, ταὶ Διὶ πατρὶ | ὑμνεῦσαι τέρπουσι μέγαν νόον κτλ.

[2] The following remarks on the hymn are suggested by C. Autran, *Homère et les origines de l'épopée grecque*, I, 40.

[3] κλέεα προτέρων ἀνθρώπων, *Theog.* 100.

[4] This appears clearly in the oral literature of Polynesia, for example.

They will tell how the gods took possession of Olympus under the supreme kingship of Zeus, who apportioned to them their several provinces and honours (111–13).

The episodes forming the mythical history of Zeus and his exploits will concern us later. For the present we must fix our attention on the brief cosmogony with which the story opens after the prelude. We shall find that it is built upon the same pattern as those we have been considering. It runs as follows:

First of all Chaos came into being, and next broad-bosomed Earth, for all things a seat unshaken for ever, and Eros, fairest among the immortal gods, who looses the limbs and subdues the thought and wise counsel of all gods and of all men.

From Chaos were born Erebus and black Night; and from Night in turn Bright Sky (*Aether*) and Day, whom Night conceived and bore in loving union with Erebus.

And Earth first gave birth to the starry Heaven, equal to herself, that he might cover her all round about, that there might be for the blessed gods a seat unshaken for ever.

And she bore the high Hills, the pleasant haunts of the goddess Nymphs who dwell in the wooded hills.

Also she bore the unharvested deep, with raging flood, the Sea (*Pontos*), without the sweet rites of love.

Here follows the marriage of Heaven and Earth. At this point a change comes over the story: Ouranos and Gaia become supernatural persons, who, with their children, the Titans, the Cyclopes, and the Giants, are involved in a series of biographical adventures. But in the cosmogony itself, which tells how the main divisions of the existing cosmos came into being—earth and the starry sky, the dry land and the sea—the veil of mythological language is so thin as to be quite transparent. Ouranos and Gaia are simply the sky and the earth that we see every day. Apart from the passing mention of the nymphs, the only mythological figure is Eros, and he is evidently no more than a bare personification of the love or attraction uniting in marriage all the parents who figure in the subsequent genealogies. Here, however, until we reach the marriage of Heaven and Earth at the end, the only birth which is (as a birth should be) the result of a marriage is the birth of light out of darkness; and even here the duplication of darkness into Erebus (male) and Night (female) and of light into Aether (male) and Day (female) is transparent allegory. The other births, or becomings—of Chaos, Earth, the Starry Heaven, the Hills, and the Sea—are 'without the sweet rites of love' (ἄτερ φιλότητος ἐφιμέρου, 132). This is a remarkable feature. It means that the cosmogonical process is a separating apart of the great departments of the ordered world, such as we have found in the Orphic and philosophical cosmogonies.

What, then, is the starting-point? 'First of all Chaos came into being.' In the modern mind the word Chaos has come to be associated with a primitive disorder in which, as the Ionian pluralists said, 'all things were together'. This is not the sense of the word in sixth- and fifth-century Greek. 'Chaos' meant the 'yawning gap',[1] between the fiery heaven and the earth, which could be described as 'empty' or as occupied by the air. Hesiod himself uses it in this sense at *Theog.* 700, where, when the ordered world already exists, 'chaos' is filled with a prodigious heat in the battle of Zeus and the Titans ((καῦμα θεσπέσιον κάτεχεν χάος). It is so used by Ibycus, Bacchylides, Aristophanes and Euripides,[2] in

---

[1] Boisacq, *Dict. Etym.* connects χάος, χάζω, χαίνω, χωρίς, χώρα all with a root meaning 'opening', 'separation', 'hollow', etc.

[2] Suidas: Χάος· καὶ ὁ ἀὴρ παρ' Ἀριστοφάνους ἐν Ὄρνισι (192)·

διὰ τῆς πόλεως τῆς ἀλλοτρίας καὶ τοῦ χάους
τῶν μηρίων τὴν κνίσσαν οὐ διαφρήσετε,

καὶ Ἴβυκος (*frag.* 29)· πωτᾶται δ' ἐν ἀλλοτρίῳ χάει. Bacchyl. v, 27: νωμᾶται δ' ἐν ἀτρώτῳ χάει λεπτότριχα σὺν ζεφύρου πνοαῖσιν ἔθειραν. Aristophanes, *Clouds* 627: μὰ τὴν Ἀναπνοὴν μὰ τὸ Χάος μὰ τὸν Ἀέρα; 424: τὸ χάος τουτί. (Schol. R *ad loc.*: Χάος λέγει τὸν Ἀέρα.) Eurip. *frag.* 448=Probus in Virg. *Ecl.* 6, 31: accipere debemus aera, quem Euripides in Cadmo χάος appellavit sic...τόδ' ἐν μέσῳ τοῦ οὐρανοῦ τε καὶ χθονός, οἱ μὲν ὀνομάζουσι χάος (the reading is uncertain, but the meaning is clear). In the sixth century 'air' and 'void' were synonymous. Aristotle (*Phys.* IV, 208 b 30) explains Hesiod's χάος as the empty place (τόπος) or room (χώρα) supposed to be required before anything could exist to occupy it. Cf. [Ar.] *MXG.* 976 b 15: εἶναί τι κενόν, οὐ μέντοι τοῦτό γέ τι σῶμα εἶναι, ἀλλ' οἷον καὶ Ἡσίοδος ἐν τῇ γενέσει πρῶτον τὸ χάος φησὶ γενέσθαι, ὡς δέον χώραν πρῶτον ὑπάρχειν τοῖς οὖσι. Most modern discussions of the term are vitiated by the introduction of the later idea of strictly infinite empty space (see above, p. 175). I do not think chaos is ever called ἄπειρον, and if it were, that would mean no more than 'immense', as applied to earth and sea.

a way that shows it was familiar to their contemporaries. The later ancients falsely derived *chaos* from χεῖσθαι, but remembered that it meant 'the empty space between heaven and earth'.[1] It is probable that in the sixth and fifth centuries the word *chaos* still carried its true etymological associations with χάσμα 'yawn', χάσκειν, χασμᾶσθαι 'to gape', 'yawn'.

Now, if cosmogony begins with the coming into being of a yawning gap between heaven and earth, this surely implies that previously, in accordance with Melanippe's formula, 'Heaven and Earth were once one form', and the first thing that happened was that they were 'separated apart from one another'. Hesiod can hardly have meant anything else. He does not say that Earth was born of Chaos, but that Earth came into being 'thereafter' (ἔπειτα). The first distinct body was the earth, 'broad-bosomed', probably conceived as a broad flat disk. We shall see later[2] why the '*starry* Heaven' (filled with the visible heavenly bodies) is said to have arisen afterwards, born from the Earth. Finally the separating process is completed, as in the cosmogonies we reviewed earlier, with the distinction of the dry land, raised up into hills and the sea.

When the gap has come into being, between the sundered opposites appears the figure of Eros, a transparent personification of the mutual attraction which is to reunite them. We have seen how Eros held the same place in the Orphic cosmogony. According to Pherekydes (*frag.* 3) Zeus, when about to fashion the world, was transformed into Eros, because (adds Proclus) he brought into agreement and love the opposites of which he was framing the cosmos.[3]

In the Milesian cosmogony this mythical personality disappears, but only to re-emerge in later systems which again avail themselves of the language of poetry. In the *Symposium* (178 A) Phaedrus argues that Eros is the eldest of the gods, for no writer in poetry or prose has spoken of his having any parents. He quotes Hesiod's lines about Chaos, Earth and Eros, and cites Acusilaus as agreeing

---

[1] *Etym. Gud.* p. 562: χάος παρὰ τὸ χεῖσθαι, ὁ κενὸς τόπος μεταξὺ γῆς καὶ οὐρανοῦ...δηλοῖ δὲ τὸ χάος τὸ μέγα καὶ ἀπέραντον χώρημα.
[2] Below, p. 197.
[3] Compare the physical account of Eros by Eryximachus in Plato's *Symposium*.

that after Chaos, Earth and Eros came into being. 'And Parmenides says of his birth: "First of all the gods she devised Eros."' With this passage in mind, Aristotle remarks that one might suspect that the need for a moving cause was first felt by Hesiod and by 'whoever else posited love or desire as a principle among things, for example Parmenides, on the ground that there must exist some cause which will move things and draw them together' (συνάξει, *Met.* A4, 984b 23). The Love of Empedocles has the same function of uniting unlike or opposite elements. Aristotle was not slow to recognize the mythical or poetical antecedents of philosophic concepts. Opening his discussion of friendship, he recalls in the same breath Heracleitus' declaration that the fairest harmony is composed of differing elements, and that all things come into being through strife, and Euripides' lines describing how the parched Earth desires (ἐρᾶν) the rain, and the majestic Heaven, filled with rain, desires to fall upon the Earth.[1] Euripides was imitating Aeschylus (*Danaids, frag.* 44): 'Love moves the pure Heaven to wed the Earth; and Love takes hold on Earth to join in marriage. And the rain, dropping from the husband Heaven, impregnates Earth, and she brings forth for men pasture for flocks and corn, the life of man.'

These fragments, again, are imitated by Lucretius (II, 991 ff.): 'We are all sprung from a heavenly seed; all have that same father by whom mother Earth the giver of increase, when she has taken in from him liquid drops of moisture, conceives and bears goodly crops and joyous trees and the race of man, bears all kinds of brute beasts, in that she supplies food with which all feed their bodies and lead a pleasant life and continue their race; wherefore with good cause she has gotten the name of mother.'

We can now see why the Milesians identified the living stuff of the world with the intermediate element—water, cloud, mist (air)—between the fiery heaven and the solid Earth. They drop

---

[1] Aristotle, *Eth. Nic.* 1155 b 1; Eurip. *frag.* 898: ἐρᾶ μὲν ὄμβρου γαῖ', ὅταν ξηρὸν πέδον | ἄκαρπον αὐχμῷ νοτίδος ἐνδεῶς ἔχῃ | ἐρᾶ δ' ὁ σεμνὸς οὐρανὸς πληρούμενος | ὄμβρου πεσεῖν ἐς γαῖαν 'Αφροδίτης ὕπο· | ὅταν δὲ συμμιχθῆτον ἐς ταὐτὸν δύο, | φύουσιν ἡμῖν πάντα καὶ τρέφουσ' ἅμα, | δι' ὧν βρότειον 3ῇ τε καὶ θάλλει γένος. Cf. Eur. *Chrysippus, frag.* 839.

the language of poetical personification, substituting for Eros his physical equivalent or medium, the moisture which rises from earth under the sun's heat and falls back in the rain, to fertilize the dry earth and enable it to produce living things. Anaximander dissipates the thin disguise of mythical imagery and keeps the indubitably natural factors—the hot and the cold, the moist and the dry, fire, water and earth. He thinks he has got hold of the real factors and processes which will furnish a prosaic and rational account of what goes on in the sky and of the origin of life. But the earlier history of these factors is revealed by comparison with the mythical cosmogonies, by their behaviour in the philosophic systems, and by the fact that they are used to explain everything in a way that innocent observation of Nature would never suggest. Even in Aristotle's system the two primary pairs of opposites— hot and cold, wet and dry—remain as the basic qualities of which the four simple bodies are composed. All other differences, such as heaviness and lightness, density and rarity, roughness and smoothness, are secondary, 'for it seems clear that these (the four primary qualities) are the causes of life and death, sleeping and waking, maturity and old age, health and disease; while no similar influence belongs to roughness, smoothness and the rest'. A long history, stretching back into the mythical epoch, lies behind the statement that this reason for their primacy 'seems clear'.

To return to Hesiod: a second consequence of the opening of the gap between Heaven and Earth is the birth of light out of darkness. Erebus and Night are the parents of Aether (the bright region of the sky) and Day. In the Orphic system Eros has another name, Phanes, the Bright One; and it is even suggested that the word Eros is primarily to be connected with a root meaning 'light'.[1] In physical terms the lifting up of the sky from the earth lets in the light of day where before there was darkness. We note that this appearance of light precedes the formation of the heavenly bodies. For the next event is that Earth gives birth to the *starry* Heaven.

[1] A. Sarić Rebac, *Wiener Studien*, LV, 1937. I take this reference from the summary in C.Q. XXXIII, 1939, p. 127.

The order of events in Anaximander's scheme is closely parallel. We first heard of 'a sphere of flame growing round the "air" (dark mist) encompassing the earth'. Thus the earth wrapped in mist was the first solid body, as in Hesiod. Then, when the sphere of flame was torn off into rings the heavenly bodies were formed. The Heaven which was separated from the Earth when the gap came into being was not a heaven of stars. The stars, in both accounts, appear to be formed of fire rising from the Earth and afterwards fed by exhalations of the moist element. So Earth gave birth to the starry Heaven 'that he might cover her all round about'. In the last words we recognize that bright Aether on high, which Euripides spoke of as 'holding Earth in the moist embrace of his arms' and identified with Zeus. The Earth mother is to be embraced by her husband Heaven. When the dry land has been separated off from the seas, to complete the world order, this Marriage follows and the eldest gods are born. The whole mythical theogony which begins here has, of course, no place in the Ionian systems, for these ignore the personal gods. In natural philosophy the intercourse of heaven and earth, heat and moisture, results in the birth of plant and animal life.

It is exactly at this point, where the formation of the physical cosmos is complete, that a significant change comes over Hesiod's story. The cosmogony we have reviewed is not a myth, or rather it is no longer a myth. It has advanced so far along the road of rationalization that only a very thin partition divides it from the early Ionian systems. Eros is the only mythological name, having no connexion here with religion or cult. Gaia and Ouranos are simply the earth and the sky, not mythical figures. But no sooner is the cosmos framed, to serve as a stage for the action which follows, than they are transformed into supernatural persons, indulging human passions of jealousy and hate in those 'violent deeds' which caused so much scandal later to religious minds.

In wedlock with Ouranos, Gaia brought forth the Titans, of whom 'the youngest, Kronos of crooked counsel, was the most terrible and hated his lusty father'. At once we are plunged back into the world of myth, and the rest of Hesiod's story moves in this supernatural atmosphere. Before we follow it further, we will pause to note a curiously close parallel, in another literature, to this sudden shift from rationalized cosmogony to myth.

The first three chapters of Genesis contain two alternative accounts of creation. The first account (Gen. i–ii. 3), in its present form, was composed not earlier than the exile; it is considerably later than Hesiod, and may even be later than Anaximander. In this Hebrew cosmogony, moreover, we find nearly the same sequence of events. Let us recall what happened on the six days of creation.

(1) 'The earth was without form and void; and darkness was upon the face of the deep; and the spirit of God moved upon the face of the waters.' Then light appeared, divided from the darkness, as Day from Night.

(So, when Hesiod's gap opened, there was earth and the moving spirit of life, Eros; and then Night gave birth to Day.)

(2) The heaven, as a solid firmament (στερέωμα), is created as a roof to divide the heavenly waters, whence comes the rain, from the waters below.

(This corresponds to Hesiod's Earth generating the starry Heaven as 'an unshaken seat for the blessed gods'. In later Ionian systems the solid crystalline sphere of heaven reappears, in place of Anaximander's sphere of flame which burst into rings. It is the shell of the world-egg.)

(3) The dry land is separated from the seas, and clothed with grass and trees.

(In Hesiod, Earth generates the hills and *Pontos* (the sea). Note that Empedocles made the trees, the first living creatures, spring up from the earth 'like embryos in the mother's womb', before the sun existed, *Vors.*[5] vol. i, p. 296.)

(4) The sun, moon, and stars are created to divide day from night and to 'be for signs and for seasons and for days and years'.

(As in the Greek cosmogonies, the heavenly bodies are formed later than the earth. Their function is to serve as 'signs', both for purposes of divination and to mark the distinctions of time in the calendar. As Plato says, 'the sight of day and night, of months and the revolving years, of equinox and solstice, has caused the

invention of number and bestowed on us the notion of time',
Timaeus 47 A.)

(5) and (6). The waters brought forth the 'moving creatures
that have life', birds and fishes and all the beasts that creep on the
earth; and finally man was made, both male and female, to be
fruitful and multiply and to have dominion over all living things.

(Thus 'creatures having life', distinguished from plants and trees
by their power of motion, arose from the moist element, when
the cosmic frame was complete. So it was in Anaximander, where
the action of the sun's heat on moisture reproduces in physical
terms Hesiod's marriage of Heaven and Earth.)

The most striking difference from the Greek cosmogonies is that
Hebrew monotheism has retained the divine Creator as first cause.
Otherwise there are no mythical personifications like Eros or
Phanes. And the action of Elohim is limited to the utterance of the
creative word. He has become extremely abstract and remote. If
we eliminate the divine command, 'Let there be' so-and-so, leaving
only the event commanded, 'There was' so-and-so, and then link
these events in a chain of natural causation, the whole account
becomes a quasi-scientific evolution of the cosmos. The process is
the same as in the Greek cosmogonies—separation or differentiation
out of a primitive confusion. As measured by the absence of personifications, Genesis i is less mythical than Hesiod, and even
closer to the rationalized system of the Milesians.

The foregoing argument will perhaps have made clear the
nature of Anaximander's achievement. We can see that his thought
was at work on a scheme of cosmogony already provided by
Hesiod and other poetical cosmogonies. He took the final step
in the process of rationalization, divesting the scheme of the last
traces of mythical imagery. It was not for nothing that his book
was one of the earliest written in prose, the proper language for
literal statements of fact.

In particular the figure of Eros vanishes. This means the elimina-
tion of the imagery of sex, and with it goes the representation of
cosmogony as a series of births forming a genealogical tree. He
speaks in abstract terms of the 'separating out of opposites',
followed by their interaction and recombination. These opposites

are the hot and the cold, the moist and the dry. Without the evidence of the mythical cosmogonies we could hardly guess that the primary 'opposites' were male and female, though, as we shall see, the tradition persisted elsewhere. What we claim to have established so far is that the pattern of Ionian cosmogony, for all its appearance of complete rationalism, is not a free construction of the intellect reasoning from direct observation of the existing world. There is nothing in the obvious appearances of Nature to suggest that the sky ever had to be lifted up from the earth, or that the heavenly bodies were formed after the earth, or indeed that the present order of the world has not existed for ever.

CHAPTER XII

HESIOD'S HYMN TO ZEUS

ESIOD'S cosmogony, reviewed in the last chapter, is the Muses' prelude to their Hymn to Zeus, 'who is king in heaven, himself holding the thunder and the smoking bolt, having by his might overcome his father Kronos and duly appointed their portions to all the immortals and designated their privileges' (*Theog.* 71). The rest of the theogony gives a number of episodes in the story of Zeus, but they are dislocated and interrupted, in a bewildering manner, by genealogies, not to mention some later interpolations. Our purpose in this chapter is to disentangle the story of how Zeus came to be king and to allot to the other gods their provinces and honours. We shall find in it the debris of a creation myth immeasurably older than the rationalized cosmogony.

At *Theog.* 132 occurs the transition we have already noted, where Gaia ceases to be merely the earth and becomes a supernatural person, who, in wedlock with Ouranos, gives birth to the eldest gods, the Cyclopes, and the Giants.

When we turn to the second account of creation in Gen. ii. 4 ff., there is the same abrupt transition to the atmosphere of myth. The utterly remote Elohim of the first chapter is replaced by an anthropomorphic Lord God, who moulds man (without woman) out of dust and breathes life into his nostrils, plants a garden containing the Trees of Life and of Knowledge, forms beasts and fowls out of the ground, fashions a woman out of the man's rib, walks in the garden in the cool of the day, and speaks to Adam with a human voice. The substance of the story, too, consists of genuine myths, and so continues, through the 'prehistoric' episodes borrowed by the Hebrews from Babylonia, down to the call of Abraham. These myths form the continuation of some earlier myth of creation, which was partly suppressed by the priestly compilers of Genesis when they substituted for it their own rationalized and semi-philosophical cosmogony of the first chapter. But, though suppressed in Genesis, the myth has left traces elsewhere in the Bible which have enabled scholars to restore its outline and trace it to its source in ritual. We shall return to it later.

In Hesiod the case is somewhat different. He has preserved, in the Hymn to Zeus, the mythical account of the origin of an ordered world, thus duplicating the semi-philosophical account which precedes it, though including also much anthropomorphic material. The first episode, in particular, repeats in mythical terms the opening of the gap with which cosmogony began.

Gaia lay with Ouranos and brought forth (1) the elder gods, afterwards called Titans, the youngest of whom, Kronos, hated his father; (2) the three Cyclopes, Brontes, Steropes and Arges; (3) the three hundred-armed Giants, Kottos, Briareos, and Gyes.

The children hated their father, because as soon as any of them were born 'he hid them all away in a secret place of the Earth and would not allow them to rise up into light'. 'Giant Gaia was stifled and groaned within herself.' She created grey adamant and made of it a sickle. Summoning her children, she asked them to take vengeance on their father. All were afraid, except Kronos. Gaia hid him in an ambush, armed with the sickle. 'And now great Ouranos came, bringing on night, and longing for love he laid himself upon Gaia and embraced her all round about.' Kronos, from his ambush, cut off his father's privy parts with the sickle and flung them behind him. Gaia received all the drips of blood, and as the years revolved brought forth the Erinyes, the armed Giants, and the Nymphs called Meliai. Kronos threw the privy parts into the sea, and from the white 'foam' (seed) coming from them was born Aphrodite, in whose train were Eros and Desire. Aphrodite received, as her privilege and portion, all the works of love.

Ouranos called his children Titans, because they had 'Strained' (τιταίνοντας) in doing their awful deed, for which vengeance (τίσις) would follow.

Hesiod's myth is somewhat confused and he seems hardly to understand its significance, much less its origin. It is possible that several elements of diverse origin have been combined in it.

More than fifty years ago Andrew Lang pointed out that we have here 'a myth of the violent separation of the earth and sky, which some races, for example the Polynesians, suppose to have originally clasped each other in a close embrace'. These words are quoted from Frazer,[1] who adds that 'in Egyptian mythology the separation of heaven and earth was ascribed to Shu, the god of light, who insinuated himself between the bodies of Seb (Keb) the earth-god and of Nut the sky-goddess. On the monuments Shu is represented holding up the star-spangled body of Nut on his hands, while Seb reclines on the ground.'

The cosmogonical myths of the Oceanic peoples were classified by Professor R. Dixon into two chief types—the evolutionary and the creative. 'The distinguishing features of the evolutionary theme are its postulation of an original darkness; and the genealogical manner in which, through a series of abstractions and concrete things, it traces the development of the cosmos from that chaotic night.' Almost invariably also, the cleaving-together of heaven and earth, and their ultimate separation, form a dramatic scene in the story; not quite invariably, but in so great a majority of versions that we may take this feature also as a characteristic of the evolutionary creation theme.

The creative type of myth has no genealogical tendencies, nor in its pure form does it give any hint of the cleaving-together of the elements. With few exceptions, it begins by assuming the existence of a certain amount of original matter, plus an original god (Na Arean). The latter inhabits a heavenly region of light and space, which is and always has been separate from the waste of waters beneath; at a given moment, he sets to work on original matter, and the universe takes shape.

Mr A. Grimble,[2] from whom I quote this passage, gives the following myth from the Central Gilberts as a specimen in which the evolutionary idea of the Universe predominates over the creative:

> In the beginning was Darkness and therein was a Cleaving-together of earth and heaven; no man dwelt therein.

[1] *Adonis*, vol. I, p. 283, where the references are given. Lang's explanation is adopted by M. P. Nilsson, *History of Greek Religion*, p. 73.
[2] 'Myths from the Gilbert Islands', *Folk-lore*, vol. XXXIII, 1922, pp. 91 ff.

But the Darkness lay with the Cleaving-together; their child was the Land (*te Aba*).

The Land lay with the Sky (*Karawa*); their child was the Void (*te Akea*).

The Void lay with the Sundering (*te Rawe*); their child was Na Arean.

Na Arean lay with the Rock (*te Ba*); their child was the Night (*te Bong*).

The Night lay with the Daylight (*te Ngaina*); their child was the Lightning (*te Iti*).

The Lightning lay with the Thunder (*te Ba*); their child was Na Arean.

At this point [adds Mr Grimble], the myth assumes narrative form, and tells how Na Arean the second raised land from the sea. But of course it does not show the god as the separator of heaven and earth, because the sundering of the elements is curiously assumed to have taken place genealogically. From the Sundering and the Void sprang the elder Na Arean. Thus the triumph of the evolutionary theme has cost the one his title of original being, and the other his prestige as the supreme lord of creation; while for all that we may discern of Na Arean's claim to be a light god in this text, it may as well have been swallowed up in the black darkness of the evolutionary hypothesis.

The best known version of the Polynesian creation myth is the Maori story recorded by Grey.[1]

Rangi' and Papa', the heaven and the earth, were regarded as the source from which all things, gods, and men originated. There was darkness, for these two still clung together, not yet having been rent apart; and the children begotten by them were ever thinking what the difference between darkness and light might be. They knew that beings[2] had multiplied and increased, and yet light had never broken upon them, but ever darkness continued. At last the children of Rangi' and Papa' consulted whether to kill their parents or rend them apart. The fiercest son was for killing them; but Tane-mahuta, the father of forests, said 'Nay, not so. It is better to rend them apart, and to let Rangi' stand far above us and Papa' lie beneath our feet. Let Rangi' become as a stranger to us, but the earth remain close to us as a nursing mother.'

[1] I quote the summary in J. C. Andersen's *Myths and Legends of the Polynesians*, 1928, p. 367. Cf. Tylor, *Primitive Culture*, vol. i, p. 322.

[2] It appears later that *human* beings are meant.

The brothers consented, all except Tawhiri-matea, father of winds and storms.

The five brothers who had consented then tried to separate Rangi' and Papa'. Four of them failed. Then Tane-mahuta arose and struggled with his parents; in vain with hands and arms he strove to rend them apart. He paused; firmly he planted his head on his mother Papa', the earth, and his feet he raised up against his father Rangi', the sky; he strained his back and his limbs in mighty effort.[1] Now were rent apart Rangi' and Papa', and with reproaches and groans of woe they cried aloud, 'Wherefore do you thus slay your parents? Why commit so dark a crime as to slay us, to rend us, your parents, apart?' But Tane-Mahuta forced them apart. Hence the saying of old time, 'It was the fierce thrusting of Tane' which tore the heaven from the earth, so that...darkness was made manifest, and light made manifest also.' At once was discovered the multitude of human beings they had begotten, who had hitherto lain concealed between the bodies of the two.

The story continues with the warfare waged by the Storm-god against his brothers to avenge the rending apart of their parents.

In China...the oldest and holiest books of the empire teach that the universe consists of two souls or breaths, called *Yang* and *Yin*, the *Yang* representing light, warmth, productivity and life, also the heavens from which these good things emanate; and the *Yin* being associated with darkness, cold, death, and the Earth.... Chaos, before it split into *Yang* and *Yin* and became the *Tao*, occupies the principal place in the pantheon (of Taoism) under the name of Pan-ku.... The *Yang* and the *Yin*, in the order of the world, are in an eternal struggle, manifested by alternation of day and night, summer and winter, heat and cold.[2]

'Whether or not there is historical connexion here between the mythology of Polynesia and China', says Tylor[3], 'I will not guess, but certainly the ancient Chinese legend of the separation of heaven and earth in the primaeval days of Puang-Ku seems to have taken

[1] This straining recalls Hesiod's derivation of Titan from τιταίνειν to stretch or strain, which is completely unintelligible as it stands, since it is not explained *what* the Titans strained. Tane' stands on his head, because he is the forest god and the 'head' of a tree is its root, the branches are its feet, as in Plato, *Tim.* 90A (F. M. Cornford, *Plato's Cosmology*, p. 354; J. C. Andersen *op. cit.* p. 404).

[2] J. J. M. Degroot, *The Religion of the Chinese*, 1910, pp. 3, 152, 19.

[3] *Primitive Culture*, vol. I, p. 325.

the very shape of the Polynesian myth: "Some day a person called Puang-Ku opened or separated the heavens and the earth, they previously being pressed down close together."'

If the Maori myth is a safe guide, certain features of Hesiod's account become clear. The children who were hidden in the dark womb of Earth, with no room to be born into the light, were human beings, and this chapter of the story should end with the birth of mankind. Here we may note the parallel between the rending apart of the Heaven-father and the Earth-mother and the separation of the sexes in mankind.

In Gen. ii we read:

These are the generations of the heavens and of the earth when they were created, in the day that the Lord God made the earth and the heavens, and every plant of the field before it was in the Earth, and every herb of the field before it grew: for the Lord God had not caused it to rain upon the earth, and there was not a man to till the ground; but there went up a mist from the Earth, and watered the whole face of the ground.

The Lord God then formed man of the dust of the ground, and breathed into his nostrils the breath of life. He set man to till the garden of Eden; created the animals; and finally fashioned the woman out of the rib he took from Adam.

On this passage the *Zohar* comments as follows:[1]

[Man was made in the image of God, and consequently was at first bisexual.] 'That is why the Scriptures say: Male and female created he them; he blessed them and gave them the name of man (Adam).' God divided this man into two, a male and a female. 'Adam had been created with two faces; therefore he was not alone. He could not find a helpmeet in her, seeing she was in his ribs and was joined to the back of him.... God cut him open, separating the female from him, as it is written: "And he took one of his ribs (*ahath*)." *Ahath* denotes the female. "And he brought her unto Adam." And he decked her as a bride and led her to Adam so that she might lie with him.'

[There is thus a correspondence, and even an interdependence, between the cosmic union in creation and the union of man and woman.] 'Adam and Eve were in the beginning created joined the one to the side of the

---

[1] I quote Denis Saurat, *Literature and Occult Tradition*, London, 1930, pp. 102 ff.

other. Why were they not created joined face to face? By reason of the words of the Scriptures: "For the Lord God had not yet caused it to rain upon the earth." The union of man, a being higher than all the other works of creation, the union of man, we say, with his wife, had to be modelled upon nature. Therefore it is only when the union of heaven and earth took place for the first time, a union which was made manifest by the rain, that man was united face to face with his wife.... Therefore the Scriptures add immediately afterwards: "And there went up a mist from the earth and watered the whole face of the ground." That is the desire felt by the female for the male: mists rise first of all from the earth to the heavens; and after forming clouds, the heavens water the earth. Notice that it is the same with the works of man.'

The *Zohar*, whether independently or not, has here presented the myth of the separation of male and female by the splitting of an original bisexed figure, parallel to the separation of Father-Heaven and Mother-Earth from a single form. This myth lies behind Aristophanes' speech in the *Symposium* and Empedocles' 'whole-natured forms', which, in the period of world-formation by strife, are divided into the two sexes.[1] In the Ionian systems the propagation of man by the union of the distinct sexes comes later than the origin of living creatures from the Earth-mother. It was true of man and woman, as of Heaven and Earth, that they were 'once one form, and then when they were separated apart, they gave birth' to their progeny.

The castration of Ouranos and its connexion with the birth of Aphrodite from the seed of the severed member point to the worship of the Phrygian Mother-goddess Cybele and of her consort Attis by her self-castrated priests.[2] As in Hesiod Earth first gives birth to the starry Heaven, and then is united with him in marriage, so in the Phrygian mythology the Mother (Nana) produces Attis by a virgin birth, and Attis (as Father, Papas) then becomes her lover. This is one expedient for providing the first parents of all living things from a single form. An alternative is found where the original divine being is thought of as male. This

[1] This matter is fully discussed and illustrated by K. Ziegler, 'Menschen- und Weltenwerden', *Neue Jahrb. f. das klassische Altertum*, 1913, pp. 529 ff. Cf. also F. Schwenn, *Die Theogonie des Hesiod*, Heidelberg, 1934.

[2] See Frazer, *Adonis*, vol. I, pp. 287 ff.

also occurs in the *Zohar*, which teaches that creation can only be accomplished by the union of male and female. 'He who is on high is the father of all; he it is who created everything, who fecundated the earth which grew big and brought forth fruits (*tholdoth*). It was fecundated as a female is fecundated by a male.' But since there is only one God, the female principle emanated from God, as his daughter. Creation then resulted from the sacred incest of Father and Daughter.[1]

The same doctrine occurs in the Indian *Brahmanas* (Satapatha and Aitaxeya), in the story of Prajapati, the creator of the world, and his daughter Ushas.[2]

'Prajapati conceived a passion for his own daughter....May I pair with her! Thus thinking he united with her. The lord of beings was the master of the house, and Ushas was his mistress....The lord of beings laid seed into Ushas. There a boy was born in a year.'

This son is Agni, who may be identified with the world: 'That boy entered into the forms one after another; for one never sees him as a mere boy, but one sees those forms of his....' As is explained elsewhere, this refers to the creation of the different kinds of animals by the union of Prajapati and Ushas. Ushas takes the female forms and Prajapati the male forms.

Now Ushas is the issue of Prajapati, is part of him, and an invocation to him runs thus: 'May these two, Heaven and Earth, the all-shaped, come to me! for Prajapati is Heaven and Earth. May Father and Mother come to me! for Prajapati is both father and mother.' We are now, therefore, dealing with the divine Hermaphrodite, who divides himself into male and female, then fecundates himself and thus produces the world, as in the Cabala. And the natural consequence of these conceptions is, as in Neoplatonism and the Cabala, the theory of the reconstitution of the Total God, who divided himself up into creatures, by the reassembling of the separated fragments. 'By offering up his own self in sacrifice, Prajapati becomes dismembered, and all those separated limbs and faculties of his come to form the universe, all that exists, from the gods...down to the worm, the blade of grass, and the smallest particle of inert matter. It requires a new, and ever new sacrifice to build the dismembered Lord of Creatures up again.' This reconstitution

---

[1] D. Saurat, *op. cit.* pp. 94 f.
[2] *Op. cit.* pp. 152 ff.

is carried out by Agni, and the ceremonies of the Sacrifice are the reconstitution of Prajapati. 'The real purport of all sacrificial performances is the restoration of the dismembered Lord of Creatures and the reconstruction of the all.'

In the Maori myth of Tane' and Rongo, Tane', having created trees and birds, desired offspring of his own form, but mortal. He fashioned a body out of sand and breathed life into it. This first mate produced an egg from which birds came; but the second child was a maiden, whom, when she had matured, Tane' took as his wife. 'In the same way Rongo of the Mangaian legend took his daughter Tavake to wife....Such consanguineous unions were not always regarded with reproach; in Hawaii, on the contrary, they were rather regarded with favour, a chief wedding with his sister, or his niece, or his daughter, often thereby exalting the royalty of his line, and adding honour to his house.'[1]

Such being some of the ways in which the origin of the first parents was conceived, Hesiod's story of the violent deed of Kronos seems somewhat confused. It appears to have combined two distinct motives. One is the forcing apart of Heaven and Earth, in order that the living beings engendered by their embrace may have an intermediate region of light and air to be born into; the other is the castration motive, leading on to the birth of Aphrodite, the goddess of marriage and birth, from the severed genitals. Her appearance should be followed by the birth of men and other living creatures from the drops of blood sprinkled on the earth. There may be two reasons why Hesiod stops short of this conclusion. One valid reason is that he has embarked on a theogony, and all the generations of the gods have to be recounted before the time comes for the appearance of human beings and other mortal animals. The other may be that he shrank from connecting the origin of mankind with the impious action of Kronos. However this may be, scholars have seen in the independent

---

[1] J. C. Andersen, *op. cit.* p. 408. McLennan's explanation of the custom of royal incest is given and illustrated by Frazer, *Adonis*, vol. I, chap. III. Where the royal blood was traced through women only, a prince would marry his sister, or, on the death of his wife, his daughter, in order to obtain or keep the crown.

castration motive a link between this story of the birth of Aphrodite and the myth and ritual of the oriental goddess whose province likewise is the union of the sexes and consequent fertility of man and of nature in general.

The chief festival of this Asiatic mother-goddess, who is also the Syrian Goddess and the Babylonian Ishtar, was held at the Spring Equinox. The Phrygian ritual has been reconstructed from accounts of the ceremonies as practised at Rome after the importation of the cult in 204 B.C.[1] On 22 March a pine-tree, swathed like a corpse and decked with wreaths of violets (for violets were said to have sprung from the blood of Attis), was brought into the sanctuary of Cybele. An effigy of Attis as a youth was tied to the stem. The third day (24 March) was known as the Day of Blood. The high-priest or Archigallus offered blood drawn from his own arms. Other priests danced and slashed themselves with knives, to bespatter the altar and sacred tree with their blood, perhaps to strengthen the dead Attis for his resurrection.

Further, we may conjecture, though we are not expressly told, that it was on the same Day of Blood and for the same purpose that the novices sacrificed their virility. Wrought up to the highest pitch of religious excitement they dashed the severed portions of themselves against the image of the cruel goddess. These broken instruments of fertility were afterwards reverently wrapped up and buried in the earth or in sub-terranean chambers sacred to Cybele, where, like the offering of blood, they may have been deemed instrumental in recalling Attis to life and hastening the general resurrection of nature, which was then bursting into leaf and blossom in the vernal sunshine. Some confirmation of this conjecture is furnished by the savage story that the mother of Attis con-ceived by putting in her bosom a pomegranate sprung from the severed genitals of a man-monster named Agdestis, a sort of double of Attis.

This conjecture is supported by the evidence of similar rites practised by eunuch priests in the service of the great Artemis of Ephesus and the Syrian Astarte of Hierapolis.

The day of mourning, on which the effigy of Attis was buried, was followed by the festival of Joy (Hilaria) for his resurrection

---

[1] I follow Frazer, *Adonis*, vol. I, pp. 267 ff.

on 25 March, reckoned to be the Spring Equinox. The ceremonies closed two days later with a procession to a brook where the image of the goddess was washed.

I have quoted this account because it furnishes a clue which will guide us to the conclusion of our argument. After mentioning the evidence for Attis being regarded as a sky-god or heavenly father like Zeus, with whom the Bithynians identified him under the name of Papas, Frazer suggests that the myth of Cybele and Attis might be connected, through the emasculation motive, with the castration of the old sky-god Ouranos by his son Kronos, and of Kronos himself by his own son, the younger sky-god Zeus; and so with the violent separation of earth and sky in the Polynesian mythology. He then continues:

> yet it seems unlikely that an order of Eunuch priests like the Galli should have been based on a purely cosmogonic myth: why should they continue for all time to be mutilated because the sky-god was so in the beginning? The custom of castration must surely have been designed to meet a constantly recurring need, not merely to reflect a mythical event which happened at the creation of the world. Such a need is the maintenance of the fruitfulness of the earth, annually imperilled by the changes of the seasons. Yet the theory that the mutilation of the priests of Attis and the burial of the severed parts were designed to fertilize the ground may perhaps be reconciled with the cosmogonic myth if we remember the old opinion, held apparently by many peoples, that the creation of the world is year by year repeated in that great transformation which depends ultimately on the annual increase of the sun's heat. However, the evidence for the celestial aspect of Attis is too slight to allow us to speak with any confidence on this subject.

Frazer is unquestionably right in refusing to believe that an order of priests and a fertility cult could be founded on 'a purely cosmogonic myth', or indeed on any myth. This would be to reverse the true order of events. The myth of the self-castration of Attis and of his union with the Mother-goddess is aetiological; that is to say the rites existed in the first place and were carried on for their practical purpose; the myth is a secondary projection of them on to the divine plane, justifying by an imaginary precedent ceremonies which, in more civilized times, would otherwise have been regarded with horror and disgust. It has been pointed out that this mother-goddess, later called Artemis Agrotera, is the huntress, the goddess of wild nature, associated with the tree-worship of the forest before the introduction of agriculture and with the fertility of men and animals, not of crops.[1] The ceremonies of the Day of Blood presumably date from this very early period, and with them the myth that the goddess herself was born from the severed genitals of the Sky-father. Such a conception of the origin of the female principle of life and fertility could only arise as a reflexion of the ritual actually practised. There is evidence that the cult of the goddess of wild nature existed in Crete in Minoan times, as well as in Asia. The myth of her birth comes from a stratum more primitive than the civilization we associate with Knossos. The complete absence of sexual symbols in the monuments of Minoan religion so far discovered[2] suggests that the myth came to Greece, not through Crete, but from the Asiatic mainland or from Cyprus.

If we take Hesiod's myth as a whole, it appears that his story of the castration of the Sky-father is a very ancient mode of conceiving the first act in cosmogony, the separation of Heaven and Earth to provide the male and female parents of all life. It also seems that this cosmogonical myth must have its ultimate source in a ritual practised in pre-agricultural times to promote the fertility of men and animals.[3] These rites continued to be celebrated, in Asia and at Rome itself, as a New Year festival of the Spring Equinox. Herein lies their significance for our purpose. The question still to be answered is: Why is the birth of the world conceived on the pattern of a New Year festival of fertility? The answer will become clearer as we examine other episodes in Hesiod's Hymn to Zeus.

[1] See M. P. Nilsson, *Minoan-Mycenaean Religion*, p. 433 (2nd ed. 1950, p. 503).

[2] Noted by Nilsson, *ibid.* p. 502 (2nd ed. p. 573).

[3] If the myth is older than agriculture, the 'Kronos' who emasculates Ouranos cannot have been originally 'an old harvest god', as we are commonly told. Must he not have been Attis himself, the self-castrated heavenly father, lover, and son of the Earth Goddess? In agricultural times the myth was interpreted as symbolic of the reaping of the corn with the sickle and the sowing of the new crop; and then the principal actor could be fused with a god of the reapers and sowers. But in the Golden Age of Kronos men lived in abundance without tilling the ground.

CHAPTER XIII

LIFE STORY OF ZEUS

IN the last chapter we traced the parallel between the separation of Heaven and Earth in the myth of the castration of Ouranos and the opening of the yawning gap, Chaos, in the semi-philosophical cosmogony which precedes the myth. When the gap had come into being, Earth became visible, Eros appeared between Earth and Heaven, and light broke into the primaeval darkness. After this first stage, the cosmic order is further articulated by the same process of the separation of opposites: the heavenly fires form the stars, and the dry land becomes distinct from the seas. Cosmogony proper thus ends in the establishment of the four popular elements—fire, air, water and earth—in their several provinces. In Hesiod's story taken as a whole, cosmogony provides the stage on which the mythical drama next to be recounted is played. The action must take place somewhere; and we find, as we proceed, that although the topography of these divine events is naturally vague, they are enacted within the framework of the cosmos.

We have now to consider the rest of the story which the Muses promised to tell, how the gods were born and took possession of Olympus, under the leadership of Zeus, who became King and apportioned to the other gods their provinces and honours. The parallel with cosmogony is still traceable here. As cosmogony ends with the establishment of a physical order, so the Hymn to Zeus ends with the institution of a social or political order, in which Zeus, as overlord, distributes to his subordinates their functions and privileges. Zeus is the hero of this action. We must now disengage from the tangle of genealogies the scattered episodes of his story. The episodes are, it is true, dislocated and even inconsistent in points of detail; but it is, I believe, a mistake to treat them as wholly unconnected, or to reject first one and then another because they are incoherent. The following is a list of those which will concern us:

(1) The Birth of the hero, Zeus.
(2) The Battle of the Gods and Titans.
(3) The Battle of Zeus with the Dragon, Typhoeus.
(4) The Enthronement of the victorious Zeus as King.
(5) The Allotment of the Gods' provinces.
(6) The Marriage of Zeus.
(7) The Creation of Animals and Mankind.

We shall find reason to think that these episodes are the scattered debris of a single Creation myth, and, further, that the myth itself is a reflexion of the New Year ritual.

(1) *The Birth of the Hero*

The first children born of the marriage of Heaven and Earth are certain figures who will take part in the coming action: the Titans, among whom Kronos is the only solid figure; the three Cyclopes, who will furnish Zeus with his thunder; and the three hundred-armed Giants. The forcible separation of Heaven and Earth follows, and then a string of genealogies. Among these we need to note only the granddaughter of Ocean, the half-nymph, half-snake Echidna, who in marriage with Typhaon produces a brood of monsters.

The narrative is resumed with the marriage of Kronos and Rhea (*Theog.* 453). Their first children, Hestia, Demeter, Hera, Hades and Poseidon, were swallowed by Kronos, who feared that one of them would rob him of the kingship; for Heaven and Earth had told him that he was fated to be subdued by one of his own sons. But Rhea, when about to bring forth Zeus, consulted Ouranos and Gaia how she might conceal his birth. They foretold[1] the fate of Kronos, and conveyed her to Lyctos in Crete. Gaia took the child from Rhea to rear him, and she hid him in a cave on the wooded hill Aigaion (Goat-mountain). She gave Kronos a swaddled stone, which he swallowed, mistaking it for the child who would one day deprive him of his kingdom. The young Zeus rapidly

[1] The oracular function of Earth (ἡ πρωτόμαντις) recurs later in the story.

grew up. Overcome by the might and craft of his son, Kronos vomited up the stone and Zeus set it up for a memorial at Pytho.

The sources and significance of this myth have been analysed in a masterly manner by Nilsson.[1] It came to the Greeks from Crete and there is reason to infer that it held a place in Minoan religion. The Greek Zeus, the bearded father of gods and men, the Olympian thunderer, had little in common with the child-god, who is born and dies, and whose tomb was shown in Crete. The motives of the hero swallowed and disgorged by a monster, and of the exposure of the child taken from its mother and suckled by animals, are to be connected with the ideas of death and rebirth. These and other elements in the Cretan and Mycenaean mythology point to the conclusion that the god is a fertility spirit, who is born annually; grows up quickly with the advance of the Spring season; becomes a youth attended by his band of dancers, the Couretes, protectors of hunters and herdsmen; is married to a tree-goddess; and dies, to be reborn in the next year. The difficulty is to see how a god of this type came to be identified by the Greeks with their Olympian thunderer. The only visible link is the common function of promoting fertility. The death and resurrection, which are the central feature in the ritual of the fertility spirit, could form no part of the story of the Greek Zeus. Accordingly they were suppressed, but only to reappear in the mysteries of Dionysus, the son of Zeus. Nilsson observes that the strength of the ecstatic cult of Dionysus, which spread all over Greece in the archaic age, is

better understood, if we assume that it was not an importation of a completely foreign god and form of religion but the revival of old Minoan and Mycenaean religious ideas, and perhaps also rites, which had for a time fallen into the background....The characteristic peculiarity of this movement is its mysticism, which combines with the belief in the re-born and dying god, who is by origin the spirit of vegetation. Thus the old religious idea acquires a deep emotional value, when the god appears as the divine prototype of the inexorable fate of man, whose birth and decay form so salient a feature of the mysteries. This idea would seem more natural if it originated in the Minoan religion, where the tree (that is the vegetation) cult seems to find ecstatic expression in

[1] *Minoan-Mycenaean Religion*, ch. XVI.

sacred dances and lamentations. These ideas were elaborated, sometimes in the form of strange rites and myths, in Orphism, which too is a creation of the religious movement in the archaic age.[1]

The Cretan myth, however, furnished Hesiod with the only available account of the birth of Zeus, and so finds a place in the story of the young king who wrests the sovereignty from his father.

(2) *The Battle of the Gods and Titans*

From the birth of Zeus we pass to the story of how he became King.

The hundred-armed Giants and the Cyclopes had been bound by Ouranos beneath the earth. Zeus and the other sons of Kronos set them free, because Earth had foretold that with their help Zeus and his brothers would conquer the Titans. The Cyclopes gave Zeus the lightning and thunder (*Theog.* 501 ff., 617 ff.).

For ten years the Titans from Mount Othrys had fought the gods from Olympus. Zeus now gave nectar and ambrosia to the hundred-armed Giants and asked for their help to decide the issue. They consented. There followed a terrific battle in which the Giants helping the Olympians hurled rocks at the Titans. All nature was convulsed: the sea roared, earth crashed, and heaven groaned; Olympus was shaken to its base. Then Zeus, armed with lightning and thunder-bolt, came from Olympus to join the gods. In the storm which filled all the space between earth and sky, the Titans were beset with flame and blinded by the lightning-flashes. At last they were overwhelmed by the Giants and hurled beneath the Earth, where they were bound in Tartarus. The Hundred-armed keep guard over them there.

It seems impossible to identify the Titans who assail Olympus with the first children born to Ouranos by Gaia: Ocean, Koios, Krios, Hyperion, Iapetos, Theia, Rhea, Themis, Mnemosyne, golden-crowned Phoebe, lovely Tethys and Kronos (*Theog.* 132). With the exception of Kronos and Rhea, these figures are empty names, and we cannot suppose that Themis and Mnemosyne, who later become brides of Zeus, were imprisoned in Tartarus, or that

[1] *Ibid.* p. 504 (2nd ed. p. 575).

they and the golden-crowned Phoebe can have fought with the rock-hurling Giants.[1] In the battle with the Titans Kronos is not even named, though at *Theog*. 851 (in the Typhoeus episode) he is mentioned as being with the Titans in Tartarus. The assailants of Olympus are nameless demons or powers of evil and disorder. Hesiod has not succeeded in harmonizing this episode with the overthrow of the old King, Kronos, by the young King, Zeus. But the episode is not to be excised on that account. It has its place in the tradition.

(3) *The Battle of Zeus and the Dragon*

After the Titans had been expelled, Earth, in union with Tartarus, bore her youngest son, Typhoeus. The monster had a hundred serpent heads, flashing fire from their eyes. His various heads uttered cries of all sorts, sometimes intelligible sounds, sometimes roaring, as of a lion or bull, or hissing, as of a snake. He would have become King of mortals and immortals, if Zeus had not intervened. The god thundered and Olympus shook under his feet. Earth, sea and sky were filled with the heat of the thunder and lightning from Zeus, and of the fire and storm from the monster. Zeus armed himself with thunder, lightning and thunderbolt, and leapt upon him from Olympus and scorched his heads. Overcome and scourged with stripes, Typhoeus fell lamed. The earth was melted by the blazing fire. Zeus hurled Typhoeus into Tartarus. From him come the storm-winds which sink ships and ravage the earth.[2]

This dragon is obviously identical with the Typhaon, mentioned

[1] Cf. Nilsson, *ibid.* p. 464 (2nd ed. p. 536); F. Schwenn, *Die Theogonie des Hesiod*, 7.

[2] In the continuation of the Rangi' and Papa' myth, the storm-god plays a leading part. 'No sooner were Rangi' and Papa' rent apart than was discovered the multitude of human beings they had begotten, who had hitherto lain concealed between the bodies of the two. Then also there uprose in the breast of Tawhiri-matea, the god and father of winds and storms, a fierce desire to wage war with his brothers, because they had rent apart their common parents.' He sent forth a whole brood of winds, clouds, and storms, and ravaged the forests of Tane-mahuta and the seas of Tangaroa, god of the ocean. He vanquished all his brothers save one who successfully resisted him. J. C. Andersen, *Myths and Legends of the Polynesians*, p. 369.

earlier, who was united with the half-serpent nymph Echidna, granddaughter of Ocean. Their marriage resulted in a brood of monsters. He is first mentioned by the poet of the Catalogue (*Il.* II, 781 ff.), who speaks of earth groaning under the lash of wrathful Zeus because of Typhoeus, 'in the country of the Arimi, where they say is the bed of Typhoeus'. This allusion, to which Hesiod seems to refer,[1] is sufficient reason for not dismissing the Typhoeus episode as a late addition to the *Theogony*.

Pherekydes of Syros is said to have told of 'the birth of Ophioneus and the battle of the gods'. Two hosts, led by Kronos and Ophioneus, challenged one another, agreeing that whichever should fall into Ogenos should be the vanquished, and their conquerors should hold the heaven.[2] This story reappears in Apollonius Rhodius (I. 503) after the Orphic cosmogony. Ophion and Eurynome, daughter of Ocean, held Olympus. By force Ophion yielded his position to Kronos, Eurynome hers to Rhea, and both fell into the waves of Ocean. Kronos and Rhea ruled over the blessed Titan gods, while Zeus was still a child in the Dictaean cave, not yet armed by the Cyclopes with thunderbolt and lightning.

Farther to the east we find traces of a fuller version of this episode, in which the Dragon is at first victorious over the god. The myth is associated with the Corycian cave in Cilicia by Pindar (*Pyth.* I, 16) and Aeschylus (*P.V.* 353) as well as in this fuller version narrated by Apollodorus (I, 6, 3).

Typhon had the head and trunk of a man, but he out-topped the mountains and his head brushed the stars. His hands reached to east and west and from them projected a hundred dragons' heads. From the thighs downwards he had coils of vipers. His body was winged and fire flashed from his eyes. Hurling rocks, he attacked heaven. The gods fled to Egypt, and being pursued changed into animal forms.[3] Zeus pelted Typhon with thunderbolts and struck

---

[1] *Il.* II, 783: εἰν ᾽Αρίμοις ὅθι φασὶ Τυφωέος ἔμμεναι εὐνάς (cf. 781). Hes. *Theog.* 304: ἡ δ᾽ ἔρυτ᾽ εἰν ᾽Αρίμοισιν ὑπὸ χθόνα λυγρὴ ῎Εχιδνα (cf. 843).

[2] *Vors.*[5] Pherek. v. Syros, A11, B4 (vol. I, 46, 49).

[3] This transformation is supposed to have been invented by the Greeks to explain the Egyptian worship of animals, Lucian, *de Sacrif.* 14 (Frazer on Apollod. 1.6.3). But may it not be a reminiscence of the part played by priests with animal masks in the original festival, not only in Egypt?

him with an adamantine sickle. Having chased him 'as far as Mount Casius which overhangs Syria', he grappled with the wounded monster. Typhon twined his coils about Zeus, wrested the sickle from his hands, and cut the sinews of his hands and feet. He carried Zeus through the sea to Cilicia and left him in the Corycian cave. The sinews he hid in a bearskin to be guarded by a she-dragon. Hermes and Aegipan restored them to Zeus, who pursued Typhon in a winged chariot, until at last he overwhelmed him and threw Mount Etna upon him. Hence the volcanic eruptions.

The oriental exaggeration of the story is in keeping with other indications pointing to its Asiatic origin. A Hittite parallel has been adduced,[1] in which the weather-god of the sky is at war with the Dragon of the deep. The Dragon captures the heart and eye of the god, to disarm him. They are recaptured by the help of a maiden, the Dragon's daughter, who marries the god's son and gives them to him. The god then conquers the Dragon.

In the Babylonian myth of the Battle of Marduk and Tiamat which we shall consider later, there is reason to believe that the Dragon of the waters was similarly victorious at first and even killed the god, who afterwards was restored to life. As Mr Gadd remarks, 'there is nothing of this in the Creation Epic, but in a text very recently published there is actually a hint of Tiamat's victory over Marduk. If this did occur, it would merely be the parallel to the work of a monster which brings about the god's death in the other Tammuz-stories.'[2] Like the authors of the Creation Epic, Hesiod or his authorities have suppressed the disablement or death of the god as unworthy of the supreme king of the immortals. With the astonishing persistence of such themes, it still reappears in those simpler versions of the battle of summer and winter which have kept closer to the original fertility rites, and are still enacted in the Mummers' play.

---

[1] By W. Potzig, *Illujankas u. Typhon* (Kleinasiat. Forsch. hrsg. Sommer u. Ehelolf, vol. I, 1930, pp. 379 ff. Sommer, *Die Achijawa-Urkunden*, Abh. Münch. 1932, pp. 382 f.). I take these references from Dornseiff, *Archäische Mythenerzählung*, pp. 25 ff.

[2] *Myth and Ritual*, ed. S. H. Hooke, Oxford, 1933, p. 59.

(4) *Zeus becomes King*

After the victory over Typhoeus, Hesiod continues (*Theog.* 881):
'Now when the blessed gods had made an end of their toil and had
decided the issue of honours with the Titans by force, then, by the
counsel of Gaia, they urged Zeus of the far-seeing eyes, Lord of
Olympus, to be King and rule over the immortals.'

The kingly function of Zeus, as the overlord of the other
immortals, was so familiar in Homeric mythology that Hesiod
has no need to dwell further on his accession to the throne. But
for our purpose of tracing the ritual pattern underlying this myth
it is a point of cardinal importance that the principal actor should
be the King, who has wrested the sovereignty from his father and
won his position by triumphing over the enemies of the gods.

(5) *The Dasmos*

'And Zeus apportioned to the gods their honours' (*Theog.* 885).
This was the first act of the newly appointed King. It is not further
described because, all through the *Theogony*, we have already been
told of the provinces and functions held by various deities in the
new order. Before the battle with the Titans, when Zeus summoned the gods to Olympus, he had promised to confirm the
existing rights of any gods who would join him in the fight, and
to re-establish any who had been deprived of their honours by
Kronos. First came Styx, bringing her children, including Victory,
Mastery and Force, to dwell with Zeus for ever. Zeus assigned her
the privilege of being the great Oath of the gods. And he fulfilled
all the promises he had made to the gods, himself enjoying the
mastery and lordship over them.

These arrangements are mentioned again in the probably inter-
polated account of Hekate, who is said to have received a portion
of the honours of all the sons of Heaven and Earth. 'The son of
Kronos did her no violence, nor robbed her of any portion allotted
to her among the former Titan gods, but she holds her privilege
in earth, sky, and sea, according to the distribution (δασμός) first
made at the beginning' (*Theog.* 421 ff.).

The allegory of the Oath of the gods, bringing Victory, Mastery, and Force to the newly enthroned King, is transparent enough. Zeus takes an oath, at his coronation, to confirm the rights and privileges of his courtiers, and his own rule will last so long as he keeps his pledge. We shall return to this feature later. The King's act has a cosmic significance, for his courtiers are gods. The social order which he thus confirms or institutes is based upon the physical order which came into being when heaven and earth had been separated apart and the elemental provinces became distinct. We hear of another distribution, whereby heaven, sea and earth were allotted to the three sons of Kronos.[1] The cosmogonical process thus once more appears as reduplicated in the superhuman drama of Zeus' accession to sovereignty. Or, to put it otherwise, the cosmogony is seen to be an abstract and philosophical scheme from which the mythical elements of the drama have been expurgated.

(6) The Marriage of Zeus

The *Theogony* ends with the marriage of the new King, multiplied into a whole series of marriages to accommodate the genealogies of his numerous descendants. The first of these unions reproduces the archaic features of the story of Kronos—swallowing his children to secure his own power. When his first wife Metis was about to bear Athena, Zeus, by the advice of Gaia and Ouranos, swallowed her, because her second child would be a son, who would become King of Gods and men in his stead.

His next partner is transparently allegorical. Themis (Law) bears to him the Seasons, named Good Government (Eunomia), Justice (Dike), and Peace (Eirene); and the Fates (Moirai), Klotho, Lachesis and Atropos, who determine the good or evil destinies of mortal men. Here once more we find associated the physical order of the Seasons, the social order of the King's government, and the 'portions' (μοῖραι) allotted to men.

---

[1] In Apollodorus' version of the myth (1.2.1), the gods, after conquering the Titans, cast lots for the sovereignty. The dominion of sky, sea and Hades fell to the lot of Zeus, Poseidon and Pluto respectively. This is the *dasmos* mentioned by Homer, *Il.* xv, 187.

(7) *Creation of Animals and Mankind*

In the Ionian philosophic cosmogonies, as in Genesis i, the institution of the world-order is followed by the formation of animals and men, to people the air, the waters and the dry land. This final feature is preserved by the poets, who, in Melanippe's formula, tell how the marriage of Heaven and Earth, mediated by the rain, brought living things into the light.

Hesiod's cosmogony stops short of this episode, because it introduces the generations, not of mortal creatures, but of the gods, and the whole supernatural story of how Zeus became King must be told before there can be any question of the beginning of human history. The story ends at the point we have reached, in the sacred marriage of Zeus with his various partners—the mythical equivalent of the marriage of sky and earth. But the only trace of any connexion between these unions and the fertility of earth and of mankind is in the birth of the Seasons as children of Zeus and Themis, and of Persephone, the ravished corn-maiden, as daughter of Zeus and Demeter, the bountiful giver of nourishment (πολυφόρβη, *Theog.* 912).

With the exception of one episode, the whole of Hesiod's story takes place on the supernatural plane of theogony. The exception is the tale of Prometheus, which was omitted in the foregoing summary because it is obviously out of place. Structurally, it is a digression arising out of the genealogy of the descendants of Ocean. Clymene, daughter of Okeanos and Tethys (who in one pre-Homeric system were the first parents of the gods), in union with the Titan, Iapetos, gave birth to Atlas, Menoitios, Prometheus and Epimetheus; and Hesiod is led on to describe the fate of these four sons. Prometheus' offence was that he cheated Zeus of the meat of the sacrifice 'at the time when there was contention[1] between gods and mortal men at Mekone'. So we suddenly find ourselves translated from the supernatural world to an earthly city where men are sacrificing to the gods. Zeus, in his anger, withheld fire from men; but Prometheus stole it and brought it to

[1] *Theog.* 535, ἐκρίνοντο. Does this mean a contention for their several rights in the sacrificial victim?

earth in the fennel-stalk. Zeus retaliated by causing Hephaestus to mould out of earth the first of that race of women who plague mankind. But of the origin of man Hesiod has no consistent account. In the *Works and Days*, the first man was created by the Olympians in the golden age of Kronos, 'when he was King in heaven'. This race and the silver race who followed vanished beneath the earth, to be succeeded by the bronze race, born of the Meliai, the tree-nymphs. Here we reach historical ground. Hesiod had discovered the bronze age, before the use of iron, and earlier than the fourth race, the heroes who fought at Thebes and Ilium.[1] It does not appear at what point in this sequence of races woman is supposed to have appeared, though the men of the silver race are spoken of as having mothers.

After the Prometheus episode in the *Theogony*, Hesiod returns to the release of the hundred-armed Giants and the battle with the Titans. If man had existed then, he could not have survived this struggle, in which all Nature was convulsed. But obviously the stage is once more clear of all but the divine beings. We hear nothing more about mankind.

Reviewing this series of episodes, we get the impression that they are the somewhat disjointed debris of a cosmogonical myth, not of Hellenic origin, but derived by the Greeks from oriental sources and current in Crete and Asia Minor before the Greeks came with their Sky-god Zeus from the North.

When set beside the humanized mythology of the Olympians in Homer, the myth with its hundred-headed and half-bestial monsters appears as archaic, crude and barbarous. The astonishing thing is that so much of it should have been preserved by Hesiod as the life story of Zeus; it is not at all astonishing that he should have failed to understand the material he was dealing with or to weave it into a wholly consistent narrative. It remains for us to look farther eastwards and restore the outline into which the fragments will fit.

[1] See Nilsson, *History of Greek Religion*, p. 184, on these races.

CHAPTER XIV

COSMOGONICAL MYTH AND RITUAL

W E have now traced back the abstract scheme or pattern of Anaximander's physical system to the type of cosmogony which appears in Hesiod and Genesis, in a form already far advanced along the road to complete rationalization. We have also seen that the life story of Zeus, from the first separation of Gaia and Ouranos to the enthronement and marriage of the new King, covers the same ground as the cosmogony, which ended in the marriage of Heaven and Earth. It is the same tale, told in the language of authentic myth, a drama of creation on the supernatural plane, where the actors include giants and monsters of a kind which had been almost completely eliminated from the humanized theology of Homer. The impression is irresistible that the gracious forms of Homer's Olympians are ludicrously out of place in this warfare of elemental powers. We have only to consider, for instance, the shock we experience when we pass from the picture of the goddess spawned from the seed of the Heaven-father's mutilated genitals to the concluding lines, telling us that the portion allotted to her is 'the dalliance of maidens, smiles and deceits, and sweet delight, love and kindliness'. We cannot guess how much of an effort it cost Hesiod to reconcile in his syncretistic theology the functions of the Homeric Aphrodite with such a story of her origin; nor can we say whether he had any inkling that the myth was to be connected with the worship of the Asiatic and Cyprian Astarte and her eunuch priests.

The Cretan legend of the birth of the child-god identified with Zeus has furnished modern scholarship with another clue linking Hesiod's myth of the creation with the rites of a fertility spirit, who, like Astarte's lover, dies and rises again. We have now to seek further light on the question: what is the true connexion between the cosmogonical myth and the type of ritual whereby the life of nature and of mankind is annually renewed in a drama of death and resurrection?

All the elements of an answer to this question are to be found in a section of the *Golden Bough*, dealing with the slaughter of the Dragon.[1] The battle of Zeus with Typhoeus was the episode immediately preceding his elevation to the Kingship. Two other Greek legends of the slaying of a water-dragon have been connected by Frazer and Dr A. B. Cook with the octennial tenure of the Kingship. The dragon-slayer at Thebes was Cadmus; at Delphi Apollo kills the Python. Both victories were celebrated originally every eighth year at nearly the same season. After stating a theory to account for these facts, Frazer remarks that it is difficult to separate these legends of the dragon from

those similar tales of the slaughter of a great dragon which are current in many lands, and have commonly been interpreted as nature-myths, in other words as personifications of physical phenomena. Of such tales the oldest known versions are the ancient Babylonian and the ancient Indian. The Babylonian myth relates how in the beginning the mighty god Marduk fought and killed the giant dragon Tiamat, an embodiment of the primaeval watery chaos, and how after his victory he created the present heaven and earth by splitting the huge carcass of the monster into halves and setting one of them up to form the sky, while the other half apparently he used to fashion the earth. Thus the story is a myth of creation. In language which its authors doubtless understood literally, but which more advanced thinkers afterwards interpreted figuratively, it describes how confusion was reduced to order, how a cosmos emerged from chaos. The account of creation given in the first chapter of Genesis, which has been so much praised for its simple grandeur and sublimity, is merely a rationalized version of the old myth of the fight with the dragon, a myth which for crudity of thought deserves to rank with the quaint fancies of the lowest savages.

Frazer then turns to the Indian story of how Indra released the waters by slaying the dragon Vṛtra, and observes that its association with ritual designed to help the god in his struggle points to its being an account not so much of creation as of some regularly

---

[1] J. G. Frazer, *The Dying God*, 1911, ch. II, §6, pp. 105 ff.

recurring phenomenon, 'the bursting of the first storms of rain and thunder after the torrid heat of an Indian summer'. 'Such a battle of the elements might well present itself to the primitive mind in the guise of a conflict between a maleficent dragon of drought and a beneficent god of thunder and rain.' In other climes the dragon might stand for the winter, the dragon-slayer for the genial summer.

Similarly it has been held with much probability that the Babylonian legend of Marduk and Tiamat reflects the annual change which transforms the valley of the Euphrates in spring. During the winter the wide Babylonian plain, flooded by the heavy rains, looks like a sea, for which the Babylonian word is *tiamtu, tiamat*. Then comes the spring, when with the growing power of the sun the clouds vanish, the waters subside, and dry land and vegetation appear once more. On this hypothesis the dragon Tiamat represents the clouds, the rain, the floods of winter, while Marduk stands for the vernal or summer sun which dispels the powers of darkness and moisture.

Along this line of thought the next step is to suppose that the cosmogonical significance of the myth as an account of creation must have been an 'after-thought'. 'The early philosophers who meditated on the origin of things may have pictured to themselves the creation or evolution of the world on the analogy of the great changes which outside the tropics pass over the face of nature every year.' It would be natural to imagine that the same great hostile powers of life and death had been at war from the beginning, and that 'the formation of the universe as it now exists had resulted from the shock of their battle. On this theory the creation of the world is repeated every spring.... The ceremonies which in many lands have been performed to hasten the departure of winter or stay the flight of summer are in a sense attempts to create the world afresh.' We are to remember how small a place the world seemed to the savage, who might easily imagine that he himself could 'annually repeat the work of creation by his charms and incantations'. And 'once a horde of savages had instituted magical ceremonies for the renewal or preservation of all things, the force of custom and tradition would tend to maintain them in practice long after the old narrow ideas of the universe had been superseded by more adequate conceptions, and the tribe had expanded into a nation'.

If we pause at this point to reflect upon the alleged workings of the 'primitive mind', we may feel, as Frazer himself seems to have felt, that this account is in some way thin and unsubstantial. It starts from the familiar annual transformation of nature. A horde of savages institutes ceremonies to promote this transformation, and at the same time their 'quaint fancy' conceives it in mythical form as a battle between a god and a dragon. Then, as an 'afterthought', the savage, in his capacity of early philosopher meditating on the origin of things, invests the myth with a cosmogonical significance, and announces that the world was created by cutting a dragon in half. Finally, both the magical ceremonies and the cosmogonical myth are perpetuated by force of custom in the highly civilized urban communities of Babylonia.

When we turn, as we presently shall, to the details of the Babylonian New Year festival and the so-called Epic of Creation, we shall find it hard to believe that a ceremonial so elaborate and impressive can have had so meagre an origin. The above account, which, it is only fair to say, evidently did not satisfy Frazer, is radically vitiated by a misconception of the relation between myth and ritual. In this book I have laboured to prove that the Ionian philosophy of nature did not spring straight out of an unprejudiced observation of natural processes. It is an analogous mistake to imagine that the whole complex of religious rites and doctrines that we are now considering has its sole ultimate root in a thinly veiled description of the advent of spring.

Frazer proceeds to bring forward the conjecture, already made by H. Zimmern and other orientalists, that the myth of the slaughter of the Dragon may have been recited and acted at the great New Year Festival of Marduk, held at Babylon, 'as a charm to dispel the storms and floods of winter, and to hasten the coming of summer'. He continues:

Wherever sacred dramas of this sort were acted as magical rites for the regulation of the seasons, it would be natural that the chief part should be played by the King, at first in his character of head magician, and afterwards as representative and embodiment of the beneficent god who vanquishes the powers of evil. If therefore the myth of the Slaughter of the Dragon was ever acted with this intention, the King would appropriately figure in the play as the victorious champion, while the defeated monster would be represented by an actor of inferior rank. Where the tenure of the regal office was limited to a fixed time, at the end of which the King was inexorably put to death, the fatal part of the dragon might be assigned to the monarch as the representative of the old order, the old year, or the old cycle which was passing away, while the part of the victorious god or hero might be supported by his successor and executioner.

This conjecture has been confirmed and elaborated by more recent research. It is now known that the Babylonian ritual was on a much larger and more impressive scale than a mimic battle between a royal magician and a priest impersonating a dragon; and that similarly the Creation myth which accompanied the ritual was something much more than the quaint fancy of a horde of savages. We are dealing with the religious ideas and institutions of highly civilized states. Thus Mr Breasted, after describing the organization of the Egyptian state during the first two or three centuries of the Old Kingdom, from about 3400 B.C., remarks that 'in the thirtieth century before Christ it had reached an elaborate development of state functions under local officials, such as was not found in Europe until far down in the history of the Roman Empire....Art and mechanics reached a level of unprecedented excellence never later surpassed.'[1] Somewhat similar statements might be made about the Mesopotamian cities from which we derive our evidence for the worship of Marduk. It is consequently ill-advised, in this connexion, to talk about the primitive mind. We do well to remember that the recitation of the early chapters of Genesis still forms part of the ceremonies in our own churches. There are other considerations also to be borne in mind. In discussing the separation of earth and sky, we have set beside Hesiod's myth some illustrations from Polynesia. The Polynesians, in view of their rich inheritance of oral literature, including poems of great beauty, are certainly not to be classed as primitive savages. If some of their cosmogonical myths seem

[1] *A History of Egypt*, 1906, pp. 83, 15.

to us extremely crude, there is always the possibility that European inquirers have heard only a 'fireside' version, which has degenerated into a folk-tale as far removed from the original form as the battle of St George and the Dragon in the Mummers' play is from the Battle of Marduk and Tiamat. As Mr J. C. Andersen remarks, 'we do not know how much of these fire-side versions was deliberately permitted; the *tohunga* were well aware of them, but took no trouble to contradict them or replace them with the higher teaching. Nor is this without parallel in modern religion; the higher truths would, to many, be only bewilderment.'[1] The existence of a higher teaching is sufficiently proved by Mr Andersen's examples of semi-philosophized creation myths which will bear comparison with the Upanishads.

Even more important than this warning is the need to correct the conception, which seems to be implied in Frazer's account, of the relation of myth to ritual.[2] The Greeks distinguished, as the two elements of a mystery, the things done (*dromena*) and the things said (*legomena*). The primary factor is the thing done. It is also the proper starting-point for inquiry. Instead of picturing a hypothetical horde of savages, at no particular time or place, sitting round a camp-fire and speculating on the origin of the world, we can take as our point of departure a set of rites which we know to have been performed in the cities of Mesopotamia at the date of the earliest records we possess. As we have remarked, the rites are already extremely elaborate; behind them must lie a very long prehistoric period of development through simpler phases of society, leading back into the palaeolithic age and terminating, no one knows when or where, in something that might be called 'primitive'. But, as Professor Hooke observes, 'the term "primitive" is a purely relative one. The only kind of behaviour or mentality which we can recognize as "primitive" in the strict sense is such as can be shown to lie historically at the fountain-head of a civilization. The earliest civilizations known to us are those of Egypt and Mesopotamia, and the earliest evidence which

---

[1] *Myths and Legends of the Polynesians*, p. 366.
[2] In this matter I follow Professor S. H. Hooke and the other writers in *Myth and Ritual*.

we can gather concerning the beliefs and practices there prevalent constitutes for us what is "primitive" in the historical sense.'[1] The particular beliefs and practices which concern our argument are those of the Babylonian New Year Festival, dating from a time when the arts of agriculture were firmly established and the King ruled over a number of great cities engaged in trade and commerce.

When we have reviewed the things done—the ritual—it will be time to consider more closely the relation between the things done and the things said—the myth. For the moment it is enough to note as certain facts that the Creation myth was connected with the New Year festival in two ways: (1) it was recited in the course of the ceremonies, to reinforce their efficacy, and (2) it 'consists of a description of what is being done, it is the story which the ritual enacts'.[2] Accordingly, the myth can be used to fill gaps in the documents describing the ritual actions performed.

The New Year festival at the opening of spring occupied the first eleven days of the month Nisan at Babylon. The observances of Nisan 2–5 are recorded; those of the later days have been partially reconstructed from indirect evidence.[3] On Nisan 2 the high-priest recited before the statue of Marduk a long prayer referring to the god's triumph over Tiamat and invoking his favour towards his temple, E-sagil, and the people of the city. Other priests and singers were then admitted. Another prayer called upon Marduk's aid against all enemies, natural and supernatural.

On Nisan 3 two figures, holding respectively a serpent and a scorpion, were fabricated for use on the sixth day. They are supposed to have represented malignant powers threatening injury to Bel-Marduk.

More prayers to Bel and his wife Bettia followed on Nisan 4 before sunrise. In particular the goddess was implored to plead with Marduk for the life and prosperity of the King and his people, and to take by the hand 'the servant who blesses thee' and lead him before the god:

'In need and danger take his hands, in sickness and lamentation

---

[1] *Loc. cit.* p. 1.   [2] *Loc. cit.* p. 3.

[3] The following account is summarized from Mr C. J. Gadd's essay in *Myth and Ritual*, pp. 47 ff., and S. Langdon's *The Babylonian Epic of Creation*, Oxford, 1923.

grant him life, that he may walk ever in joy and gladness, and proclaim thy excellent acts to all the world.'

The chief priest, at dawn, addressed a prayer or incantation to the constellation whose heliacal rising announced the spring. In the evening, after the daily services, he recited the 'Epic of Creation' from beginning to end.

Nisan 5 was marked by a series of remarkable ceremonies. The temple was purified by an enchanter or priest of incantation. He sprinkled water and smeared the doorposts with oil and the walls with the blood of a sheep, whose carcass was then thrown into the river to carry away all defilement. The craftsmen then began to cover the chapel of Nebo in E-sagil with a canopy called 'the golden sky'. Marduk and other deities were invoked to cast out malign influences before the arrival of Nebo from Borsippa on the following day.

The ceremonies so far described appear to be of a preliminary nature, consisting of invocations and lustrations preparing the scene for the appearance of the principal human actor.

The King now entered for the first time. Escorted in by priests he was immediately left alone before the statue. Soon the high-priest appeared and took away from him his regalia, his sceptre, ring, and crooked weapon, and his crown, which he placed upon a stool before Marduk. Next he struck the King a blow on the cheek, pulled his ears, and forced him to kneel before the god. In this humiliation the King had to recite a sort of 'negative confession':

I have not sinned, O Lord of the lands, I have not been unregardful of thy godhead,
I have not destroyed Babylon, I have not commanded her ruin,
I have not shaken E-sagil, her rites I have not forgotten,
I have not smitten the cheek of the people in my charge...nor caused their humiliation,
I take thought for Babylon, I have not beaten down her walls.

To this the chief priest replied with a message of comfort and blessing from the god; he would hear his prayer, increase his majesty, and strike down his enemies. Hearing these words, the King might now reassume his sovereign bearing, and at once received back from the god, by the priest's hands, his insignia of royalty. Once more, however, the priest was to strike him upon the cheek, and that not softly, for a sign to follow—if tears came into his eyes, Bel was gracious, if not, Bel was wroth; the enemy would arise and work his ruin.

At the end of the day, the king and the priest joined in burning a bundle of reeds in a trench, in presence of a white bull. A prayer beginning, 'Divine Bull, glorious light which lightens the darkness', is interpreted as a survival from the time when the sun was in the sign of the Bull at the opening of spring.

It is unfortunate that the tablets describing the ritual break off here, where the king has just begun to take his part. If we had a full account of the remaining six days, he would no doubt appear as the central figure of the whole festival. There are, however, remains of a commentary on the ritual explaining certain actions of the king as symbolic of what Marduk did when, as the Creation myth tells, he burnt Kingu, the husband of Tiamat, lifted his weapon to consume the sons of Enlil and Ea, and so on.

It is interesting to note how, in the ceremonial humiliation of the king, the emphasis already falls on his social function as upholder of justice and defender of his people against their enemies. Much of his religious function as priest-king has devolved upon an elaborately organized priesthood which takes complete charge of the ritual, though the king still plays his central part as the embodiment of the god.

On Nisan 6 the important event was the arrival of the god's son, Nebo, from his own temple at Borsippa. The two figures prepared on Nisan 3 were decapitated and burnt before his face. On the same day all the gods, including Anu from Erech and Enlil from Nippur, came to Babylon in order to 'take the hands of the great lord Marduk' and join in his procession to the Festival House. The ultimate purpose was to 'fix the fates' of the coming year, on two separate occasions (Nisan 8 and 11), in the Assembly Room situated in the part of the temple dedicated to Nebo. Nebo's duty, as scribe of the gods, was to write down on the tablets of destiny the good and evil fates decreed by the gods. Here the correspondence between the ritual and the Creation myth is remarkable; for 'in the Creation Epic there is a double fixing of the fates; first by the gods for Marduk, when he is appointed their champion against Tiamat, and secondly in E-sagil itself, which the Anunnaki had built for Marduk after the creation of mankind....Every year at Babylon a new "fate" of supremacy was decreed by the gods to Marduk, and by a parallel acceptation no doubt to the king of Babylon as his earthly vicegerent.'[1]

There are traces of other significant rites belonging to these later days. One is the Ritual Marriage, 'symbolically of the utmost importance, being in fact the cult-act of the old agricultural religion upon which the fruitfulness of the year depended'. Evidence from the Sumerian period confirms Herodotus' account of the god's bridal chamber on the top of the stage-tower, and 'we know something of the ceremonious arrival of the goddess-bride, the giving of wedding presents, and the beneficial effect which the divine union was thought to produce, particularly the rise of the waters which irrigated the land and brought forth its fruits'. In this aspect the New Year festival was a local version of a rite practised in every one of the old cities, the local ruler impersonating the local god. The ceremony is generalized in the mythical marriage of Tammuz and Ishtar.

Something, too, is known about the Procession in which the King 'took the hand of Bel' to conduct him along the Sacred Way from E-sagil to the Festival House outside the city. Anxious watch was kept to guard against untoward accidents and unfavourable omens.

We are not told what Marduk and the other gods did during the three days (Nisan 8–11) at the Festival House. It is inferred that there must have been dramatic representations of the Battle of Marduk and Tiamat.

The enactment of the Death and Resurrection of Bel is attested by fragments of a commentary, purporting to reveal 'the inner meaning of certain dramatic acts which were performed in the course of the New Year festival'. Mr Gadd gives a short summary:[2] 'Bel was imprisoned in the mountain, or realm of the dead; he was smitten, wounded, and his clothing taken from him. With him a certain "Sinner" was led away and put to death. After Bel's

---

[1] C. J. Gadd, *Myth and Ritual*, p. 55.
[2] The text is printed and translated by Professor S. Langdon in *The Babylonian Epic of Creation*, Oxford, 1923.

disappearance the city fell into strife, but he was finally brought back by the intervention of his wife, who stood at the door of the tomb bewailing him and beseeching the help of the gods, who at last bored a hole and released him.'

This episode is completely suppressed in the Creation Myth, but a recently published text hints at a victory of Tiamat over Marduk, which, if it did occur, 'would merely be the parallel to the work of a monster which brings about the god's death in the other Tammuz-stories'.

The extreme complexity of the ritual incompletely summarized above may be partly due to the transfer to the city of a number of simpler ceremonies originally practised in the countryside. Agricultural rites intended to promote fertility are naturally spaced out over the course of the year, some at the time of the sowing, others when the corn begins to spring up, others at the ingathering of the crop. When detached from the soil, the whole series may be condensed into a single festival inaugurating the new year, or into two, in spring and at the autumn sowing, as at Eleusis.[1] In the present case, the core of the whole festival is evidently the renewal of the life of nature by the death, resurrection and marriage of the fertility spirit, embodied in the King. Traces are still discernible of a much earlier phase in which the human representative of the spirit may have been annually slain and succeeded by his slayer, or deposed when his strength waned to give place to his son. But at Babylon the King has become a very important figure, the head of a great hierarchy of officials, ruling over many cities. The connexion between his physical powers and the fertility of men, animals, and crops is not forgotten; but it sinks into the background. In place of a literal death or deposition we find the symbolic humiliation of the King and restoration of his sovereignty carried out in private by the high priest; and the death and resurrection of Bel disappearing from the Creation Myth, to be preserved only in a mystical drama.[2] All the emphasis now falls on other aspects

---

[1] In Mesopotamia and in Hebrew religion also a New Year Festival occurs both in spring and in autumn. S. H. Hooke, *Origins of Early Semitic Ritual*, Oxford, 1938, p. 51.

[2] On this subject see Hooke, *Origins of Early Semitic Ritual*, pp. 10 ff.

of the royal function: the maintenance of the social order by the King's righteousness and the preservation of the people by his victory over their enemies. According to the astrological principle so prominent in Babylonian thought—'on earth as it is in heaven'—the social order has its counterpart in the celestial order of the stars and thus extends outwards to embrace the cosmos. The divine King is at the centre, not merely of a city or a nation, but of the universe. And his victory over the enemies of his people has its counterpart in the victory of Marduk over the powers of darkness and disorder which established the boundaries of the world and set the stars in their courses.

These are the aspects which dominate the so-called Epic of Creation. The term 'epic' is a misnomer. The document, known from its opening words as the *Enuma eliš*, is essentially a Hymn to Marduk. It fulfils the original purpose of a hymn, which is not merely an utterance of praise celebrating the god's glorious deeds, but an incantation, reinforcing the effect of the ritual which it accompanies and at the same time reflects on the magnified scale of divine action. As the ceremonies of the spring festival renew or recreate the life of man and nature and secure for another year the continuance of the physical and social order, so in the beginning Marduk instituted the order and created the life which moves within it.

There is a persistent tradition that the world was created at the spring equinox.[1]

> Non alios prima crescentis origine mundi
> inluxisse dies aliumve habuisse tenorem
> crediderim: ver illud erat, ver magnus agebat
> orbis, et hibernis parcebant flatibus Euri
> cum primum lucem pecudes hausere, virumque
> ferrea progenies duris caput extulit arvis,
> inmissaeque ferae silvis et sidera caelo.[2]

Professor Hooke remarks that the Fixing of Destinies by the gods during the last three days of the Babylonian festival was clearly the end to which all the New Year ritual tended.

---

[1] Frazer, *Adonis*, vol. I, p. 307; *Dying God*, p. 108.
[2] Virgil, *Georg.* II, 336.

It was, in a literal sense, the making of a New Year, the removal of the guilt and defilement of the old year, and the ensuring of security and prosperity for the coming year. By this ceremony was secured the due functioning of all things, sun, moon, stars and seasons, in their appointed order. Here lies the ritual meaning of Creation, there is a new creation year by year, as the result of these ceremonies. The conception of creation in this stage of the evolution of religion is not cosmological but ritual. It has not come into existence in answer to speculations about the origin of things, but as a ritual means of maintaining the necessary order of the things essential for the well-being of the community.[1]

When once it has been realized that the ritual is prior to the myth, we can formulate in more precise terms the relation of the New Year Festival to the story of Creation. On any given occasion the rites are performed by some individual King with his attendant priests for the particular year then being inaugurated. But they must be repeated year after year, outlasting for centuries any set of individual celebrants. Inevitably a distinction is felt between the man who is priest or King at any given moment and the office which he bears for a while and then transmits to a successor. It is by virtue of his office, not as an individual person but as 'His Majesty', that the King performs his role. Thus the function of the King comes to be detached from his personality, and related to it somewhat as the timeless Platonic Idea is related to the many particulars which embody it in time. It has been conferred upon him, and he can be deprived of it, as in the humiliation ceremony of Nisan 5. In the same way the ritual action which is *always* performed is detached, as it were in the aorist tense, from any and all of the particular occasions. The function, consisting of all those magical powers which distinguish the King from a common man, acquires an archetypal or paradigmatic character. The divinity of the King becomes a god on the supernatural plane, and his official action is 'idealized' into an exploit of that god. The relation of cause and effect is now reversed. The narrative of the god's exploit becomes an aetiological myth. We are told that the human king carries out his yearly duties as the representative on earth of his divine prototype, the incarnation or 'son' of the god. He renews

[1] *Origins of Early Semitic Ritual*, p. 18. Cf. A. M. Hocart, *Kingship*, Oxford, 1927, pp. 194 ff.

the physical and social order every spring *because* the god instituted that order; and the action of the god, from being properly timeless and universal, comes to be an unique historical event located 'in the beginning'. Such is the process whereby the New Year ritual generates the cosmogonical myth. Transferred to the supernatural plane, the action is deliberately transfigured and embroidered by the prophetic and poetical imagination with every circumstance that can enhance its impressiveness.

The King becomes the supreme god, and the enemies of his people terrific giants and monsters. Their contest is on a scale to convulse the universe. The narrative develops into the biography of the god, and the hymn celebrating his triumphant exploits will now be used as an incantation, assuring a renewal of his favour and inviting his present help to enhance the efficacy of every fresh performance of the rite.[1]

It remains to note an inevitable consequence of this origin of the aetiological myth. The rites which it reflected will, sooner or later, fall into disuse; or the myth may travel to other lands where different practices prevail. In such a case the details, whose primary significance is now forgotten and lost, may appear grotesque and even revolting. The poetical exaggeration may cause the whole story to be mistaken by the modern scholar for the 'quaint fancy' of a horde of savages credited with an astonishing degree of mental disorder. Finally, it may be relegated to the nursery and classed as 'folklore'. The ancients stopped short of this conclusion; but the choice for them was either to reject the myth as unworthy of the gods, or, if they still obscurely felt its significance, to explain it allegorically or to rationalize it by expurgating the features which seemed monstrous and incredible. The results of this last procedure can be seen in the first chapter of Genesis, when we set it beside the Babylonian Hymn to Marduk, and similarly, as we have argued, in the cosmogony of Hesiod set beside his Hymn to Zeus.

---

[1] A faint survival of this function of the myth may be seen in Pindar's Odes of Victory, where the poet normally passes from a brief mention of the particular victory he is celebrating to a much more important mythical precedent set by some ancestor of the house.

CHAPTER XV

THE HYMN TO MARDUK AND THE HYMN TO ZEUS

W E have now to compare the plan and contents of the two Creation myths as presented in Hesiod's Hymn to Zeus and the Babylonian Hymn to Marduk, to see whether the resemblance is sufficient to justify the inference that Hesiod's version is ultimately derived from the other.

(1) *The Primitive Confusion and the First Parents of the Gods*

The Babylonian myth (*Enuma eliš*) opens with a description of the original state of things in which nothing existed except the primaeval waters. Heaven and Earth were not yet parted from one another:

> When on high the heavens were not named,
> And beneath a home bore no name.

The male and female forms of water (Apsu and Tiamat) 'mingled their waters together', before there were any sacred buildings or marshlands to be seen, or any gods existed, or the fates were fixed. We hear also of Mummu, who acts later as the messenger of Apsu. Professor Langdon interprets Mummu as 'Word', the Logos of Babylonian thought.

'Then were created the gods in the midst thereof.' The first pair were Lahmu and Lahamu; then Anšar and Kišar (explained by Lukas[1] as the Upper and Lower World, two separate parts of the whole), and their sons Anu (the Heaven-god) 'the rival of his fathers', and Ea surnamed Nudimmud as the creator of man, whose province is the water. Enlil, the deity of the third province, earth, seems to have been expurgated by the authors of this

[1] Franz Lukas, *Die Grundbegriffe in den Kosmogonien der alten Völker*, Leipzig, 1893, p. 8.

version.[1] The three appear in Damascius' account as Ἀνός (Anu), Ἴλλινος (Enlil), and Ἀός (Ea), *de Princip*. 125. Ea was even stronger than his father Anšar, and 'had no rival among the gods, his brothers'.

The pattern of Hesiod's cosmogony is recognizable here. There is primal unity; the separation of Heaven and Earth and of the first parents (cf. Oceanus and Tethys); and the distinction of the three provinces—sky, sea and earth. The cosmogony, as we remarked, provides the stage on which the subsequent drama is enacted.

(2) *The Victory of Ea over Apsu*

The brother gods rebelled against Apsu and Tiamat. Apsu with Mummu, his messenger, went to consult Tiamat, and declared his intention to destroy their children. Tiamat was distressed and protested; but Mummu advised Apsu to execute his plan. The gods wept when they heard of this decision. But Ea devised a curse, whereby he bewitched Apsu and Mummu and caused them to sleep. He castrated Mummu, severed his sinews, and tore off his crown. He bound both Apsu and Mummu and killed them. Then he fixed his dwelling upon Apsu. In this temple he founded his secret chamber (where the rites were performed). The female, Tiamat, remains to avenge the deed.

This episode corresponds to the first act of Hesiod's myth: the emasculation of Ouranos by Kronos, the only one of his sons who dared to resent his father's not allowing the children of Heaven and Earth to be born into the light. It is very curious that the castration motive should occur in both episodes. In both also we find the succession of the gods: Apsu, Ea, Marduk, Nebo, and Ouranos, Kronos, Zeus, (Dionysus?). On this point Mr Gadd writes:[2]

From very ancient times the Sumerians had regarded the earthly king as no more than the shadow, or 'tenant' as they called it, of the divine

---

[1] Langdon, *op. cit.* p. 12, note: 'Enlil of the older Sumerian myth is completely suppressed in the Semitic version. The earth god Enlil and his son Ninurta were replaced by Ea and his son Marduk.' This occurred when Marduk, god of Babylon, took over the mythology of Eridu, whose god Ea had founded his temple on the *abzu*. (E. Burrows, *The Labyrinth*, ed. S. H. Hooke, London, 1935, p. 50.) [2] *Myth and Ritual*, p. 61.

king, i.e. the local god, as whose representative he ruled. As things were in heaven, so on earth, but the converse is more significant—as on earth, so in heaven. On earth there comes a time when the king grows old and feeble, no longer fit to govern, and it is hardly too much to presume that originally, at any rate, when such a time came and the king, on the 5th Nisan, surrendered his regalia to the city-god, and was humbled before him, he may not have received them back with the divine blessing, but may have been dismissed in favour of his son. Now in the Creation Epic there is a plain instance of this kind of thing: Ea, who in his time was able to cope with and vanquish Apsu and Mummu, was powerless to deal with their new avenger Tiamat, against whom he was forced to rely upon the fresh strength of his son Marduk. We find, however, that Marduk himself had a son, Nebo, who played a part in the New Year ritual which has always been difficult to understand. It is evident from the drama that Nebo came from Borsippa in some way as the helper and rescuer of Marduk when he was held imprisoned in the 'mountain', and it has been observed that Nebo seems partly to duplicate the part of his father as a champion against the powers of evil; may we say he is an embryo champion? Of course it would never have been admitted in theology that Marduk might pass in his turn, and his kingdom be taken by his son Nebo, but at least there was a point in the ritual when the earthly counterparts of these gods, namely the king and his son, could formally accomplish, or could once have accomplished, the acts of abdication and accession. It must, however, be insisted upon that we have no direct evidence for this, but it is quite according to Babylonian ideas that the natural succession of son to father should be sanctified by imagining and even representing the same process at work in the kingdom of the heavens.

The parallel here with the Greek myth is extraordinarily close. In particular, the suggestion that Marduk might be threatened with supersession by his son Nebo recalls the fear which led Zeus to swallow his wife Metis, lest she should bear a son destined to be King of gods and men in his stead. By acting thus on the advice of Gaia, he secured his own rule for ever. There was no one to trick him, as his father Kronos had been tricked, with a swaddled stone.

On the other hand, it must be recognized that this motive of the young king succeeding his father is combined with a secondary and compatible succession which occurred in historical fact. We are told that the story of the conflict with Apsu and Tiamat was originally told of Ea, who after his victory founded his temple at Eridu. When the story is transferred to Marduk and his temple at Babylon, that earlier conflict remains; but it is duplicated by a second conflict, magnified to a much greater scale, between Marduk and Tiamat. The remarkable thing is that this reduplication is preserved in Hesiod's myth. There the succession of the gods has been interpreted as reflecting the supersession of the gods of an older religion by the gods of an invading people. But, if we are right in supposing that Hesiod's myth is derived ultimately from the Babylonian, no such inference to historical facts on Greek soil will be justified. The only historical event required is the shift from Eridu to Babylon. If there were any historical parallel on Greek soil, it would be only a happy coincidence. In its original form, however, the myth is capable of both interpretations at once; for they are not incompatible. The transference of the story from Ea to Marduk and from Eridu to Babylon could very well be accommodated by a priestly theologian by making Marduk the son of Ea, outdoing his father's exploit on a grander scale. Ea's victory is restricted to the conquest of Apsu; Tiamat is left as the more terrific adversary still to be overcome by Marduk.

(3) *The Birth of the Hero, Marduk*

As in Hesiod's story the next episode is the birth of the hero, Zeus, so the victory of Ea is followed by the birth of his son, Marduk, 'in the midst of the nether sea'. The child was suckled at the breast of goddesses and tended by a nurse who 'filled him with terribleness'. (It is not clear whether this means that, like Zeus and other heroes, he was taken from his mother to be nursed by others.) Like Zeus, he grew up quickly: 'virile became his growth, he was given to procreation from the beginning'. (This is characteristic of fertility spirits, who must pass from infancy to early manhood in a very short time.) He became tall, surpassing all the gods. He had four eyes and four ears, and fire blazed from his lips.

Nothing is said of any attempt by Ea to make away with his son. On the contrary, Ea perfects him and endows him with 'double godhead'. Similarly, as we have seen, the death of Marduk, perhaps caused by Tiamat at their first encounter, and his resurrection are completely passed over in the Hymn.

(4) Tiamat and the Brood of Monsters

The death of Apsu is reported to Tiamat by a god or gods who urge her to revenge him. Mother Hubur (the world-encircling stream of salt water) gives birth to a brood of monsters (identified with constellations) of terrific appearance to reinforce her host of gods. Tiamat exalted Kingu among her first-born to dominion over all the gods, and took him for her husband. She fastened the tablets of fate on his breast, saying: 'Thy command is not annulled; the issue of thy mouth is sure.' Kingu fixed the destinies among the gods, saying: 'Open ye your mouths; verily it shall quench the fire-god. He who is strong in conflict may humiliate might.'

All that corresponds in Hesiod to this episode is the account of how the dragon-nymph of the waters, Echidna, granddaughter of Ocean, in union with Typhaon, gave birth to monsters, Cerberus, Chimaera, Hydra and others. Hesiod does not connect these monsters with the battle between Zeus and Typhoeus. Some of them were slain by Heracles.

(5) Marduk becomes King

Ea, hearing of Tiamat's preparations, becomes faint and reports to his father Anšar. Anšar in terror appeals to Ea to use his curse to defeat Tiamat, as he had defeated Apsu. Ea went up against Tiamat, but fled and reported his failure to Anšar. Anu is then sent, but he also is put to flight. The assembled gods are in despair; but Anšar remembers the might of Marduk. Summoned by his father Ea, Marduk promises to subdue Tiamat on condition that, if victorious, he shall be made a great god and decree fates like Anšar himself. Anšar's messenger summons all the gods to assemble for a banquet and to decree fate for Marduk. After the banquet the gods found for him a princely chamber and make him a great god. 'From this day shall thy word not be changed. To exalt and to humble—this is thy power. Verily the issue of thy mouth is sure, not uncertain is thy commandment. Not one among the gods shall transgress thy boundary.' Marduk is to be patron of the upkeep of temples. He is given 'kingship of universal power over the totality of all things'. His word shall prevail, and he will be victorious over his enemies. His power is then proved by the performance of a miracle: at his word a garment is destroyed and made whole again. The gods then do homage saying, 'The King is Marduk.'[1] They give him a sceptre, a throne, and a hatchet, and ask him to go and kill Tiamat. They determine the successful issue.

Standing as it does so much closer than Hesiod's story to the original ritual, the myth here enlarges on the exaltation of Marduk to the kingship over the gods, reflecting the enthronement of the human representative identified with him. In Hesiod the final recognition of Zeus as King of the Olympians comes as the reward of his victory over the Titans and Typhoeus. But before these battles Zeus had already taken the lead and promised to confirm the honours of the other gods as their prospective king.

(6) *The Battle of Marduk and Tiamat*

Marduk is armed with bow and arrow, a toothed sickle, lightning and flame, and a net to enfold Tiamat. He takes control of the four winds and creates seven storm-winds to trouble her inward parts. With his great weapon, the cyclone, he drives the chariot of the storm. The gods hastened to him. Peering into the inward parts of Tiamat, he saw the open jaws of Kingù, her husband, and he faltered. The gods also turned faint. Marduk replied to Tiamat's curse with a challenge, and she defied him. Catching her in his net, he caused the winds to fill her belly and killed her with an arrow in her heart. Her host of gods was scattered and sought to flee, but Marduk bound them and they are imprisoned in the underworld. He also bound the monsters and their chief Kingù, from whom he took the tablets of fate, sealed them, and fastened them to his own breast.

Hesiod has two distinct battles, one with the Titans for the possession of Olympus, the other with the Dragon after Olympus

[1] Tablet IV, 28. Not 'Marduk is King'. Langdon calls attention to this phrase, which identifies the king with the god.

has been taken. In the Babylonian myth the two conflicts appear to be combined in one. Tiamat's host consists of all the gods save those created by Anšar; these would correspond to the Titans led by Kronos, if the Titans are identified with that elder generation of gods. The monsters are created to reinforce this host, as in the Greek myth the Hundred-armed are called in to help the Olympians.

The Titans, however, are capable of another interpretation, as will appear later.

(7) *The Ordering of the Heavens*

Marduk returned to the bound Tiamat, and, treading on her hinder part, split her scalp with his sickle. Her blood was carried away by the north wind. He then divided the monster into two parts. 'Half of her he set up and made the heavens as a covering. He slid the bolt and caused the watchmen to be stationed. He directed them not to let her waters come forth. He explored the heavens, he paced the spaces.'[1] Over against the heavens he set the abode of Ea on the face of the deep (Apsu); and as its counterpart he fixed Ešarra (the earth). He caused Anu, Enlil and Ea to occupy the three abodes, heaven, earth and the deep.

He constructed stations for the great gods (viz. the signs of the zodiac in which the several planets have most influence), and fixed the constellations. He fixed the year and the signs of the zodiac, placing three stars for each of the twelve months, and determined the motions of the planets in the ecliptic, the motions of the moon, etc. The gods sang in praise of the heavens so created. (A large part of this astronomical section is lost.)

In Hesiod the lifting up of the starry heaven from the earth occurred in the cosmogony, after the opening of the gap, the appearance of the earth, and the birth of light. In Genesis i the firmament dividing the waters above from those below, and the heavenly bodies, are created at the corresponding point. This

---

[1] In the coronation ceremony of the Indian King (according to the *Satapatha Brahmana*), 'after the crowning the King takes three steps in imitation of the god Vishnu and thus paces out the three worlds, earth, air, heaven, and ascends to the region of the gods'. Hocart, *Kingship*, p. 80.

curious order of events can only be explained by the myth which must begin with a preliminary separation of parts of the world to form a scene for the action, although this action leads up to the formation of the heavenly bodies and the fixing of their motions, determining the order of the year and the seasons. In the Babylonian account of creation, all the emphasis falls on these astral arrangements, on whose regular working the fertility of the earth and consequently the life of man depend. The maintenance of this celestial order is a chief part of the king's function. Its institution is accordingly the principal work of the god whom he represents on earth.

(8) *The Creation of Man*

Marduk now told Ea that he would create man to serve the gods. Ea replied: 'For the pacification of the gods, let one of their brothers be given. He shall perish and man be fashioned. Let the great gods assemble. Let this one be given and as for them may they be sure of it.' Marduk assembled the great gods and declared, 'he who caused Tiamat to revolt and join battle shall bear his transgression that the gods may be in peace'. The gods denounced Kingù, who was brought bound before Ea. His arteries were severed and with his blood Ea made mankind.

According to Langdon,

there were in fact two Sumerian traditions, one from Nippur in which the earth-goddess created man from clay, and one from Eridu in which Ea created man in the same manner. The legend of the slaying of a god and mixing his blood with clay is probably later and worked into both versions. Marduk had originally no connexion with the tale....The legend of a god who was sacrificed to create man is extremely old.

The Greek tradition wavers between the creation of man from clay by a god, and the birth of mankind and of all living creatures from the Earth-goddess, fertilized by the seed of the Heaven-father. The latter idea persists in the philosophic systems. It is curious that in Hesiod mankind first appears in connexion with the sacrifice, when Prometheus cheated Zeus of the better portion, as if sacrifice to the gods were, as in the Babylonian doctrine, man's primary function. In Genesis also the first sin committed after the expulsion of our first parents from Eden was occasioned by the sacrifices offered by Abel and Cain.

In interpreting the notion that the creation of man was the result of a sacrifice we must apply the same principle that applied to the creation of the world as the result of cutting a Dragon in half. The root fact is the annual sacrifice of a human being or of some substitute in order to renew the vitality of the human group. The custom generates an aetiological myth, which converts this renewal into an unique event on the supernatural plane—the sacrifice of a god 'in the beginning' in order that his blood might be used to 'create' mankind.[1]

(9) *The Division of the Gods and the Fixing of Fates*

Marduk next divided the gods into two groups: the Igigi, deities of the upper world, and the Anunnaki, of the lower world, or the gods of heaven and the gods of earth. He issued laws to the gods.

In gratitude the gods offered to make a shrine for Marduk where they would assemble. (The reference is to the coming of the gods in their sacred boats to Marduk's temple at Babylon for the New Year festival.) Marduk directs them to build the city of Babylon and a temple. The gods obeyed and erected the stage-tower, E-sagil, with chapels for themselves. Marduk is installed in his dwelling at Babylon.

The gods feasted in E-sagil; and then 'laws were fixed and plans designed.... The stations of heaven and earth were arranged among the gods, all of them. The great gods (of the lower world) who are fifty sat down. The gods of fates who are seven (Igigi, of the upper world) fixed the fates for all men.' The weapons of Marduk were assigned places in the sky as constellations.

Anu, the Heaven-god, defines the powers of Marduk. He is to be shepherd of the peoples, and to maintain the cult of the gods. The gods celebrate the exploits of Marduk and enumerate his fifty names in a hymn.

The closing act in Hesiod's story of Zeus is the distribution to the Olympians of their provinces and honours by the newly

[1] See Mr Hocart's chapter on The Creation in *Kingship*, pp. 189 ff.

installed king. This is the institution of a social order under its religious aspect, embracing the physical order of the cosmos. It is symbolized by the obviously allegorical marriage of Zeus with Themis (Law) and the birth of their children, the Seasons, whose names are Good Government, Justice, and Peace, and the Fates (Moirai), who give to mortal men their portions of good and evil. By Eurynome, daughter of Ocean, Zeus becomes father also of the Charites, Aglaia, Euphrosyne and Thalia.

It will hardly be denied that we have here the divine counterpart of the installation of a new earthly king, or the annual renewal of his authority over his people and of his power over nature. In our own country at this day the whole constitution is suspended at the death of the king until the Privy Council has proclaimed his successor. In India, as Mr Hocart points out,[1] the Vedic doctrine is that 'all the gods abide in Indra'.

The King is Indra, therefore the King is all the gods, and in him are deposited their 'desirable embodiments and favourite abodes', namely, the chief military command, the chaplaincy, and so forth; he unites in himself all the powers which are separately exercised by his officials and his queen. The Egyptians were evidently also of opinion that the King included in himself the deities that were severally represented by minor personages....In Cambodia after the lustration the officials return to the new king all the seals and powers they received from his predecessor. The king touches the seals and returns them to the officials who... resume their appointments, titles, and functions....The King is the fount of all honours, and when he dies all honours have to return to the new king, who issues them again. Our own coronation ritual...is scarcely less definite. 'As soon as the King is crowned the Peers etc. put on their coronets and caps', and 'the Queen being crowned all the Peeresses put on their coronets'. Thus our Peers have to derive anew their authority from the new sovereign.

In spite of discrepancies, it is perhaps sufficiently clear that Hesiod's cosmogonical myth is derived ultimately from the Babylonian. The discrepancies are less striking than the coincidences, and less than we might expect when we consider that the story reached Hesiod in fragments detached from the ritual

[1] *Kingship*, p. 116.

which explained it and gave it coherence. It must be remembered, too, that the *Enuma eliš* is only one version of the Babylonian myth, which happens to have reached us in a fairly complete form. It is known to be a revision of an earlier Sumerian version, and traces remain of other variants on Eastern soil.[1]

Subsequent discoveries may prove that some form of the ritual existed in Minoan religion, as indeed the Cretan legends of the birth and death of Zeus and the Palaiokastro hymn to the greatest Kouros suggest.[2] In that case the myth would have passed through a Cretan phase before reaching Hesiod.

[1] (Note by Professor E. R. Dodds.) Cornford's hypothesis of a connexion between the Hesiodic *Theogony* and the Babylonian myth has now been greatly strengthened by the publication of the fragmentary Hittite-Hurrian *Epic of Kumarbi* (Hittite text in *Keilschrifturkunden aus Boghazköi*, XXXII, 1943, German translation and commentary by H. G. Güterbock, Zürich, 1946). This Hurrian tale of wars in Heaven, which the Hittites took over, seems to provide a link between the Babylonian story (some of whose characters appear in it under their Babylonian names) and the Greek adaptation. Features common to all three are the forcible separation of Heaven and Earth (*Kumarbi*, p. 27, Güterbock), the conflict of divine generations, the old god's attempt to destroy his children (in *Kumarbi* and Hesiod by eating them), and the castration motif. But as R. D. Barnett has pointed out (*J.H.S.* LXV, pp. 100 f.), *Kumarbi* has additional resemblances to Hesiod, some of which are very striking, particularly the fertilization of Earth by the severed genitals of the old god, the introduction of a stone-baby, and the figure of Upelluri, a Hurrian Atlas who supports sky and earth. Barnett, like Cornford, suggests the traders of Ugarit (or at a later date those of al-Mina) as possible intermediaries who may have carried these myths into the Aegean world.

[2] See Nilsson, *Minoan-Mycenaean Religion*, ch. XVI.

CHAPTER XVI

THE CANAANITE MYTH AND THE PALESTINIAN RITUAL

A GENERATION ago, before Sir Arthur Evans's discoveries at Knossos had opened up a new vista into the pre-Homeric past, classical scholars were, on the whole, disposed to treat Greek religious and philosophic thought as independent of oriental influence. They thought of the Aegean coasts as enclosing a little isolated world, accessible indeed to the occasional visit of a Phoenician trader or pirate such as Homer describes, but not to the importation of ideas. More recent discoveries in the near East ought finally to banish this illusion.

The Cilician story of the battle of Zeus and Typhon told how the god pursued the dragon 'as far as Mount Casius which overhangs Syria', and there the adversaries came to grips. Within sight of Mount Casius, now called Jebel Akra, lies the region of Ras Shamra, the site of the ancient city of Ugarit. Here, from the fourth millennium onwards, was one of the principal stopping-places on the oldest and most important trade route between East and West, linking Crete, by way of Cyprus and the Southern coast of Asia Minor, with Syria and its immediate Mesopotamian hinterland.[1]

The painted pottery of the fourth millennium in Syria shows a high level of civilization, and is obviously related to the main group of painted pottery which flourished at this time on the Iranian plateau and as far east as the valley of the Indus. This culture formed part of the great civilizations of the upper Euphrates and Mesopotamia. After a period of increasing Mesopotamian influence and a time of unrest, the Semitic Canaanites, who were finally to master Babylon, migrated northwards and probably

[1] C. F. A. Schaeffer, *The Cuneiform Texts of Ras Shamra-Ugarit*, 1939, p. 3, gives a full account of what is known of the history of Ugarit and of the texts found there.

reached Ras Shamra. 'Ugarit now became once more, not only an outpost of Mesopotamia and a trading station for the export of Asiatic merchandise, but soon a gateway through which an ever-increasing flow of Mediterranean commerce could penetrate into Asia.' At the beginning of the second millennium Ugarit was an important town, containing temples of Dagon, whose son, Baal or Adad, the god of thunder and rain, had previously been worshipped there by the Hurrites under the name of Tesub. Objects of distinctly European character now make their appearance. 'Their centre of distribution is probably the Balkans and the region round the middle Danube, whence they were carried by trade and migrations westward to the Rhine valley, eastward to the Caucasus, and southward to the Syrian coast.' Ugarit now came more within the sphere of Egyptian influence. The Pharaohs of the XIIth dynasty allied themselves with the kings of Palestine and Syria to safeguard their Asiatic frontiers and trade routes. At the same time 'the Minoan Sea Empire was gaining a footing in Ugarit; modest compared with the sway held by Egypt, but more lasting. Cretan merchants had set up their offices in Ugarit.' Products of the Middle Minoan period have been found in tombs. 'It is clear that Ras Shamra was one of the most important centres of Cretan trade in Syria.' In the fifteenth and fourteenth centuries the safety of land and sea routes caused a great development of trade and consequent prosperity. Vaulted tombs of Cretan type have yielded late Mycenaean types of pottery from Cyprus or Rhodes. 'The presence in the town of many Aegeans and Mycenaeans, amongst them artisans of every kind, sculptors, jewellers, and bronze-smiths, explains the patent closeness of their work to the art of their native lands.' Ugarit was overwhelmed by an earthquake and tidal wave about the middle of the fourteenth century.

We need not follow the history of Ugarit further. It is enough that a single partly excavated site should yield such abundant proof of the opportunities for intercourse between the Aegean lands and Syria, Egypt and Mesopotamia. That this intercourse was no mere matter of the exchange of goods is further shown by the library of King Nigmed. During his reign, in the middle of the second millennium, 'a college of learned priests existed, where the poetical works and myths of the ancient Canaanites or proto-Phoenicians were recorded on clay tablets to be preserved in the library'. This library was housed in the same building with the high priest's dwelling. Attached to it was a school of scribes who were set to copy documents and to learn the sacred literature. The writing is cuneiform, but in a hitherto unknown alphabetic script, the earliest yet discovered. When deciphered the language proved to be a Semitic dialect; and the majority of the texts recovered have been published. They have 'shed a vivid light on the origin of the Phoenicians, their myths and their ancestral legends'. It is now possible to form a much clearer idea of the Canaanite religion which the immigrant Hebrews found in possession of the promised land and which their prophets strove to suppress.

Before turning to that subject, we may note that the library shows what careful provision was made for intellectual intercourse between the nations represented at Ugarit. Several rooms contained only dictionaries and lexicons. One gives the Babylonian equivalents of Sumerian words, Sumerian being already a dead language, Babylonian the diplomatic language used by the kings of Mesopotamia, Asia Minor, Syria and Egypt in official correspondence and by the chief merchants in business letters. There is also a dictionary giving the equivalents of Sumerian words in an unknown tongue. Thus with the Proto-Phoenician or Canaanite of the alphabetic scripts, four languages written in almost as many different systems were taught in the scribes' school. When we add to these the inscriptions in Egyptian hieroglyphic, in Hittite, and in Cypriot, 'we can show that no less than seven different languages were in use at Ugarit in the middle of the second millennium B.C. Nothing could indicate more effectively the cosmopolitan character of the inhabitants of this truly international port of Ugarit.' In the light of all this evidence, it seems unreasonable to doubt that myths and legends of Mesopotamian, Egyptian, or Syrian origin could have made their way to Crete long before the fall of Knossos.

In the Canaanite mythology disclosed by the Ras Shamra tablets, the supreme god, who reigns over the other gods and bestows wisdom and eternal life, is El. In the form of a bull he is united with the chief mother-goddess, Asherat of the Sea, as in the Cretan legend the bull Zeus is united with Europa, who gives birth to Minos. Asherat of the Sea, like Hesiod's Gaia, acts as counsellor of the gods. She bears seventy sons.

The chief of El's sons is Baal, identified with the Phoenician Hadad, the Syrian-Hittite Teshub, and the Egyptian Seth or Sutekh. He is a god of the heights, of lightning and thunder, and of the beneficent fertilizing rain.[1] A myth of his adventures,[2] obviously based on a fertility ritual, shows many points of contact with the myth and ritual of Marduk and the Hesiodic story of Zeus.

The Battle with the Dragon Leviathan

The texts containing this myth open with Baal's instructions to his messenger, Gepen-Ugar, to slay Lotan (a contracted form of the biblical Leviathan), the swift serpent, the crooked dragon with seven heads, and to obtain a certain magical object. The messenger seems to have failed in this task. The record of his attempt and of the final victory over Leviathan does not appear in the fragments quoted.

Professor Hooke remarks a curious parallel here: 'neither in the Canaanite myth, so far as our knowledge goes at present, nor in the Babylonian myth, is the manner of the death of the god (Baal), which must have formed part of the ritual, described. In both there is the trace of a possible defeat and death of the god at the hands of an opponent, symbolized by some dragon, or other bestial form.' We have already remarked that the death of the Cretan Zeus remained equally mysterious.

The Death of Baal

Baal's messenger was also charged to visit Mot, the Lord of the Underworld, and to seek reconciliation. In reply Mot invited Baal to a banquet. Baal disappears and vegetation withers. His son Aleyan-Baal laments him. A fragmentary passage describes a banquet. Aleyan-Baal is instructed to bring Baal's attributes,

---

[1] Schaeffer, *Cuneiform Texts*, pp. 59 ff.
[2] Hooke, *Origins of Early Semitic Ritual*, pp. 30 ff.

clouds, winds, and rain, and his attendants to the underworld. 'The next scene appears to describe, in symbolic form, a fertility rite, a sacred marriage. Aleyan-Baal loves a heifer and a child is born named Mes or Mos, a name which is not yet explained.' The death of Aleyan-Baal is announced; mourning and funeral rites follow. Anat, Aleyan's sister and mistress (in the form of the heifer), searches for Baal and buries him.

The Resurrection of Aleyan-Baal

Anat, continuing her search, comes to Mot to demand her brother and lover, Aleyan. Finding his body, she carries it up Mount Zaphon (perhaps Jebel Akra, Mount Casius) and buries it there with a sacrifice of 420 beasts of various kinds.[1] She then goes to Mot, implores him to restore Aleyan to her, and, when he refuses, kills him. 'Then follows a curious scene in which Anat splits Mot with the *harpé*, or ritual sickle, winnows him, roasts him, grinds him, sows him, and gives him to the birds to eat.'

After Mot's death Ltpn-Eldpd hears in a dream that Aleyan is alive and fertility is about to return. Rejoicing, he carries the news to Anat. The search continues with the assistance of Shapash, the sun-goddess and guardian of the dead.[2]

An account follows of the victory of Baal over Mot and his followers. Mot threatened Aleyan that after seven years he would undergo the same fate that Anat inflicted on Mot himself.

Aleyan returns and sits on the throne of Baal. Shapash announces the doom of Mot, who goes down to the underworld.

The text ends with an invocation of Shapash and a ritual casting of two objects into the sea.

The agricultural significance of Mot becomes curiously transparent in the treatment he receives from Anat. It is compared with the treatment of the last sheaf at harvest-time, abundantly illustrated by Frazer. Mr Schaeffer[3] describes the rite as consisting of 'taking from him his sacred character to allow of his profane

[1] For this episode see Schaeffer, p. 71.
[2] Cf. Demeter's search for Persephone, assisted by Helios.
[3] *Cuneiform Texts*, p. 72.

usefulness. By dispersing Mot's flesh, that is by scattering corn, the goddess restores to the fields the spirit of vegetation and so assures crops in the coming year.' Part of the corn is roasted and ground for eating; part is reserved to be sown in the fields.

Mot is both the harvested corn and the lord of the underworld. He is the Greek Pluto, the king of the dead and also the 'wealth' stored in the underground silo during the months of summer drought after the harvest, when the fields are scorched and all vegetation disappears. The suggestion in the text that Aleyan-Baal with his father on the one hand, and Mot on the other, rule for alternate periods is explained as referring to the two periods of the agricultural year in Canaan: summer heat and drought when Mot reigns, and the rains, the revival of vegetation and the filling of the streams, marked by the resurrection and reign of Aleyan-Baal.[1] The parallel with Eleusinian ritual and myth is extraordinarily close. As I have pointed out elsewhere,[2] the period during which Persephone, carried off by Pluto in early summer, remains in the underworld is not, as is commonly supposed in northern climates, the winter, but the summer drought after harvest. She returns to the upper world as the seed-corn to be used at the autumn sowing, the time of the chief Eleusinian festival. She is symbolized by the ἀπαρχαί of the harvest sent by the Greek states to Eleusis. Thus she 'descends' into the underground store of Pluto at harvest-time and 'ascends' (ἄνοδος) in the autumn, when the treasured seed, on which the life of the community depends, is brought out for sowing the new crop. Her sacred marriage with Pluto takes place while she is beneath the earth. She is a maiden (Kore) at her descent, but returns as the mother of the new crop (Demeter) in autumn.

[1] Hooke, *Origins of Semitic Ritual*, p. 40.
[2] *The* ᾽Απαρχαί *and the Eleusinian Mysteries* in Essays presented to Sir W. Ridgeway (1913), pp. 153 ff. My theory was accepted by Nilsson, 'Die Eleus. Gottheiten', *Arch. f. Religionswissenschaft*, vol. XXXII, p. 107; *Geschichte der griechischen Religion*, 1941, pp. 443 ff.

The Battle of Baal with Mot and his host

As lord of the underworld, Mot, like Pluto-Hades, has a second aspect, symbolizing the powers of Death. Accordingly, he and his followers appear again in the myth as the enemies whom Baal has to fight and banish to the underworld before his son Aleyan can be enthroned. Under this aspect Mot recalls Kronos, in his character of harvest god, leading the Titans against Zeus and his Olympians.

The foregoing myth is closely related to the myths of Ishtar and Tammuz, of Isis and Osiris, and of the death and resurrection of Bel. As we have seen, this part of the story had fallen into the background in the New Year festival at Babylon, where the agricultural significance of the rites has almost faded out in an advanced urban civilization. The emphasis there fell on the triumph of the god-king over the Dragon, Tiamat-Leviathan, the institution of the social and physical order, and the installation of the divine king in his temple.

APPENDIX

The text ends here. The author's notes suggest that although he might have added more material for comparison, e.g. from the Far East, the argument of the book was virtually complete and lacked only a summing-up. The following summary is based on material found among the notes for Chapter XIV and only partly used in the text. Though primarily referring to Part II, these notes do something to draw the two parts of the book together and perhaps indicate the lines along which the whole would have been concluded.

The notes outline the author's view of the origin and development of anthropomorphic religious beliefs and their subsequent dissolving away in philosophy. The older, and still widely current, explanation of the rise of anthropomorphic gods is that primitive man, confronted with powers of nature which are beyond his control, projects his own nature into them and so 'personifies' them. This explanation assumes a clear distinction between man and nature such as we now possess, but which cannot plausibly be attributed to man at this early stage. Against it is maintained the view that one at least, if not the only, starting-point of anthropomorphism is the *divine man*, the king who also represents the god, who combines in himself individual personality and impersonal functions. As individual he is mortal, but as The King (i.e. in respect of his function) he is more. The functions are impersonal and also divine, because they survive the individual holder of them and are indeed everlasting. This distinction between individual and function is realized in that the function is *conferred* on the individual at his installation and *transmitted* to his successor. (Their relationship is aptly illustrated by the comparison with Platonic Ideas and particulars on p. 237.) The functions include both natural processes connected with human welfare and also powers exercised by the social group, the maintenance of internal order and safety against external enemies, i.e. political powers.

From the notion of divine and eternal functions to their embodiment in a divine being or beings is no long step. Then in the annual ritual, the purpose of which is the renewal of powers both in universal nature and in the human society, the King is the representative of the God and his actions are symbolical re-enactments of universal and in themselves timeless events, detached from individual actors and temporal occasions. These universal actions finally take shape in men's minds as events of long ago in time, and form an aetiological myth of what happened 'in the beginning'. The gods have personal names and as much individuality as is necessary to enable them to act. The names may be very transparent, e.g. Gaia and Ouranos, but from these beginnings, under literary treatment at the hands of priests and poets, they easily become more and more individual persons like Zeus and Hera, and accumulate biographical details from other sources. Thus they develop into fully anthropomorphic gods.

The provinces and powers of nature which they still retain (Zeus as Sky-god etc.) are survivals of the spheres in which the powers of the King-God and his entourage were originally exercised.

The King-God was originally responsible for the whole business of the weather as it affected human life. Thus he was at once sun-god, rain-god, thunder-god, etc., besides wielding the political powers which were also in his province. Later the complex might split into parts, but on the view here given it is a mistake to suppose that he was either sun-god or fertility-spirit or thunder-god or anything else *exclusively*, or to say, for instance, that the King was originally the sun-god (only) triumphing over darkness in the dawn. That is only one aspect of his functions. This mistake leads to the false notion that the whole development starts from the observation of the natural phenomenon of dawn, that then the sun is 'personified' or 'deified' and rites are performed 'in his honour', and that finally the King somehow comes to represent the already existing sun-god.

On the view here given there are two distinct kinds or stages of anthropomorphism:

(i) *The man who is also god*: the early stage when the individual person and the divine function are still united in the divine man, but yet distinguishable.

(ii) *The god who becomes (supernatural) man*: the later stage, when the universal function has become detached in myth, as archetype acting in supposed historical events 'in the beginning', and has acquired more or less independent existence and a personal character. The character is at first relevant to the functional action which he (for the former function is now a person) performs, but later perhaps gets embroidered with irrelevant personal and biographical features.

The material at all stages is both human and superhuman.

When the gods are established, another consequence is the setting aside of priests to attend upon them. These were originally assistants of the King in his ritual duties, but now become separated from him. As a result the King is deprived of his religious importance and only his political functions are left to him. Occasionally the separation may work the other way, as at Athens, where new civil magistrates were created and the *basileus* retained only his religious functions.

Eventually there comes a time when the more enlightened members of the community begin to lose their belief in divine kings who 'created', and now maintain the world in the spring ritual, and then in the gods who grew out of their functions. The functions of these gods may be said in general terms to have been twofold: (i) the institution of order, both of the world and of society; (ii) the control of the seasonal powers, of the weather and of fertility (which in their turn are of course dependent on the *ordered* movement of the heavenly bodies). Thus when the earliest philosophical thinkers seek to replace religious explanations of the world with a rational one, the problems which seem to demand their attention are (i) that of the cosmic order of the elements and its causes, which the Greeks temporarily detached from its connexion with social order although retaining many social conceptions (like those of justice and war) which they transferred to non-human nature; (ii) the causes of τὰ μετέωρα, i.e. of such phenomena as rain and storm, thunder, lightning, meteors, earthquakes. These are the things which now demand to be explained by natural causes, without the action of gods, and particularly the second class, since it was in them that the direct intervention of the gods in human affairs was commonly recognized, so that signs and omens were drawn from them.

Thus the questions asked by these men are determined by the religious framework which they have inherited and are seeking to supplant. More than that, the abandonment of personal accretions which is the aim of this early philosophical speculation entails a kind of rediscovery of the impersonal universal functions and factors which were originally involved in the renewal-('creation'-) drama and now appear once again stripped of their picturesque anthropomorphic dress. A fairly far advanced stage of this rationalizing process is illustrated by the semi-philosophical cosmogony of Hesiod when compared with the equivalent mythical story of Gaia and Ouranos, the assault of Kronos on his father and so forth, which follows it. In the philosophers Gaia sheds what human character she possessed (it was always slight), and becomes plainly and simply the Earth. The relationship to their mythical counterparts of other notions of the Milesian natural philosophers (especially the four opposed 'powers' of hot and cold, moist and dry) has been made sufficiently clear in the text of the book.

The danger of ending with this inadequate summary is that it may convey the false impression that the earliest Greek philosophers (and of ancient peoples it was only among the Greeks that this transition from myth to philosophy was achieved) did no more than repeat the lessons of myth in a changed terminology. A reminder is therefore perhaps necessary, first, that so far as the Ionians are concerned this point is dealt with at the beginning of Chapter x, and secondly that (as is made clear in the first chapter) Milesian speculation by no means represents the whole achievement of early Greek scientific thought. There remains the medical tradition, practical in aim, tentative and experimental in method, gradually building up a body of systematic knowledge based on repeatedly observed facts, and openly hostile to the more dogmatic pronouncements of the philosophers.

GENERAL INDEX

Abaris, 89, 104, 108
Achilles, 74
Acusilaus, 195
Adad, 251
Adam, J., 147, 149
Aeschylus, 106, 145, 153
    Eum., 76; (*v.* 62), 75; (*v.* 104), 150
    P.V. (*v.* 353), 219; (*frag.* 44), 196;
        (*frag.* 379), 176; (*frag.* 390), 115
Aesop, 68, 69
Aether, 193, 197, 198
Agathocles, 107
Agdestis, 211
Agni, 209, 210
Aigaion, Mount, 215
Aigipan, 220
Air, 136, 153, 167, 179
Alcmaeon, 35, 37, 40, 42, 122, 172
Aleyan-Baal, 253 ff.
Ammianus Marcellinus: (xx, 9, 8),
    91
Ammon (well of Juppiter A.), 17
Amos, 77, 99, 105
Anamnesis, Ch. IV, 63, 81
Anat, 253
Anaxagoras, use of experiment by, 6,
    43; 'Mind' in, 14, 151, 152f., 154,
    172, 178, 179; on the sun and
    moon, 132, 136; Socrates con-
    fused with, 134, 135; pluralism of,
    171; cosmogony of, 181
Anaximander, 34, 147, Ch. x, 189,
    197, 198, 200
Anaximenes, 6, 153, 161, 166, 167,
    179
Andersen, J. C., 205, 206, 210, 218,
    230
Annunaki, 234, 247
Anšar, 239, 240, 243, 245
Anthropomorphism, rationalist ob-
    jections to, 153; rise and decline
    of, 257–9
Anu, 233, 239, 243, 245, 247

Aphrodite, 82, 203, 208, 210, 211, 225
Apollo, 68, 69, 73, 74, 75, 76, 87, 88 f.,
    100, 101, 128, 226
Apollodorus: (I, 6, 3), 219; (I, 2, 1), 222
Apollonius Rhodius: (I, 496 ff.), 191;
    (I, 503), 219
Apsu, 239, 240, 241, 242, 243, 245
Archilochus, 115
Aristeas, 89, 104, 108
Aristophanes: *Birds*, 163, 191; (*v.* 192),
    194
    Clouds (*v.* 365), 134; (*v.* 627), 194
    Frogs, 128; (*v.* 355), 113; (*v.* 1030),
    107
Aristotle, use of experiment by, 3; as
    natural scientist, 18; believed in
    divinity behind nature, 20; em-
    piricism in, 39 f.; organization of
    research by, 43; on Socrates and
    Plato, 45, 46; on 'theologians',
    105; on divination, 142; on his
    predecessors, 159, 160, 167; pri-
    mary elements in, 167, 197; be-
    lieved world to be eternal, 188
    An. Post. (100a7), 41; (95b38), 169
    de An. (405a29), 172
    de Caelo (A5), 182; (A9), 174; (B1),
        180; (286a9), 81
    de Resp. (480b22), 38
    de Sensu (442a29), 14; (436a18), 38
    Eth. Nic. (1113a15 ff.), 83; (1155b
        1 ff.), 197
    Gen. et Corr. (336b34), 169; (338
        a15), 169
    Metaph. (A1), 40; (984a27), 181;
        (984b23), 196; (986a22), 35;
        (997b35), 48; (1071b26), 191;
        (1074b1), 174
    Meteor. init., 185; (A14), 183; (353
        b5 ff.), 182
    MXG. (976b15), 194; (978b1 ff.),
        175
    Part. Anim. (640b5), 160

261

INDEX OF GREEK WORDS

Revised October 31, 1965

hARPER ✦ TORChBOOKS

HUMANITIES AND SOCIAL SCIENCES

American Studies: General

THOMAS C. COCHRAN: The Inner Revolution: *Essays on the Social Sciences in History* TB/1140

EDWARD S. CORWIN: American Constitutional History. *Essays edited by Alpheus T. Mason and Gerald Garvey* TB/1136

A. HUNTER DUPREE: Science in the Federal Government: *A History of Policies and Activities to 1940* TB/573

OSCAR HANDLIN, Ed.: This Was America: *As Recorded by European Travelers in the Eighteenth, Nineteenth and Twentieth Centuries. Illus.* TB/1119

MARCUS LEE HANSEN: The Atlantic Migration: 1607-1860. *Edited by Arthur M. Schlesinger; Introduction by Oscar Handlin* TB/1052

MARCUS LEE HANSEN: The Immigrant in American History. *Edited with a Foreword by Arthur M. Schlesinger* TB/1120

JOHN HIGHAM, Ed.: The Reconstruction of American History TB/1068

ROBERT H. JACKSON: The Supreme Court in the American System of Government TB/1106

JOHN F. KENNEDY: A Nation of Immigrants. *Illus. Revised and Enlarged. Introduction by Robert F. Kennedy* TB/1118

RALPH BARTON PERRY: Puritanism and Democracy TB/1138

ARNOLD ROSE: The Negro in America: *The Condensed Version of Gunnar Myrdal's An American Dilemma* TB/3048

MAURICE R. STEIN: The Eclipse of Community: *An Interpretation of American Studies* TB/1128

W. LLOYD WARNER and Associates: Democracy in Jonesville: *A Study in Quality and Inequality* || TB/1129

W. LLOYD WARNER: Social Class in America: *The Evaluation of Status* TB/1013

American Studies: Colonial

BERNARD BAILYN, Ed.: The Apologia of Robert Keayne: *Self-Portrait of a Puritan Merchant* TB/1201

BERNARD BAILYN: The New England Merchants in the Seventeenth Century TB/1149

JOSEPH CHARLES: The Origins of the American Party System TB/1049

LAWRENCE HENRY GIPSON: The Coming of the Revolution: 1763-1775. † *Illus.* TB/3007

LEONARD W. LEVY: Freedom of Speech and Press in Early American History: *Legacy of Suppression* TB/1109

PERRY MILLER: Errand Into the Wilderness TB/1139

PERRY MILLER & T. H. JOHNSON, Eds.: The Puritans: *A Sourcebook of Their Writings*
Vol. I TB/1093; Vol. II TB/1094

KENNETH B. MURDOCK: Literature and Theology in Colonial New England TB/99

WALLACE NOTESTEIN: The English People on the Eve of Colonization: 1603-1630. † *Illus.* TB/3006

LOUIS B. WRIGHT: The Cultural Life of the American Colonies: 1607-1763. † *Illus.* TB/3005

American Studies: From the Revolution to the Civil War

JOHN R. ALDEN: The American Revolution: 1775-1783. † *Illus.* TB/3011

RAY A. BILLINGTON: The Far Western Frontier: 1830-1860. † *Illus.* TB/3012

GEORGE DANGERFIELD: The Awakening of American Nationalism: 1815-1828. † *Illus.* TB/3061

CLEMENT EATON: The Freedom-of-Thought Struggle in the Old South. *Revised and Enlarged. Illus.* TB/1150

CLEMENT EATON: The Growth of Southern Civilization: 1790-1860. † *Illus.* TB/3040

LOUIS FILLER: The Crusade Against Slavery: 1830-1860. † *Illus.* TB/3029

DIXON RYAN FOX: The Decline of Aristocracy in the Politics of New York: 1801-1840. ‡ *Edited by Robert V. Remini* TB/3064

FELIX GILBERT: The Beginnings of American Foreign Policy: *To the Farewell Address* TB/1200

FRANCIS J. GRUND: Aristocracy in America: *Social Class in the Formative Years of the New Nation* TB/1001

ALEXANDER HAMILTON: The Reports of Alexander Hamilton. ‡ *Edited by Jacob E. Cooke* TB/3060

THOMAS JEFFERSON: Notes on the State of Virginia. ‡ *Edited by Thomas P. Abernethy* TB/3052

BERNARD MAYO: Myths and Men: *Patrick Henry, George Washington, Thomas Jefferson* TB/1108

JOHN C. MILLER: Alexander Hamilton and the Growth of the New Nation TB/3057

RICHARD B. MORRIS, Ed.: The Era of the American Revolution TB/1180

R. B. NYE: The Cultural Life of the New Nation: 1776-1801. † *Illus.* TB/3026

---

† The New American Nation Series, edited by Henry Steele Commager and Richard B. Morris.

‡ American Perspectives series, edited by Bernard Wishy and William E. Leuchtenburg.

* The Rise of Modern Europe series, edited by William L. Langer.

|| Researches in the Social, Cultural, and Behavioral Sciences, edited by Benjamin Nelson.

§ The Library of Religion and Culture, edited by Benjamin Nelson.

ᵘ Not for sale in Canada.

Σ Harper Modern Science Series, edited by James R. Newman.

American Studies: Since the Civil War

Anthropology

Art and Art History

Business, Economics & Economic History

2

THOMAS C. COCHRAN & WILLIAM MILLER: The Age of Enterprise: *A Social History of Industrial America* TB/1054

ROBERT DAHL & CHARLES E. LINDBLOM: Politics, Economics, and Welfare: *Planning & Politico-Economic Systems Resolved into Basic Social Processes* TB/3037

PETER F. DRUCKER: The New Society: *The Anatomy of Industrial Order* TB/1082

EDITORS OF FORTUNE: America in the Sixties: *The Economy and the Society* TB/1015

ROBERT L. HEILBRONER: The Great Ascent: *The Struggle for Economic Development in Our Time* TB/3030

FRANK H. KNIGHT: The Economic Organization TB/1214

FRANK H. KNIGHT: Risk, Uncertainty and Profit TB/1215

ABBA P. LERNER: Everybody's Business: *Current Assumptions in Economics and Public Policy* TB/3051

ROBERT GREEN MCCLOSKEY: American Conservatism in the Age of Enterprise, 1865-1910 TB/1137

PAUL MANTOUX: The Industrial Revolution in the Eighteenth Century: *The Beginnings of the Modern Factory System in England* ° TB/1079

WILLIAM MILLER, Ed.: Men in Business: *Essays on the Historical Role of the Entrepreneur* TB/1081

PERRIN STRYKER: The Character of the Executive: *Eleven Studies in Managerial Qualities* TB/1041

PIERRE URI: Partnership for Progress: *A Program for Transatlantic Action* TB/3036

Contemporary Culture

JACQUES BARZUN: The House of Intellect TB/1051

JOHN U. NEF: Cultural Foundations of Industrial Civilization TB/1024

NATHAN M. PUSEY: The Age of the Scholar: *Observations on Education in a Troubled Decade* TB/1157

PAUL VALÉRY: The Outlook for Intelligence TB/2016

Historiography & Philosophy of History

SIR ISAIAH BERLIN et al.: History and Theory: *Studies in the Philosophy of History. Edited by George H. Nadel* TB/1208

JACOB BURCKHARDT: On History and Historians. *Intro. by H. R. Trevor-Roper* TB/1216

WILHELM DILTHEY: Pattern and Meaning in History: *Thoughts on History and Society.* ° *Edited with an Introduction by H. P. Rickman* TB/1075

H. STUART HUGHES: History as Art and as Science: *Twin Vistas on the Past* TB/1207

RAYMOND KLIBANSKY & H. J. PATON, Eds.: Philosophy and History: *The Ernst Cassirer Festschrift. Illus.* TB/1115

JOSE ORTEGA Y GASSET: The Modern Theme. *Introduction by Jose Ferrater Mora* TB/1038

SIR KARL POPPER: The Open Society and Its Enemies
Vol. I: *The Spell of Plato* TB/1101
Vol. II: *The High Tide of Prophecy: Hegel, Marx and the Aftermath* TB/1102

SIR KARL POPPER: The Poverty of Historicism ° TB/1126

G. J. RENIER: History: Its Purpose and Method TB/1209

W. H. WALSH: Philosophy of History: *An Introduction* TB/1020

History: General

L. CARRINGTON GOODRICH: A Short History of the Chinese People. *Illus.* TB/3015

DAN N. JACOBS & HANS H. BAERWALD: Chinese Communism: *Selected Documents* TB/3031

BERNARD LEWIS: The Arabs in History TB/1029

SIR PERCY SYKES: A History of Exploration. ° *Introduction by John K. Wright* TB/1046

History: Ancient and Medieval

A. ANDREWES: The Greek Tyrants TB/1103

P. BOISSONNADE: Life and Work in Medieval Europe: *The Evolution of the Medieval Economy, the 5th to the 15th Century.* ° *Preface by Lynn White, Jr.* TB/1141

HELEN CAM: England before Elizabeth TB/1026

NORMAN COHN: The Pursuit of the Millennium: *Revolutionary Messianism in Medieval and Reformation Europe* TB/1037

G. G. COULTON: Medieval Village, Manor, and Monastery TB/1022

HEINRICH FICHTENAU: The Carolingian Empire: *The Age of Charlemagne* TB/1142

F. L. GANSHOF: Feudalism TB/1058

EDWARD GIBBON: The Triumph of Christendom in the Roman Empire *(Chaps. XV-XX of "Decline and Fall," J. B. Bury edition).* § *Illus.* TB/46

MICHAEL GRANT: Ancient History ° TB/1190

W. O. HASSALL, Ed.: Medieval England: *As Viewed by Contemporaries* TB/1205

DENYS HAY: The Medieval Centuries ° TB/1192

J. M. HUSSEY: The Byzantine World TB/1057

SAMUEL NOAH KRAMER: Sumerian Mythology TB/1055

FERDINAND LOT: The End of the Ancient World and the Beginnings of the Middle Ages. *Introduction by Glanville Downey* TB/1044

G. MOLLATT: The Popes at Avignon: 1305-1378 TB/308

CHARLES PETIT-DUTAILLIS: The Feudal Monarchy in France and England: *From the Tenth to the Thirteenth Century* ° TB/1165

HENRI PIRENNE: Early Democracies in the Low Countries: *Urban Society and Political Conflict in the Middle Ages and the Renaissance. Introduction by John H. Mundy* TB/1110

STEVEN RUNCIMAN: A History of the Crusades. Volume I: *The First Crusade and the Foundation of the Kingdom of Jerusalem. Illus.* TB/1143

FERDINAND SCHEVILL: Siena: *The History of a Medieval Commune. Intro. by William M. Bowsky* TB/1164

SULPICIUS SEVERUS et al.: The Western Fathers: *Being the Lives of Martin of Tours, Ambrose, Augustine of Hippo, Honoratus of Arles and Germanus of Auxerre. Edited and translated by F. R. Hoare* TB/309

HENRY OSBORN TAYLOR: The Classical Heritage of the Middle Ages. *Foreword and Biblio. by Kenneth M. Setton* TB/1117

F. VAN DER MEER: Augustine The Bishop: *Church and Society at the Dawn of the Middle Ages* TB/304

J. M. WALLACE-HADRILL: The Barbarian West: *The Early Middle Ages, A.D. 400-1000* TB/1061

History: Renaissance & Reformation

JACOB BURCKHARDT: The Civilization of the Renaissance in Italy. *Intro. by Benjamin Nelson & Charles Trinkaus. Illus.* Vol. I TB/40; Vol. II TB/41

ERNST CASSIRER: The Individual and the Cosmos in Renaissance Philosophy. *Translated with an Introduction by Mario Domandi* TB/1097

FEDERICO CHABOD: Machiavelli and the Renaissance TB/1193

EDWARD P. CHEYNEY: The Dawn of a New Era, 1250-1453. * *Illus.* TB/3002

R. TREVOR DAVIES: The Golden Century of Spain, 1501-1621 ° TB/1194

DESIDERIUS ERASMUS: Christian Humanism and the Reformation: *Selected Writings. Edited and translated by John C. Olin* TB/1166

3

WALLACE K. FERGUSON et al.: Facets of the Renaissance
TB/1098

WALLACE K. FERGUSON et al.: The Renaissance: Six Essays. Illus. TB/1084

JOHN NEVILLE FIGGIS: The Divine Right of Kings. Introduction by G. R. Elton TB/1191

JOHN NEVILLE FIGGIS: Political Thought from Gerson to Grotius: 1414-1625: Seven Studies. Introduction by Garrett Mattingly TB/1032

MYRON P. GILMORE: The World of Humanism, 1453-1517.* Illus. TB/3003

FRANCESCO GUICCIARDINI: Maxims and Reflections of a Renaissance Statesman (Ricordi). Trans. by Mario Domandi. Intro. by Nicolai Rubinstein TB/1160

J. H. HEXTER: More's Utopia: The Biography of an Idea New Epilogue by the Author TB/1195

JOHAN HUIZINGA: Erasmus and the Age of Reformation. Illus. TB/19

ULRICH VON HUTTEN et al.: On the Eve of the Reformation: "Letters of Obscure Men." Introduction by Hajo Holborn TB/1124

PAUL O. KRISTELLER: Renaissance Thought: The Classic, Scholastic, and Humanist Strains TB/1048

PAUL O. KRISTELLER: Renaissance Thought II: Papers on Humanism and the Arts TB/1163

NICCOLO MACHIAVELLI: History of Florence and of the Affairs of Italy: from the earliest times to the death of Lorenzo the Magnificent. Introduction by Felix Gilbert TB/1027

ALFRED VON MARTIN: Sociology of the Renaissance. Introduction by Wallace K. Ferguson TB/1099

GARRETT MATTINGLY et al.: Renaissance Profiles. Edited by J. H. Plumb TB/1162

MILLARD MEISS: Painting in Florence and Siena after the Black Death: The Arts, Religion and Society in the Mid-Fourteenth Century. 169 illus. TB/1148

J. E. NEALE: The Age of Catherine de Medici ° TB/1085

ERWIN PANOFSKY: Studies in Iconology: Humanistic Themes in the Art of the Renaissance. 180 illustrations TB/1077

J. H. PARRY: The Establishment of the European Hegemony: 1415-1715: Trade and Exploration in the Age of the Renaissance TB/1045

J. H. PLUMB: The Italian Renaissance: A Concise Survey of Its History and Culture TB/1161

CECIL ROTH: The Jews in the Renaissance. Illus. TB/834

GORDON RUPP: Luther's Progress to the Diet of Worms ° TB/120

FERDINAND SCHEVILL: The Medici. Illus. TB/1010

FERDINAND SCHEVILL: Medieval and Renaissance Florence. Illus. Volume I: Medieval Florence TB/1090 Volume II: The Coming of Humanism and the Age of the Medici TB/1091

G. M. TREVELYAN: England in the Age of Wycliffe, 1368-1520 ° TB/1112

VESPASIANO: Renaissance Princes, Popes, and Prelates: The Vespasiano Memoirs: Lives of Illustrious Men of the XVth Century. Intro. by Myron P. Gilmore TB/1111

History: Modern European

FREDERICK B. ARTZ: Reaction and Revolution, 1815-1832. * Illus. TB/3034

MAX BELOFF: The Age of Absolutism, 1660-1815 TB/1062

ROBERT C. BINKLEY: Realism and Nationalism, 1852-1871. * Illus. TB/3038

ASA BRIGGS: The Making of Modern England, 1784-1867: The Age of Improvement ° TB/1203

CRANE BRINTON: A Decade of Revolution, 1789-1799. * Illus. TB/3018

J. BRONOWSKI & BRUCE MAZLISH: The Western Intellectual Tradition: From Leonardo to Hegel TB/3001

GEOFFREY BRUUN: Europe and the French Imperium, 1799-1814. * Illus. TB/3033

ALAN BULLOCK: Hitler, A Study in Tyranny. ° Illus. TB/1123

E. H. CARR: The Twenty Years' Crisis, 1919-1939: An Introduction to the Study of International Relations ° TB/1122

GORDON A. CRAIG: From Bismarck to Adenauer: Aspects of German Statecraft. Revised Edition TB/1171

WALTER L. DORN: Competition for Empire, 1740-1763. * Illus. TB/3032

CARL J. FRIEDRICH: The Age of the Baroque, 1610-1660. * Illus. TB/3004

RENÉ FUELOEP-MILLER: The Mind and Face of Bolshevism: An Examination of Cultural Life in Soviet Russia. New Epilogue by the Author TB/1188

M. DOROTHY GEORGE: London Life in the Eighteenth Century TB/1182

LEO GERSHOY: From Despotism to Revolution, 1763-1789. * Illus. TB/3017

C. C. GILLISPIE: Genesis and Geology: The Decades before Darwin § TB/51

ALBERT GOODWIN: The French Revolution TB/1064

ALBERT GUERARD: France in the Classical Age: The Life and Death of an Ideal TB/1183

CARLTON J. H. HAYES: A Generation of Materialism, 1871-1900. * Illus. TB/3039

J. H. HEXTER: Reappraisals in History: New Views on History & Society in Early Modern Europe TB/1100

A. R. HUMPHREYS: The Augustan World: Society, Thought, and Letters in 18th Century England ° TB/1105

ALDOUS HUXLEY: The Devils of Loudun: A Study in the Psychology of Power Politics and Mystical Religion in the France of Cardinal Richelieu § ° TB/60

DAN N. JACOBS, Ed.: The New Communist Manifesto & Related Documents. Third edition, revised TB/1078

HANS KOHN: The Mind of Germany: The Education of a Nation TB/1204

HANS KOHN, Ed.: The Mind of Modern Russia: Historical and Political Thought of Russia's Great Age TB/1065

KINGSLEY MARTIN: French Liberal Thought in the Eighteenth Century: A Study of Political Ideas from Bayle to Condorcet TB/1114

SIR LEWIS NAMIER: Personalities and Powers: Selected Essays TB/1186

SIR LEWIS NAMIER: Vanished Supremacies: Essays on European History, 1812-1918 ° TB/1088

JOHN U. NEF: Western Civilization Since the Renaissance: Peace, War, Industry, and the Arts TB/1113

FREDERICK L. NUSSBAUM: The Triumph of Science and Reason, 1660-1685. * Illus. TB/3009

JOHN PLAMENATZ: German Marxism and Russian Communism. ° New Preface by the Author TB/1189

RAYMOND W. POSTGATE, Ed.: Revolution from 1789 to 1906: Selected Documents TB/1063

PENFIELD ROBERTS: The Quest for Security, 1715-1740. * Illus. TB/3016

PRISCILLA ROBERTSON: Revolutions of 1848: A Social History TB/1025

ALBERT SOREL: Europe Under the Old Regime. Translated by Francis H. Herrick TB/1121

N. N. SUKHANOV: The Russian Revolution, 1917: Eyewitness Account. Edited by Joel Carmichael Vol. I TB/1066; Vol. II TB/1067

A. J. P. TAYLOR: The Habsburg Monarch, 1809-1918: A History of the Austrian Empire and Austria-Hungary ° TB/1187

4

5

H. J. BLACKHAM: Six Existentialist Thinkers: *Kierke-gaard, Nietzsche, Jaspers, Marcel, Heidegger, Sartre* ° TB/1002

CRANE BRINTON: Nietzsche. *New Preface, Bibliography and Epilogue by the Author* TB/1197

ERNST CASSIRER: The Individual and the Cosmos in Renaissance Philosophy. *Translated with an Intro-duction by Mario Domandi* TB/1097

ERNST CASSIRER: Rousseau, Kant and Goethe. *Introduc-tion by Peter Gay* TB/1092

FREDERICK COPLESTON: Medieval Philosophy ° TB/376

F. M. CORNFORD: Principium Sapientiae: *A Study of the Origins of Greek Philosophical Thought. Edited by W. K. C. Guthrie* TB/1213

F. M. CORNFORD: From Religion to Philosophy: *A Study in the Origins of Western Speculation* § TB/20

WILFRID DESAN: The Tragic Finale: *An Essay on the Philosophy of Jean-Paul Sartre* TB/1030

PAUL FRIEDLÄNDER: Plato: *An Introduction* TB/2017

ÉTIENNE GILSON: Dante and Philosophy TB/1089

WILLIAM CHASE GREENE: Moira: *Fate, Good, and Evil in Greek Thought* TB/1104

W. K. C. GUTHRIE: The Greek Philosophers: *From Thales to Aristotle* ° TB/1008

F. H. HEINEMANN: Existentialism and the Modern Pre-dicament TB/28

ISAAC HUSIK: A History of Medieval Jewish Philosophy TB/803

EDMUND HUSSERL: Phenomenology and the Crisis of Philosophy. *Translated with an Introduction by Quentin Lauer* TB/1170

IMMANUEL KANT: The Doctrine of Virtue, *being Part II of The Metaphysic of Morals. Trans. with Notes & Intro. by Mary J. Gregor. Foreword by H. J. Paton* TB/110

IMMANUEL KANT: Groundwork of the Metaphysic of Morals. *Trans. & analyzed by H. J. Paton* TB/1159

IMMANUEL KANT: Lectures on Ethics. § *Introduction by Lewis W. Beck* TB/105

QUENTIN LAUER: Phenomenology: *Its Genesis and Pros-pect* TB/1169

GABRIEL MARCEL: Being and Having: *An Existential Diary. Intro. by James Collins* TB/310

GEORGE A. MORGAN: What Nietzsche Means TB/1198

PHILO SAADYA GAON, & JEHUDA HALEVI: Three Jewish Philosophers. *Ed. by Hans Lewy, Alexander Altmann, & Isaak Heinemann* TB/813

MICHAEL POLANYI: Personal Knowledge: *Towards a Post-Critical Philosophy* TB/1158

WILLARD VAN ORMAN QUINE: Elementary Logic: *Revised Edition* TB/577

WILLARD VAN ORMAN QUINE: From a Logical Point of View: *Logico-Philosophical Essays* TB/566

BERTRAND RUSSELL et al.: The Philosophy of Bertrand Russell. *Edited by Paul Arthur Schilpp*
Vol. I TB/1095; Vol. II TB/1096

L. S. STEBBING: A Modern Introduction to Logic TL/538

ALFRED NORTH WHITEHEAD: Process and Reality: *An Essay in Cosmology* TB/1033

PHILIP P. WIENER: Evolution and the Founders of Prag-matism. *Foreword by John Dewey* TB/1212

WILHELM WINDELBAND: A History of Philosophy
Vol. I: *Greek, Roman, Medieval* TB/38
Vol. II: *Renaissance, Enlightenment, Modern* TB/39

LUDWIG WITTGENSTEIN: The Blue and Brown Books ° TB/1211

Political Science & Government

JEREMY BENTHAM: The Handbook of Political Fallacies: *Introduction by Crane Brinton* TB/1069

KENNETH E. BOULDING: Conflict and Defense: *A General Theory* TB/3024

CRANE BRINTON: English Political Thought in the Nine-teenth Century TB/1071

EDWARD S. CORWIN: American Constitutional History: *Essays edited by Alpheus T. Mason and Gerald Gar-vey* TB/1136

ROBERT DAHL & CHARLES E. LINDBLOM: Politics, Economics, and Welfare: *Planning and Politico-Economic Sys-tems Resolved into Basic Social Processes* TB/3037

JOHN NEVILLE FIGGIS: The Divine Right of Kings. *Intro-duction by G. R. Elton* TB/1191

JOHN NEVILLE FIGGIS: Political Thought from Gerson to Grotius: 1414-1625: *Seven Studies. Introduction by Garrett Mattingly* TB/1032

F. L. GANSHOF: Feudalism TB/1058

G. P. GOOCH: English Democratic Ideas in Seventeenth Century TB/1006

J. H. HEXTER: More's Utopia: *The Biography of an Idea. New Epilogue by the Author* TB/1195

ROBERT H. JACKSON: The Supreme Court in the American System of Government TB/1106

DAN N. JACOBS, Ed.: The New Communist Manifesto & *Related Documents. Third edition, Revised* TB/1078

DAN N. JACOBS & HANS BAERWALD, Eds.: Chinese Com-munism: *Selected Documents* TB/3031

ROBERT GREEN MC CLOSKEY: American Conservatism in the Age of Enterprise, 1865-1910 TB/1137

KINGSLEY MARTIN: French Liberal Thought in the Eighteenth Century: *Political Ideas from Bayle to Condorcet* TB/1114

JOHN STUART MILL: On Bentham and Coleridge. *In-troduction by F. R. Leavis* TB/1070

JOHN B. MORRALL: Political Thought in Medieval Times TB/1076

JOHN PLAMENATZ: German Marxism and Russian Com-munism. ° *New Preface by the Author* TB/1189

SIR KARL POPPER: The Open Society and Its Enemies
Vol. I: *The Spell of Plato* TB/1101
Vol. II: *The High Tide of Prophecy: Hegel, Marx, and the Aftermath* TB/1102

HENRI DE SAINT-SIMON: Social Organization, The Science of Man, and Other Writings. *Edited and Translated by Felix Markham* TB/1152

JOSEPH A. SCHUMPETER: Capitalism, Socialism and Democracy TB/3008

CHARLES H. SHINN: Mining Camps: *A Study in American Frontier Government.* ‡ *Edited by Rodman W. Paul* TB/3062

Psychology

ALFRED ADLER: The Individual Psychology of Alfred Adler. *Edited by Heinz L. and Rowena R. Ansbacher* TB/1154

ALFRED ADLER: Problems of Neurosis. *Introduction by Heinz L. Ansbacher* TB/1145

ANTON T. BOISEN: The Exploration of the Inner World: *A Study of Mental Disorder and Religious Experience* TB/87

HERBERT FINGARETTE: The Self in Transformation: *Psy-choanalysis, Philosophy and the Life of the Spirit.* TB/1177

SIGMUND FREUD: On Creativity and the Unconscious: *Papers on the Psychology of Art, Literature, Love, Religion.* § *Intro. by Benjamin Nelson* TB/45

6

C. JUDSON HERRICK: The Evolution of Human Nature
TB/545

WILLIAM JAMES: Psychology: *The Briefer Course. Edited with an Intro. by Gordon Allport* TB/1034

C. G. JUNG: Psychological Reflections TB/2001

C. G. JUNG: Symbols of Transformation: *An Analysis of the Prelude to a Case of Schizophrenia. Illus.*
Vol. I: TB/2009; Vol. II TB/2010

C. G. JUNG & C. KERÉNYI: Essays on a Science of Mythology: *The Myths of the Divine Child and the Divine Maiden* TB/2014

JOHN T. MC NEILL: A History of the Cure of Souls
TB/126

KARL MENNINGER: Theory of Psychoanalytic Technique
TB/1144

ERICH NEUMANN: Amor and Psyche: *The Psychic Development of the Feminine* TB/2012

ERICH NEUMANN: The Archetypal World of Henry Moore. *107 illus.* TB/2020

ERICH NEUMANN: The Origins and History of Consciousness TB/2007; Vol. I *Illus.* TB/2008

C. P. OBERNDORF: A History of Psychoanalysis in America
TB/1147

RALPH BARTON PERRY: The Thought and Character of William James: *Briefer Version* TB/1156

JEAN PIAGET, BÄRBEL INHELDER, & ALINA SZEMINSKA: The Child's Conception of Geometry ° TB/1146

JOHN H. SCHAAR: Escape from Authority: *The Perspectives of Erich Fromm* TB/1155

Sociology

JACQUES BARZUN: Race: *A Study in Superstition. Revised Edition* TB/1172

BERNARD BERELSON, Ed.: The Behavioral Sciences Today
TB/1127

ABRAHAM CAHAN: The Rise of David Levinsky: *A documentary novel of social mobility in early twentieth century America. Intro. by John Higham* TB/1028

THOMAS C. COCHRAN: The Inner Revolution: *Essays on the Social Sciences in History* TB/1140

ALLISON DAVIS & JOHN DOLLARD: Children of Bondage: *The Personality Development of Negro Youth in the Urban South* || TB/3049

ST. CLAIR DRAKE & HORACE R. CAYTON: Black Metropolis: *A Study of Negro Life in a Northern City. Revised and Enlarged. Intro. by Everett C. Hughes*
Vol. I TB/1086; Vol. II TB/1087

EMILE DURKHEIM et al.: Essays on Sociology and Philosophy: *With Analyses of Durkheim's Life and Work.* || *Edited by Kurt H. Wolff* TB/1151

LEON FESTINGER, HENRY W. RIECKEN & STANLEY SCHACHTER: When Prophecy Fails: *A Social and Psychological Account of a Modern Group that Predicted the Destruction of the World* || TB/1132

ALVIN W. GOULDNER: Wildcat Strike: *A Study in Worker-Management Relationships* || TB/1176

FRANCIS J. GRUND: Aristocracy in America: *Social Class in the Formative Years of the New Nation* TB/1001

KURT LEWIN: Field Theory in Social Science: *Selected Theoretical Papers.* || *Edited with a Foreword by Dorwin Cartwright* TB/1135

R. M. MACIVER: Social Causation TB/1153

ROBERT K. MERTON, LEONARD BROOM, LEONARD S. COTTRELL, JR., Editors: Sociology Today: *Problems and Prospects* || Vol. I TB/1173; Vol. II TB/1174

TALCOTT PARSONS & EDWARD A. SHILS, Editors: Toward a General Theory of Action: *Theoretical Foundations for the Social Sciences* TB/1083

JOHN H. ROHRER & MUNRO S. EDMONSON, Eds.: The Eighth Generation Grows Up: *Cultures and Personalities of New Orleans Negroes* || TB/3050

ARNOLD ROSE: The Negro in America: *The Condensed Version of Gunnar Myrdal's An American Dilemma*
TB/3048

KURT SAMUELSSON: Religion and Economic Action: *A Critique of Max Weber's The Protestant Ethic and the Spirit of Capitalism.* || ° *Trans. by E. G. French; Ed. with Intro. by D. C. Coleman* TB/1131

PITIRIM A. SOROKIN: Contemporary Sociological Theories. *Through the First Quarter of the 20th Century* TB/3046

MAURICE R. STEIN: The Eclipse of Community: *An Interpretation of American Studies* TB/1128

FERDINAND TÖNNIES: Community and Society: *Gemeinschaft und Gesellschaft. Translated and edited by Charles P. Loomis* TB/1116

W. LLOYD WARNER & Associates: Democracy in Jonesville: *A Study in Quality and Inequality* TB/1129

W. LLOYD WARNER: Social Class in America: *The Evaluation of Status* TB/1013

RELIGION

Ancient & Classical

J. H. BREASTED: Development of Religion and Thought in Ancient Egypt. *Introduction by John A. Wilson*
TB/57

HENRI FRANKFORT: Ancient Egyptian Religion: *An Interpretation* TB/77

G. RACHEL LEVY: Religious Conceptions of the Stone Age and their Influence upon European Thought. *Illus. Introduction by Henri Frankfort* TB/106

MARTIN P. NILSSON: Greek Folk Religion. *Foreword by Arthur Darby Nock* TB/78

ALEXANDRE PIANKOFF: The Shrines of Tut-Ankh-Amon. *Edited by N. Rambova. 117 illus.* TB/2011

H. J. ROSE: Religion in Greece and Rome TB/55

Biblical Thought & Literature

W. F. ALBRIGHT: The Biblical Period from Abraham to Ezra TB/102

C. K. BARRETT, Ed.: The New Testament Background: *Selected Documents* TB/86

C. H. DODD: The Authority of the Bible TB/43

M. S. ENSLIN: Christian Beginnings TB/5

M. S. ENSLIN: The Literature of the Christian Movement
TB/6

JOHN GRAY: Archaeology and the Old Testament World. *Illus.* TB/127

H. H. ROWLEY: The Growth of the Old Testament
TB/107

D. WINTON THOMAS, Ed.: Documents from Old Testament Times TB/85

The Judaic Tradition

LEO BAECK: Judaism and Christianity. *Trans. with Intro. by Walter Kaufmann* TB/823

SALO W. BARON: Modern Nationalism and Religion
TB/818

MARTIN BUBER: Eclipse of God: *Studies in the Relation Between Religion and Philosophy* TB/12

MARTIN BUBER: Moses: *The Revelation and the Covenant* TB/27

MARTIN BUBER: Pointing the Way. *Introduction by Maurice S. Friedman* TB/103

MARTIN BUBER: The Prophetic Faith TB/73

MARTIN BUBER: Two Types of Faith: *the interpenetration of Judaism and Christianity* ° TB/75

ERNST LUDWIG EHRLICH: A Concise History of Israel: From the Earliest Times to the Destruction of the Temple in A.D. 70 ° TB/128
MAURICE S. FRIEDMAN: Martin Buber: The Life of Dialogue TB/64
LOUIS GINZBERG: Students, Scholars and Saints TB/802
SOLOMON GRAYZEL: A History of the Contemporary Jews TB/816
WILL HERBERG: Judaism and Modern Man TB/810
ABRAHAM J. HESCHEL: God in Search of Man: A Philosophy of Judaism TB/807
ISAAC HUSIK: A History of Medieval Jewish Philosophy TB/803
FLAVIUS JOSEPHUS: The Great Roman-Jewish War, with The Life of Josephus. Introduction by William R. Farmer TB/74
JACOB R. MARCUS The Jew in the Medieval World TB/814
MAX L. MARGOLIS & ALEXANDER MARX: A History of the Jewish People TB/806
T. J. MEEK: Hebrew Origins TB/69
C. G. MONTEFIORE & H. LOEWE, Eds.: A Rabbinic Anthology TB/832
JAMES PARKES: The Conflict of the Church and the Synagogue: The Jews and Early Christianity TB/821
PHILO, SAADYA GAON, & JEHUDA HALEVI: Three Jewish Philosophers. Ed. by Hans Lewey, Alexander Altmann, & Isaak Heinemann TB/813
HERMAN L. STRACK: Introduction to the Talmud and Midrash TB/808
JOSHUA TRACHTENBERG: The Devil and the Jews: The Medieval Conception of the Jew and its Relation to Modern Anti-Semitism TB/822

Christianity: General

ROLAND H. BAINTON: Christendom: A Short History of Christianity and its Impact on Western Civilization. Illus. Vol. I, TB/131; Vol. II, TB/132

Christianity: Origins & Early Development

AUGUSTINE: An Augustine Synthesis. Edited by Erich Przywara TB/335
ADOLF DEISSMANN: Paul: A Study in Social and Religious History TB/15
EDWARD GIBBON: The Triumph of Christendom in the Roman Empire (Chaps. XV-XX of "Decline and Fall," J. B. Bury edition). § Illus. TB/46
MAURICE GOGUEL: Jesus and the Origins of Christianity.° Introduction by C. Leslie Mitton
Volume I: Prologomena to the Life of Jesus TB/65
Volume II: The Life of Jesus TB/66
EDGAR J. GOODSPEED: A Life of Jesus TB/1
ADOLF HARNACK: The Mission and Expansion of Christianity in the First Three Centuries. Introduction by Jaroslav Pelikan TB/92
R. K. HARRISON: The Dead Sea Scrolls: An Introduction ° TB/84
EDWIN HATCH: The Influence of Greek Ideas on Christianity. § Introduction and Bibliography by Frederick C. Grant TB/18
ARTHUR DARBY NOCK: Early Gentile Christianity and Its Hellenistic Background TB/111
ARTHUR DARBY NOCK: St. Paul ° TB/104
JAMES PARKES: The Conflict of the Church and the Synagogue: The Jews and Early Christianity TB/821
SULPICIUS SEVERUS et al.: The Western Fathers: Being the Lives of Martin of Tours, Ambrose, Augustine of Hippo, Honoratus of Arles and Germanus of Auxerre. Edited and translated by F. R. Hoare TB/309

F. VAN DER MEER: Augustine the Bishop: Church and Society at the Dawn of the Middle Ages TB/304
JOHANNES WEISS: Earliest Christianity: A History of the Period A.D. 30-150. Introduction and Bibliography by Frederick C. Grant Volume I TB/53
Volume II TB/54

Christianity: The Middle Ages and The Reformation

JOHANNES ECKHART: Meister Eckhart: A Modern Translation by R. B. Blakney TB/8
DESIDERIUS ERASMUS: Christian Humanism and the Reformation: Selected Writings. Edited and translated by John C. Olin TB/1166
ÉTIENNE GILSON: Dante and Philosophy TB/1089
WILLIAM HALLER: The Rise of Puritanism TB/22
JOHAN HUIZINGA: Erasmus and the Age of Reformation. Illus. TB/19
A. C. MCGIFFERT: Protestant Thought Before Kant. Preface by Jaroslav Pelikan TB/93
JOHN T. MCNEILL: Makers of the Christian Tradition: From Alfred the Great to Schleiermacher TB/121
G. MOLLAT: The Popes at Avignon, 1305-1378 TB/308
GORDON RUPP: Luther's Progress to the Diet of Worms ° TB/120

Christianity: The Protestant Tradition

KARL BARTH: Church Dogmatics: A Selection TB/95
KARL BARTH: Dogmatics in Outline TB/56
KARL BARTH: The Word of God and the Word of Man TB/13
RUDOLF BULTMANN et al.: Translating Theology into the Modern Age: Historical, Systematic and Pastoral Reflections on Theology and the Church in the Contemporary Situation. Volume 2 of Journal for Theology and the Church, edited by Robert W. Funk in association with Gerhard Ebeling TB/252
WINTHROP HUDSON: The Great Tradition of the American Churches TB/98
SOREN KIERKEGAARD: Edifying Discourses. Edited with an Introduction by Paul Holmer TB/32
SOREN KIERKEGAARD: The Journals of Kierkegaard. ° Edited with an Introduction by Alexander Dru TB/52
SOREN KIERKEGAARD: The Point of View for My Work as an Author: A Report to History. § Preface by Benjamin Nelson TB/88
SOREN KIERKEGAARD: The Present Age. § Translated and edited by Alexander Dru. Introduction by Walter Kaufmann TB/94
SOREN KIERKEGAARD: Purity of Heart TB/4
SOREN KIERKEGAARD: Repetition: An Essay in Experimental Psychology. Translated with Introduction & Notes by Walter Lowrie TB/117
SOREN KIERKEGAARD: Works of Love: Some Christian Reflections in the Form of Discourses TB/122
WALTER LOWRIE: Kierkegaard: A Life Vol. I TB/89
Vol. II TB/90
PERRY MILLER & T. H. JOHNSON, Editors: The Puritans: A Sourcebook of Their Writings Vol. I TB/1093
Vol. II TB/1094
JAMES M. ROBINSON et al.: The Bultmann School of Biblical Interpretation: New Directions? Volume 1 of Journal of Theology and the Church, edited by Robert W. Funk in association with Gerhard Ebeling TB/251
F. SCHLEIERMACHER: The Christian Faith. Introduction by Richard R. Niebuhr Vol. I TB/108
Vol. II TB/109

NATURAL SCIENCES AND MATHEMATICS

Biological Sciences

9